D0794416

# Davy Crockett's Riproarious Shemales and Sentimental Sisters

11 95

Courtesy, Harry Ransom Humanities Research Center, The University of Texas at Austin

FIGURE 1. *John Gadsby Chapman's oil portrait
of Congressman Crockett painted in 1834.*

# Davy Crockett's Riproarious Shemales and Sentimental Sisters:

*Women's Tall Tales
from the Crockett Almanacs
1835–1856*

Edited
With an Introduction by
## MICHAEL A. LOFARO

STACKPOLE
BOOKS

Copyright ©2001 by Stackpole Books

Published by
STACKPOLE BOOKS
5067 Ritter Road
Mechanicsburg, PA 17055
www.stackpolebooks.com

All rights reserved, including the right to reproduce this book or portions thereof in any form or by any means, electronic or mechanical, including photocopying, recording, or by any information storage and retrieval system, without permission in writing from the publisher. All inquiries should be addressed to Stackpole Books, 5067 Ritter Road, Mechanicsburg, Pennsylvania 17055.

Printed in the United States of America

10 9 8 7 6 5 4 3 2 1

FIRST EDITION

**Library of Congress Cataloging-in-Publication Data**

Davy Crockett's riproarious shemales and sentimental sisters : women's tall tales from the Crockett almanacs, 1835–1856 / edited with an introduction by Michael A. Lofaro.
     p.    cm.
   ISBN 0-8117-0499-8
   1. Crockett, Davy, 1786–1836—Legends.   2. Crockett, Davy, 1786–1836—Humor.
3. Tall tales—United States.   4. Women—United States—Folklore.   I. Lofaro, Michael A., 1948–

GR105.37.D3 D383   2001
398.2'0973'02—dc21

                                00-052241

*For Nancy and Ellen*
*The Best Combination of Shemales and Sentiment*
*And*
*For Christopher*
*A Source of Support and Strength*

# Contents

## THE TALES

---

An asterisk indicates that the tale does not have an illustration.
Bracketed titles have been provided by the editor.

# List of Illustrations

# Acknowledgments

There are countless people who deserve my thanks for their help with this book. It began over twenty years ago under a fellowship to the National Humanities Center and has likewise received generous support from the John C. Hodges Better English Fund of the Department of English at the University of Tennessee and photographic grants from the Office of Research of the university. Librarians and libraries have provided invaluable support, especially D. Strong Wyman of the Special Collections Library and Marie A. Garrett at the University of Tennessee, as have the many kind individuals at the American Antiquarian Society, the Library of Congress, the St. Louis Mercantile Library Association, and the University of Texas at Austin. Steven Harthorn and Dr. Claudia Milstead contributed much to this volume's completion as research assistants and friends. The encouragement of other colleagues and friends, such as Thomas J. Heffernan, D. Allen Carroll, and John Seelye, has kept the fun in humor, as has that of my family, without whose unstinting gift of time and love this book would have been a project rather than a pleasure.

# A Taste of the Tales

Do the names Florinda Fury, Katy Goodgrit, Hippotamus Zephyr, Sal Fink, Comfort Crockett, and Sally Ann Thunder Ann Whirlwind Crockett draw only a blank? Indeed, when asked to recall any of the tall tales of Davy Crockett, most people never knew that he served as the fictional narrator of often outrageous tall tales, much less that a significant number of the tales concerned the exploits and adventures of backwoods women. The question might cause a few devotees of the legendary Crockett to pause, fall back upon memories of Walt Disney, and quote "Kilt him a bar when he was only three," a line from "The Ballad of Davy Crockett." Or upon further thought, they might also remember that when hunting, his grin was often as effective as his rifle, a story the Disney production staff revived rather than created. These, however, are but pale reflections of the original legendary feats of Crockett, a nineteenth-century comic superhero who could tree a ghost, ride his pet thirty-seven-foot-long alligator up Niagara Falls, drink up the Mississippi River, and twice save the world, once by unfreezing the earth and sun from their axes with hot bear oil and once by wringing the tail off Halley's Comet. And such traits likewise hint at the extraordinary deeds performed by women, the riproarious shemales and sentimental sisters of the Almanacs whose actions nearly echoed those of Crockett himself. This tall-tale Davy and his crew of fellow half-horse, half-alligator frontier screamers had an extraordinary group of female relatives and counterparts who could be just as wild, heroic, comic, and grotesque as the male characters, but whose depictions still maintained or parodied many of the feminine traits accepted as norms in nineteenth-century America.

The unique tall-tale world of the Crockett Almanacs began as a marketing device in which the publishers attempted to gain a large share of the lucrative almanac market by giving the prospective buyer something more than simply the standard almanac data on sunrise, sunset, weather, tides, and phases of the moon. The publishers recognized the incredible popularity of Crockett and successfully incorporated the current stories circulating about him in newspapers, books, and plays into their publications as a major selling point. Their actions mirrored those of the historical David Crockett, who realized the beneficial effects of such legendary notoriety and manipulated it

FIGURE 2. *Crockett's Wonderful Escape,*
*by Driving His Pet Alligator up Niagara Falls*

to enhance his political career. After his heroic death at the Alamo on March 6, 1836, the tales mushroomed to truly epic proportions. As the best-selling and longest-running series of comic almanacs published in the United States before the Civil War, the Crockett Almanacs were a funhouse mirror turned upon the culture of antebellum America.

Politically, the tales centered upon the idea of Manifest Destiny and territorial expansion but gave little direct comment upon the issues of states' rights and slavery. Socially, they dealt primarily with safe satiric targets, groups essentially powerless in nineteenth-century America—African-Americans, Native Americans, and Mexicans—and also, and perhaps most interestingly, with the beginnings of radical changes in the status of women. The anonymous authors emphasized the "otherness" of the riproarious shemales whom they created. They overtly mocked the sentimental tradition to present a comic inversion of the then-current ideal of femininity, while still stressing the secondary status of women's traditional roles. But, perhaps ironically and unintentionally, by placing women in the savage wilderness and downplaying their civilized traits, the authors broke their female characters loose from society's strictures to act out male adventures and fantasies with a freedom that only life in the wilderness could allow.

Such reversals of the stereotypical roles of nineteenth-century women and subsequent satire were at least part of the intent of the anonymous writers who produced the Crockett Almanacs and used Crockett as their main narrator. Their portrayals of women, which range from the heroic to the satiric, from the comic to the sentimental, yield an intriguing view of this time that creates uproarious laughter and provokes serious commentary, often in the same tale. Look as deeply as you wish. The mirror they provide has the ability to reveal much about those times, about the views and beliefs of the writers and the audience that appreciated the stories, and, in true funhouse fashion, also a good deal about the preconceptions of modern readers as they react to a culture far different from their own.

Given the inherently disposable nature of almanacs, only a few of the tales about Crockett himself have survived, and most surface in scholarly publications. Even rarer are mentions of the women who peopled the Almanacs. Made easily available in their entirety for the first time in this book, these tales and the fascinating woodcuts that illustrate them bring alive a unique world. They explore the broadest possible range of women's actions, those that exuberantly break the bounds and limits of society and those that piously reinforce those same strictures. Among the highlights of the tales are Lottie Ritchers, who "war a streak of litenin set up edgeways, and buttered with quicksilver"; Katy Goodgrit, who could "grin a wild cat out of countenance"; Oak Wing's sister, who skinned a live bear with her teeth that were "as long and as sharp as nales"; Nance Bowers, who "war seven feet tall out of her stockins . . . could wipe her feet with her hair . . . [and] swing on the top of a fifty foot hickory tree"; Sal Fungus, who could "laugh the bark off a tree . . . , dance a rock to pieces, . . . [and] sing a wolf to sleep"; and Davy's sister, Comfort Crockett, who was so religious that "when she sung a psalm you'd a thought all the trees in creation war organ pipes an a harrycane blowin the bellows."

I believe that these stories are the earliest body of American tall tales about women. They are as entertaining as they are informative in bringing alive the times surrounding their publication from 1835 to 1856. These comic depictions of minorities and women can certainly be judged as cruel and offensive by today's standards as they were deemed hilarious and delightful to the majority of their original readers. The stories therefore remain a touchstone both for how much has changed and, in some cases, how little. Although the Almanacs have received relatively little scrutiny, their significance has long been established. The Grolier Club of New York included the seven "Nashville" Almanacs of 1835 to 1841 (actually published in Boston) as one of their choices for their 1946 exhibition of "One Hundred Influential American Books Printed before 1900." These Almanacs were thus placed alongside the Declaration of Independence, the Gettysburg Address, Twain's *Huckleberry Finn*, and Poe's *The Raven* as American classics.

Those who wish more information on the context of the stories, their historical and cultural background, and their place within the Humor of the Old Southwest and popular culture of the day might wish to explore the next section, "Shemales, Sentiment, and Stereotypes: A Long View of the Crockett Almanacs." Those who have whet their whistles with the taste of these tales provided by this brief preface and gathered sufficient strength for their plunge into antebellum humor are welcome to dive directly into the texts. But in either case, please do observe the warning of Ben Harding, Crockett's seagoing sidekick and editor, before launching into these "terrificashus" yarns: "You had best hoop your ribs before you reed em or you will shake your bowels out a laffing." (1839, p. 2)

# Shemales, Sentiment, and Stereotypes: A Long View of the Crockett Almanacs

## HISTORICAL VIEWS OF WOMAN

"Male and Female represent the two sides of the great radical dualism. But, in fact, they are perpetually passing into one another. Fluid hardens to solid, solid rushes to fluid. There is no wholly masculine man, no purely feminine woman." (Margaret Fuller, *Woman in the Nineteenth Century*, 1845)

"She has a head almost too small for intellect but just big enough for love." (Dr. Charles D. Meigs, *Lecture on Some of the Distinctive Characteristics of the Female*, 1847)

## VIEWS OF WOMEN IN THE CROCKETT ALMANACS

"She can jump a seven rail fence backwards, dance a hole through a double oak floor, spin more wool than one of your steam mills, and smoke up a ton of Kentucky weed in a week." ("Crockett's Mother [age 148]," 1845, p. 5)

"[Sal Tuig] stood six foot and two inches without her shoes; she had a fist like a rock, and the biggest feet in the whole cleering. Besides all this she had lost an eye at a tea-squall [tea party], and one ear had been bit off in a fite with two wolves." ("Crockett's Disappointment," 1843, p. 8)

After Mike Fink shoots half the comb out of his wife's hair, he challenges Crockett "to take a blizzard at what was left on it. The angeliferous critter stood still as a scarecrow in a cornfield, for she'd got used to Mike's tricks by long practiss. 'No, no, Mike,' sez I, 'Davy Crockett's hand would be sure to shake, if his iron war pointed within a hundred mile of a shemale, and I give up beat, Mike.'" ("Col. Crockett beat at a Shooting Match," 1840 Nashville, p. 11)[1]

5

Classifying the depictions of women is always a difficult task. Whether historical or fictional, their relation to their age often depends upon the point of view of the author who relates their story as well as that of the reader. And when the idea of the proper role of women in society is debated, as it is on several levels in the quotations above, and further, when it is presented in comic or satiric form, the confusion that results may make a Gordian knot or Rubik's cube seem simple by comparison. There is no one correct view or interpretation of the tales that compose this volume. They do, however, form part of a tradition that ranges from the classical accounts of ancient goddesses and the Amazons to television's Xena the Warrior Princess, and from such complete liberation from the bounds of a male-dominated society to total subjugation to imposed cultural roles.

There have always been tales about women who blur gender-defined roles by functioning as men. The riproarious shemales of the Crockett Almanacs, however, are perhaps best initially defined by what they are not. They are not intended as goddesses or culture heroes, beings who are worshiped or who exemplify the most cherished traits of their society. They are not evil. No Medeas making an envenomed dress and tiara for Jason's new bride and killing her children or Lizzie Borden's whacking a hatchet into the heads of her parents are in their ranks.[2] They are not child rearers. The only mothering in the Almanacs is done by Mother Nature, the wilderness. These women are not socially or politically active. Neither are they depicted as following different sexual paths such as cross-dressing, transvestism, or lesbianism. In the main, despite their occasional savagery, they are simple, sometimes innocent women who are dramatically and comically altered by living in the wilderness. They are who they are because of where they are. The authors' use of this geographical determinism reiterates the same view of the American frontier that informs the works of J. Hector St. John de Crèvecoeur and James Fenimore Cooper, among others. This belief liberates the authors to have these women act as they choose, to emulate the half-horse, half-alligator shenanigans of backwoods males or to echo the sentimental stereotypes that equate women with all things civilized. Often they fall between these poles, sample both roles, select the most outlandishly wild path, temper it with a bit of sentiment, and proceed on in their adventures to hilarious and sometimes grotesque conclusions. Through the slapdash work of their anonymous nineteenth-century creators, who, given the practices of the printing trade, are very likely male, the shemales of the Almanacs carry a great deal of cultural and comic baggage that we can unpack. The authors are as aware of classical myths and the traditional satires and comedic depictions of women as they are of the struggle over the proper sphere of women in their own day, but however interesting and informative, all this serves as mere background to their truly original creations in the Almanacs. As a part of the dominant Boston–New York–Philadelphia printing axis and likely residents of those cities, these authors seem to have followed the advice of one of their number who uses Davy Crockett to instruct us in the pecking order of manly life in the wilderness: "If he can't hunt, perhaps he can fight; and if he can't fight perhaps he can scream; and if he can't scream, perhaps he can grin pretty severe; and if he can't do that, perhaps he can tell a story." (1841, p. [29])

The women of the Crockett Almanacs do hunt, fight, scream, and more. In these activities, they are part of a continuum in the depiction of women who range from nearly equal to clearly superior to their male counterparts in all the activities that their particular culture and age deem appropriate for men. In examining the ancestors, contemporaries, and in a very brief way, the inheritors of the characteristics of women of the Almanacs, the huge range to be explored contains mythic, historical, and fictional narratives, some but not all related with a humorous intent. In so doing, this introduction is far from comprehensive. With the riproarious shemales of the Crockett Almanacs as its main focus, it seeks to examine the originality of these portrayals from 1835 to 1856 as they modify those of their precursors and incorporate and highlight the sentiment and stereotypes of antebellum America as part of the satire. The picture is never completely clear or constant. Just as the tales in this volume range from the fantastic and outrageous to the believable and mundane, as their creators quickly blend their perceptions of past and present to meet publication deadlines, so too can readers who accept the confluence of imagination and history delight in these hybrid women, who, in the hands of these same authors, twist the perceived realities of frontier life with comic gusto.

## ANCESTORS

In approaching classical myth, literature, and history as the origin of the idea of the manly or manlike woman, language is in many ways an appropriate starting point for the investigation of meaning. Perhaps the most ancient category for shemales is that of androgyny, since in its broadest conceptual sense it is two within one and is the linguistic combination of the male (*andro-*) and the female (*gyne-*).[3] In the case of the Crockett Almanacs, however, none of the physical aspects or modern connotations and mistaken associations of androgyny apply. Physical hermaphroditism, bisexuality, and homosexuality are never broached as topics or used in descriptions. Even if these women sometimes look like men in the woodcuts that illustrate the tales, the sex of the riproarious shemales is unambiguous; they simply choose to add masculine gender roles, sometimes overpowering ones, to their existing feminine roles.

Hera, the supreme goddess of the Greeks, provides another interesting point of departure, not for any assumption of masculine roles, since she was far too busy meting out punishment for her husband Zeus's sexual adventures and rapes and too smart to challenge his power directly, but because of her name. While it is open to debate, some have suggested that *Hera* is the feminine form of the word *heros,* meaning "glorified ancestor."[4] In English, the dominantly masculine connotations of the word *hero* and its feminine form, the diminutive *heroine,* now mute the original duality of heroism in terms of gender.

Moving from rudimentary philology to myth, it is clear that Athena is a far closer ancestor to the shemale than Hera. Athena is the daughter of Zeus and Metis, not Hera. Zeus swallowed the pregnant Metis, a daughter of the Titans, but developed such a severe headache that Prometheus had to split his head open with an axe to relieve it. Athena sprang fully grown—and in some later accounts, fully armed—from Zeus's head, giving dramatic emphasis to her dual roles as goddess of wisdom and of warfare. In the latter role, Athena is mainly a protectress and is most often remembered as a defender and champion of heroes—all male, of course. She tells Cadmus to plant dragon's teeth, from which spring the noblemen that help him to found Thebes, helps Bellerophon capture and bridle Pegasus, and Perseus to behead the Gorgon. She also, among others, protects and aids Heracles, Orestes, Odysseus, and his son Telemachus.[5]

It is relatively easy to place the shemales of the Crockett Almanacs under the cloak of Athena, for they also function widely as protectors and, like Athena, when they battle, it is to defend their men or themselves. Rarely do they engage in offensive or aggressive warfare. All those in the "Battles with Humans" section, for example, are attacked, mistreated, or otherwise provoked into fighting. Though they do not initiate conflict, shemales are more than willing to brawl and batter in any no-holds-barred event. Take "Sal Fink, the Mississippi Screamer," for instance, who, when captured and carried off "by about fifty Indians . . . to Roast flesh Hollow," turned the tables on them when they were asleep by slipping her bonds and tying all their heels together around the campfire. Finally, "she, with a suddenachous jerk, that made the intire woods tremble, pulled the intire lot o' sleepin' redskins into that ar great fire, fast together" to make her escape and prove out the subtitle of this tale, "How She Cooked Injuns."(172)

Noted as well throughout the Almanac stories, and particularly in the section "Battles with Animals," these shemales obviously also inherited the qualities associated with Artemis, a child of Zeus and Leto and the twin of Apollo. She is the goddess of the hunt, a figure more at home roving the mountains and forests of Arcadia with her silver bow and pack of hunting hounds than residing on Olympus. Again, shemales are in one way a tad more subdued than goddesses. Although still protectresses, they very seldom set off on a hunt. Like Davy's wife, whose full name of Sally Ann Thunder Ann Whirlwind Crockett is revealed only once in the Almanacs, they defend their loved ones and themselves or retaliate against attacks or creatures that stalk them. In "An Evening Visiter," Sally Ann rescues Davy, as he says, when she grabs his rifle, Killdevil, "like a flash and fired it in time to save my life" from a "monstopolous grate wild cat."(152, 151) In "Perilous Adventure with a Black Bear," she helped to distract the rampaging beast from her husband when "she caught up a hickory rail, and as the bear rushed at her with his mouth wide open she ran it down his throat."[6](138)

Another parallel exists between classical mythology and shemale stories in that their narratives both generally restrict the choices of women. In myth, those who marry normally die or kill their husbands and children. Those who do not marry are either transformed and fixed in some aspect of their maiden state, like Daphne, who avoids Apollo's advances by becoming a laurel tree, or cross gender barriers, as in the case of Athena and Artemis, to act like men.[7] While it is a bit of a logical leap, most shemales further reflect the qualities of their two divine virginal forebears and likewise remain unmarried. Even those who do wed (Davy's wife, Sally Ann Thunder Ann Whirlwind Crockett again serving as the most notable example) evince comparatively little subservience to their mates and surrender only some of their freedom, individuality, and roaming life in the wilderness for home and hearth. They never fall victim to Alexis de Tocqueville's astute historical judgment that in nineteenth-century America "the independence of woman is irrecoverably lost in the bonds of matrimony."[8] As many of the tales of battles with men and beasts and even the "Courting Stories and Amorous Adventures" reveal, married shemales never give up the adventurous frontier lifestyle of their single sisters, and they remain in relatively the same status in the tales.

For many, the most evocative and enduring image of this Athena-Artemis-shemale is that of the warrior-woman race of the Amazons. The long-standing argument over whether the Amazons ever existed is perhaps less important than their even longer-standing appeal to the popular mind from the time of Homer to the present day. Disappearing as a race after the

fall of Troy, the Amazons are often discussed in ancient literature and represented in ancient art. The accounts of Homer, Herodotus, Strabo, Diodorus
Siculus, and Plutarch resonate with the same depictions of the battles of the
Greeks against the Amazons visualized in art in the Athenian Treasury at
Delphi and in the Parthenon.[9] Amazons are carved on the pediment of the
temple of Zeus at Olympia and appear as a near constant theme on vases and
in paintings and sculpture. Often they are shown in combat with Heracles
and by extension are linked again to Athena, his chief protector, whose
shield in the Parthenon also bears their image.[10] The Amazons worship Ares,
the god of war, and an early version of Artemis, and conduct a society in
which men serve only as domestic slaves; further, they kill, cripple, or banish
male children. These shunned offspring are reared by their fathers, the neighboring Gargarian men, with whom the Amazons have mated at random and
in the dark until pregnant to assure the continuation of their race. Two
months of each year are reserved for mating and, to enhance their desired
gene pool, only those warriors who have killed a man in battle can participate. Amazons are also superb equestrians and bare, sear, or remove one or
both breasts to improve their prowess with bow and spear.[11] The profile of
such a warrior is unique:

> The individual Amazon was an exquisite instrument of lethality,
> combining an inbred ridicule of male-oriented society with a craving
> for the exhilaration of battle. A pitiless slayer, she liked to kill from
> a distance with arrows that reached their mark before the victim saw
> them discharged, arrows that pinioned feet to the ground and hands
> to shield, and impaled torso, neck, and limbs. Even better, she liked
> to kill at short range with sword, spear, or *bipennis*, the famed Ama-
> zon double-edged ax.[12]

The Amazons are clearly an extreme version of the shemale, far more
extreme than one can find between the covers of a Crockett Almanac, even
though they share some characteristics. Shemales are fierce too, but mainly
because of their standard of comparison—the nineteenth-century sentimental norm for women. The key to their difference hearkens back to the protectress role of Athena. Like her and unlike the Amazons, the women of the
Almanacs seldom exhibit overt aggression and a preference for offensive warfare. They are a curious amalgam of male and female traits: curious because of
their comic tall-tale presentation and an amalgam for selectively sampling
the behavior of both sexes.

Another rough parallel exists between the intentional self-mutilation of the Amazons, albeit for purposes of warfare, and the "comic" mutilation of the riproarious shemales by the authors of those tales for the purposes of satire. These are sprinkled throughout the range of the stories and concentrated in the "Wild and Grotesque Description" section. The epitome of "comic" mutilation in the Crockett Almanacs is displayed in "Gum Swamp Breeding." Davy tells us why he was so smitten with her:

> This gal was named Jerusha Stubbs, and had only one eye, but that was pritty enough for two. . . . One of her legs was a little shorter than the other. . . . She had two cancers cut out of her breast, so that she was as flat as a board up and down there, which I couldn't have got over no how, only she had a beautiful grate hump on her back, and that made up for having nothing of the kind in front.

All this, together with boils, a harelip, and the fact that most of her teeth had rotted out, are all part of Jerusha's beauty for her backwoods beau. (109–110) Strikingly, in both instances, breasts are removed and symbolically and actually sever these women from perhaps their most feminine role—that of mother and nurturer. The positing of shemales as grotesques simultaneously separates them from the norms of civilization and seems to validate them as denizens of the wilderness in the imaginations of the writers.

Although their descriptions attract the most attention, the "grotesque" shemales usually engage as well in manlike adventures in their tales. In having these women step outside of their expected roles, the authors of the Almanacs join them to a historically long chain of women who are admired and even revered for their male qualities. The logical progression of heroic traits thus runs from goddesses like Athena and Artemis to queens and warrior queens, and to crusaders, women ready to die for their beliefs and desires. Even though such historical figures tend to be aristocratic by birth, action, or thought, and rather unlike those immersed in fiction and placed in the "classless" imaginative world of the American frontier, they often reveal the same "male" attributes that are exhibited by the shemales of the Almanacs and demonstrate a long-standing tradition of powerful women who often act as men but retain their femininity. The authors of the tales (and perhaps some of the readers) were conversant enough with both classical literature and myth, particularly the patterns the life of an epic hero would follow, to have Crockett reenact the role of Prometheus in one of his adventures. They were likewise familiar with the lives of many of these great women of history, especially those who were associated with Western European culture. They had available to them Samuel Knapp's *Female Biography* (1833), for example, which featured sections on Cleopatra, Boadicea (Boudica), Joan of Arc, Isabella of Castille, Maria Theresa, and Catherine the Great, among others.[13] The Almanac authors appear, in fact, to draw upon a general sense of the power and malelike behavior of these queens and warriors as indirect support for the existence of shemales. Add in a dash of frontier savagery and pepper with nineteenth-century preconceptions about proper roles for women, and the proper recipe for the present tales results.

In sampling the stories of well-known queens, rulers who often direct wars and battles but do not actually fight in them, one can certainly begin with the Old Testament and the story of Esther from the fifth century B.C.[14] As a queen, she successfully overcomes her fear to intercede with her husband, Ahasuerus (Xerxes I), king of Persia, to stop the slaughter of the Jews. Haman, the enemy of Esther's cousin and adoptive father, Mordecai, issued an edict that the king had signed. Using her wiles to reveal Haman's plot, Esther finally identifies herself as a Jew and convinces her husband to issue another edict allowing her people to arm themselves, since under Persian law the king's edicts could not be revoked. She is somewhat less fearful and less feminine when she asks the king to have the bodies of Haman's ten sons publicly hanged (Esther 9:13). Clearly, Esther's role of protectress links her to Athena. Although the authenticity of her story has no corroborating historical evidence outside of the Old Testament, her heroism and the victory of her people are still celebrated throughout the Jewish world with the feast of Purim.

Other such notable pre-nineteenth-century queens range from Cleopatra (69 B.C.–30 B.C.) to Catherine the Great (1729–96); they exhibit extraordinary qualities of leadership and innovation in matters of state, traits that, though dominant, never erase their feminine nature. The democratic norms of the nineteenth-century American frontier keep shemales from such positions of leadership. Just like their male counterparts, for the most part these women operate as rugged individualists in their adventures and give no hint of interest in statecraft.

You find no one like Cleopatra, for example, a woman whose vaulting political ambition to keep the Egyptian dynasty of the Ptolemies independent of Rome is sometimes eclipsed by the tales of her legendary beauty (which Plutarch disputes). Likewise, her rise to power and military engagements are less well known than the stories of her suicide, her choosing death by poison or the bite of an asp before humiliation in Rome at the hands of

Octavian, the victor over her forces and those of Marc Antony at the naval battle of Actium (31 B.C.).

A ruler-queen often acts on an international scale, one far beyond the scope of the frontier Almanac women, whose boundaries for behavior, whether they seek to break these constraints or not, are drawn by the sentimental norms of the day. Activity and independence, action rather than ultimate global influence, allows these queens to reach out a hand to the Almanac shemales.

Certainly one such independent female monarch is Eleanor of Aquitaine (1122–1204). Her life as the "grandmother of Europe," Queen of France, Queen of England, mother of two kings of England, Richard the Lion-Hearted and John, is as politically significant and active as it is long. But in addition to accompanying her first husband, King Louis VII of France, on the Second Crusade, fomenting an unsuccessful rebellion with her sons against her second husband, King Henry II of England, surviving fifteen years of confinement until Henry's death, arranging Richard's marriage, governing while he fought in the Crusades and putting down John's rebellion, ransoming Richard from Austria, and supporting John as king after Richard's death, Eleanor is also known for her beauty, love of learning, and patronage of culture. The brief period from when she left Henry because of his many open love affairs and returned to her palace at Poitiers in Aquitaine in 1169, until her confinement in 1174 for her part in the rebellion against him, fostered a courtly tradition of respect and equality or superiority for women and the installing of courtesy and manners as ideals for knights. She commissioned a guidebook on the proper courting of a lady and encouraged Chrétien de Troyes to find the source of his poetic inspiration in the story of King Arthur and the knights of the Round Table. Versions of all these concepts undergird the conception of and "proper" or civilized treatment of women in the nineteenth century and are oftentimes ruthlessly parodied in the Crockett Almanacs, especially in the tales in the "Courting Stories and Amorous Adventures" section of this book.

Several parallels exist between Eleanor and her contemporary, Queen Tamara, who was given the title of "Mountain of God" by her father when he appointed her co-ruler in 1178. Tamara's military campaigns extended the boundaries of her land and secured the independence of the feudal kingdom of Georgia from the Turks. She ruled from 1184 to 1212 and, like Eleanor, inspired a renaissance in arts and letters, a golden age in Georgia that lasted until the followers of Genghis Khan destroyed the capital of Tiflis (now Tbilisi) in 1236.

The fame of Queen Isabella I of Spain (1451–1504), so firmly connected with her sponsorship of the voyages of Columbus, also finds its root in military campaigns. After the union of her kingdom of Castille with that of Aragon by her marriage to Ferdinand, her belief in her divinely inspired mission to end Muslim rule in their last strongholds on the Iberian peninsula culminated in her defeat of the kingdom of Granada and capture of the Alhambra from Boabdil, the last of the caliphs, in January 1492. Also like Eleanor and Tamara, Isabella was described as beautiful. Unlike these two earlier queens, however, Isabella and Ferdinand closed rather than opened a renaissance. To assert Roman Catholicism as the one true faith, these monarchs required nonbelievers to convert or be expelled. Many of the leading intellectuals, public servants, and artisans of Granada were Muslims and Jews. Nearly all the Jews refused conversion and began to leave Spain immediately. An edict in 1501 offered Muslims the same choice. Suspicion of those who remained as recent converts or who had turned to Catholicism over the past few centuries led to the reintroduction of the Inquisition, ostensibly to determine their religious loyalty, but realistically it was also a process used to strip them of property, wealth, and because of racial difference, their lives.

With the fall of Granada and the end of her military crusade, Isabella now had freed the funds necessary to back a highly speculative venture—Columbus's voyage to the Indies. Constant to the end, she did so in hopes of great wealth and of converting a new people to the Catholic faith. Columbus and Isabella both died in 1504—he firmly believing that he had found the Orient, and she, regretting the enslaving of the people Columbus had discovered, insisting in her last official act that they be treated fairly as people with souls. Unfortunately, the act had no real effect. This sequence of entrenched racism toward Native Americans appears as a staple of much nineteenth-century popular literature of the frontier and is redefined and reenacted in a few of the Almanac stories.

As "Good Queen Bess," Elizabeth I of England (1533–1603) also dealt with the commingled religious and political turmoil. Elizabeth had Parliament pass laws to establish the Church of England as the official church and eventually executed her cousin Mary, queen of Scots, eliminating the chance of a Catholic line succeeding to the throne, a threat effectively ended with the defeat of the Spanish Armada the next year, in 1588. She supported American colonization, both the efforts of Sir Walter Ralegh in his two Roanoke colonies and that of the Virginia Company, who named their colony after the then-deceased Virgin Queen. Likewise, she covertly encouraged her "sea dogs"—Sir Francis Drake and John Hawkins, among others—in their privateering and pillaging along the Spanish Main. All this was balanced during the Age of Elizabeth by a flowering in the science, arts, and particularly in literature through the work of John Donne, Edmund Spenser, Ben Jonson, Christopher Marlowe, and of course, William Shakespeare.

The eighteenth century saw the rise of two powerful empresses in Europe—Maria Theresa of Austria (1717–1780) and Catherine the Great of Russia (1729–1796). Both were affected by the ideas of the Enlightenment and did much to bring their peoples out of a feudal system by instituting legal and economic reforms, reorganizing political administration, and extending and improving education and medical care. Both defended and increased their huge, multinational empires and ruled them successfully. Personally, despite their support of the arts, they were quite different. Patron of the music of Haydn, Mozart, and Beethoven, mother of sixteen children, and capable of great tact and compassion, Maria Theresa, like Elizabeth I, was seen as a mother to her country. Catherine the Great was a fine horsewoman and hunter, a well-versed scholar who became famous throughout Europe for her description of an ideal government in a work she called her *Great Instruction* and who published school textbooks, including her own *Primer for Youth*, wrote for the theater and the opera, subsidized the translation of foreign books, and made St. Petersburg, and especially the Hermitage palace, a cultural center.

In their mastering of male-dominated roles, many of these queens foreshadow the shemales of the Crockett Almanacs. The grand scale of their far-ranging actions and their "feminine" side, often witnessed through their intellectual endeavors and achievements, however, place them apart from the Almanac women. These queens rule—and rule men—but they do not personally engage in battles. Their achievements come more from mental prowess, political agility, and organizational skills than from individual action. It is another group, the warrior queens and crusaders, that brings the historic parallel one step closer to the imagined American frontier shemales of the nineteenth century by actively participating in combat.

The period from the Old Testament to the time of the Almanacs again yields a memorable sample of such extraordinary warrior women. Chapter 5 of the book of Judges records "The Song of Deborah," in which she rallies the tribes of Israel to defeat Sisera, the Canaanite commander, by instructing Barak to raise ten thousand men to march against the enemy and accompanying them into battle (c. 1150 B.C.). Her "Song" also records the more active role of Jael, the wife of Heber, who kills the fleeing Sisera when he sleeps by driving a tent peg through his head.

Ancient Irish literature tells of the long and ultimately unsuccessful war that Medb (Maeve), the queen of western Ireland, fought about the time of the birth of Christ against the province of Ulster and its hero, Cuchulainn. He, perhaps ironically, had learned his martial skills from the woman warrior Scathach on the Isle of Skye and honed them in his training through combat with Aife, "the hardest woman warrior in the world." While the story of Medb's bloody aggression and guile echoes that of Athena-Artemis and perhaps the Amazons, also of interest is the way in which the conflict begins. *The Tain*, the Celtic cycle that is the source for this struggle, commences with a verbal battle of boasts, a "flyting" in literary terms, between Medb and Ailill, her husband, over superiority. While in bed engaging in their "pillow talk," they dispute the primacy of their lineage, their wisdom, generosity in gift giving, ability in combat, number of troops under their personal disposal, provinces under individual command, and even offers of marriage and wedding presents, until Ailill is so angered that he challenges Medb to prove her claims of greater wealth. They jump from bed and begin an inventory of possessions, with Medb finally admitting that the finest bull had joined Ailill's herd after refusing to be led by a woman. She then determines to best her husband by securing the finest bull in Ireland, the Brown Bull of Ulster, thus beginning the contest with Cuchulainn.[15]

In England, the reason for Boudica's ascendancy to the status of warrior queen has, to modern readers, a less frivolous origin than a battle of egos. A Briton of the royal house, this widow of King Prasutagus of the Iceni raised a mighty rebellion in 60 A.D. against the Roman emperor Nero after he annexed all the family's lands, ignoring the terms of Prasutagus's will, and after she and her daughters were tortured and assaulted by Roman soldiers and her tribesmen enslaved. Mounting a force estimated between 100,000 and 120,000 men, women, and children, Boudica destroyed Camulodunum (Colchester), laid waste to Londinium (London), and burned Veralamium (St. Albans), killing some 70,000 people. In the subsequent battle against the Roman legions under Suetonius, the governor of the province, 80,000 Britons were killed, and Boudica poisoned herself to avoid capture.[16]

Zenobia (Septima Bat Zabbai), queen of Palmyra (a city in present-day Syria), is another warrior widow who fought against Rome, not because of any personal wrong done to her but from a desire for power. A huntress who preferred horses to chariots, she declared herself queen rather than rule as her son's regent and extended her sovereignty and control of major trade routes by conquering most of Egypt, Syria, and Asia Minor as far as the Bosporus Strait by 270 A.D. A counterattack by the Emperor Aurelian eliminated these gains, and Zenobia was captured while fleeing the siege of Palmyra. He set her free, however, and after marrying a Roman senator, Zenobia lived out the rest of her life in luxury in Tibur (Tivoli) in a villa near that of Hadrian.[17]

Although not a queen, Joan of Arc (1412–1431) would be hard to exclude from any survey, however brief, of warrior women. The story of the patron saint of France whose military achievements as a "knight" reversed her country's fate in the Hundred Years' War is well known. It is recorded pictorially as well on ten beautiful stained-glass windows in the Cathedral of the Holy Cross in Orléans. Her religious visions instructed her to free that city and to liberate Rheims so that the Dauphin Charles could rightfully claim his throne; likewise, her faith allowed her to withstand imprisonment, a year of interrogation, and being burned at the stake as a heretic in Rouen by the English.[18] In part, Joan's power to lead derived from her virginity, her "marriage" to her country, echoing that of Tamara and Elizabeth I, and paralleled her devotion to God. Her purity through manlessness parallels many shemales of the Crockett Almanacs and also reflects reasonably similar states of the widowed warrior queens Boudica and Zenobia, that of the Amazons, and that of Catalina de Erauso, Queen Jinga, and Maria Augustin.

Probably the least known of these women, but one who led an extraordinary life, was Catalina de Erauso. Shortly before she was to take her vows as a nun, this young Basque novitiate escaped her convent, cut her hair, dressed as a man, and set out in 1603 to South America and the life of a conquistador. After twenty years of fighting, pillaging, and committing approximately a dozen murders, and now pursued by cutthroats, she took sanctuary with a bishop, confessed her exploits in summary by stating that she had "hustled, killed, maimed, wreaked havoc, and roamed about," and became a celebrity. On her return to Europe in 1624, the king of Spain granted her a pension and, perhaps since as part of her confession she had been examined by the Church and pronounced a virgin, the pope granted her his blessing and allowed her to continue to dress as a man. Six years later, she returned to the New World but escaped any further mention in the ledger of history.[19]

Queen Jinga Mbandi (variously spelled Nzinga, Zhinga) of Angola (c. 1580–1663) was manless only in the fact that there was no longer a king of the Ndongo when she proclaimed herself queen. She may have killed her brother to secure her title. She kept a harem of fifty or sixty young men, who in turn could take as many wives as they pleased so long as they killed all their offspring. She also dressed her favorites as women to pass freely among the women of her household. Jinga herself customarily dressed as a man in animal skins and, when practicing ritual sacrifice and drinking the blood of her victim, an act designed to solidify her alliance with the fierce cannibalistic tribe of the Jagas, she also went about armed with sword, axe, and bow and arrows for the ceremony. Although ultimately unsuccessful in her war against the Portuguese for control of the slave trade that supplied the Brazilian plantations and mines, she did win major victories in 1643, 1647, and 1648 after her further alliance with other tribal kingdoms and with the Dutch.[20] Her intelligence in establishing a pan-kingdom alliance and her bravery in fighting the forces of colonization in Angola made her both a national hero and a fit example for a nineteenth-century American abolitionist to cite regarding the ability and equality of African-American slaves. While Lydia Maria Child noted Jinga's despotism and murderous acts ("her character is stained with numerous acts of ferocity and crime"), her main points are clear: "History furnishes few instances of bravery, intelligence, and perseverance, equal to the famous Zhinga [Jinga]" and "her great abilities cannot for a moment be doubted."[21]

From 1808 to 1814, Napoleon's campaigns on the Iberian peninsula led to the rise and fame of the Spanish Joan of Arc, Maria Augustin (1786–1857), also known as the Maid of Saragossa or La Saragossa. When Bonaparte reneged on his bargain to divide a Portugal conquered with Spanish help and then attacked his former ally, he quickly succeeded in capturing Madrid. This act, however, together with his treacherous behavior, soon brought the Spanish people to revolt. One principal target of Napoleon's counterattack was the fortress of Saragossa. Eighteen-year-old Maria Augustin was bringing food to the fortress and found the soldiers abandoning their positions. She inspired them back to their duty by taking the match from the hand of a dead artilleryman, announcing that she would not leave until the French had been defeated, and firing off the cannon. She stayed in the heat of the battle for two months, rescuing the wounded and nursing the sick and disabled, until Napoleon's forces retreated. Like Joan of Arc, La Saragossa's devotion to her country made her an emblem of fierce national pride for future generations and was soon enshrined in the paintings of Goya and even in Byron's "Childe Harold's Pilgrimage."[22]

While some of these historical vignettes of women are tinged with, and in some cases enveloped by, myth, other forebears of the riproarious shemales of the Crockett Almanacs spring from the imagination and are recorded in literary fiction and folklore. They may stem from an archetype of the wild woman, from examples similar to those already discussed, or from combinations of the imaginary and the real. All tend to maintain the dual or twin nature of women who are cast as nurturers and procreators by virtue of their sex but whose actions place them within the traditional role of men in Western culture. This paradoxical union is perhaps most evident in ruthless behavior. Before Queen Margaret stabs the duke of York to death in Shakespeare's *Henry VI, Part III,* the duke gives eloquent voice and perhaps a reaction typical of the time to what he perceives as the "unnaturalness" of her behavior: "Women are soft, mild, pitiful, and flexible—/Thou, stern, obdurate, flinty, rough, remorseless" (I, iv, 141–42).

In the realm of literature, chief among the few eclectically chosen representatives who flesh out and complicate this category is Chaucer's Wife of Bath, a character who herself has more ancient roots.[23] Although in her energetic pilgrimages the Wife has no adventures comparable to the brawling and killing in which shemales revel, she is comparably more assertive in the structure of her text in that she herself is a narrator who tells her tale which, on the most basic level, focuses on her heroine's demand for sovereignty in marriage over her husband. Shemales never rule or abuse their husbands, rarely tell their own story, as the Wife does in her "Prologue," and almost never assume the controlling role of narrator in the Almanacs. Both the Wife and the shemales in the "Wild and Grotesque Description" section of this book, however, are at least in part the object of point-blank humor directed at their appearance, which diverges enough from ideals of feminine beauty to hearken back to the ancient satire directed at crones, hags, and assertive women. Recall, for example, the grotesque description of Jerusha Stubbs in the Almanacs. Similarly regarded as low or common characters and fit subjects for comedy, shemales act in an audacious and forthright manner whether the issue is domestic or sexual, behavior whose incongruity with the standards of the day leads to hilarious results.

Cumulatively, the Almanac tales set up, satirize, and invert these standards for comic effect. In "Crockett's Double-Breasted Gal-lantry" in the "Sentimental and Religious Stories" section of this volume, Davy pours forth his backwoods version of the romantic, sentimental role of women and especially mothers in the nineteenth century as an ideal object of veneration: "My mother was a woman, an' so is my sister when she gets to be a mother, an' if she don't be a mother, then she ain't no woman. Well, women are Margaret-nificent creeturs—tha're angels without feathers: the werry sugar maple jelly o' creation, an' whenever I see them scandalized, or insulted, then the volcano o' my galantry begins to rumble for overwhelmen eruption."(257) Yet rather than reinforce the norm, shemales are anything but passive and bound to their home. Davy's introductory description of his niece, Nance Bowers, in the "Battles with Animals" section is a case in point and, although less of a grotesque than Jerusha Stubbs, she is framed as a type of elemental earth god-dess run wild. Nance "war about as fair a sample of full grown female flesh, as ever flourished outside of the garden of Eden; she war seven feet tall out of her stockins, and hair comb. She could outscream a thunderbolt, outscream a dozen wild-cats, wipe her feet with her hair, swing on the top of a fifty foot hickory tree, and eat more wild cat steaks raw, than any other livin critter in creation." Where others might fall back on the stereotype of the caustic, sharp-tongued woman for an easy laugh, the authors have Uncle Davy imme-diately go on with a deft comic touch of inversion and light grotesque to praise Nance's mouth: "She had one of the most universally useful mouths in her face that ever fell to the head of humanity; she could eat victuals with one corner, whistle with the other, an scream with the middle; she could grin with her upper lip, and frown all sorts of temptation with the under one."(148) Inversion complete.

There are, of course, many other literary treatments of women who, unlike the Wife of Bath, are as warriorlike as Nance Bowers proves later in her tale. One could make the case for an entire subgenre of such Amazonian texts, but a few wide-ranging examples may suffice. Among the warrior tales of Japan is the nearly unique and striking account of Tomoe (Tomoe Gozen) in a battle in 1183 and set down in the *Heike Monogatari*, a work whose com-position dates approximately from the early thirteenth century. Tomoe is one of a small minority of *onna-musha* (warrior women) and perhaps the most famous. Her beautiful face, long hair, and white skin make for a vivid image, since description in these tales usually focuses upon weaponry and armor. An expert horsewoman who rides untamed horses over rough terrain, Tomoe is ordered to leave the side of her Lord Kiso, who anticipates defeat and does not wish the further disgrace of having a woman participate in his final bat-tle. Her relation to her master is paradoxical. She is introduced as his servant but then labeled his leading commander in battle. Tomoe reluctantly obeys Lord Kiso, but before leaving, she spurs her horse forward into the enemy's ranks, engages one of their finest male warriors in individual combat, decapi-tates him, and tosses his head away, then removes her armor and heads toward the eastern provinces.[24]

A similar exit is the fate of Gurdafrid (or Gordafarid), the warrior maid in *Sohrab and Rostam*, a portion of the Persian national epic, the *Shahname* of Abol-Qasem Ferdowsi of the late tenth century. Although the main conflict between Sohrab and his father, Rostam, proceeds because they cannot recog-nize each other, the story of Gurdafrid introduces the theme of disguise.

After young Sohrab defeats and captures Hojir, the peerless warrior and keeper of the White fortress, Gurdafrid dresses in armor, hides her hair beneath a helmet, and rides forth on a battle steed to avenge their honor. Sohrab accepts her challenge but is at first unable to defend himself from the hail of arrows flying from her bow, a tactic reminiscent of the Amazons. He unseats her with a lance and throws her to the ground in a rage. She shatters his lance with her sword, but, feeling that victory is beyond her reach, mounts her horse and speeds back to the fortress. Sohrab follows, but when he captures her, she snatches off her helmet and he sees that this new champion is a woman. Gurdafrid guilefully plays upon his astonishment and shame to escape into the fortress she has previously promised to surrender, but when he returns the next day to attack the stronghold, Gurdafrid and all the inhabitants have fled through an underground passage, escaping as well from further mention in the tale.[25]

The Scandinavian legend of Brynhild is a classic warrior-woman tale that is recorded most fully in the *Volsunga Saga* and normally referred to as the legend of Sigurd (or Siegfried, in the German *Niebelungenlied*). Since Brynhild has slain Odin's favorite, Hjálm-Gunnarr, she is condemned to marry, a state that is the antithesis of her warlike existence, and she swears an oath to marry only a man who knows no fear. Sigurd is smitten with her beauty and successfully woos her and gets her with child. In the German variants of the legend, Brynhild's supernatural strength is assured only through her virginity, the same link between martial prowess and maidenhood that is evinced in so many stories, including those of the riproarious shemales. Through prophecy, fate, and then deception on Sigurd's part, they marry others. When Brynhild learns of Sigurd's trickery, she plots to have him killed. Her love-hate relationship with him culminates first in her successful revenge, which reclaims her honor, and next in her grief-stricken suicide, a merger of heroic and romantic themes that casts her as the triumphant victim.[26]

Two other examples are contained in the epic poetry of Western culture. Female knights provide readers with one of the fiercest battles in Edmund Spenser's *The Fairie Queene* as they fight over a man. The Amazon-like Radigund has imprisoned Artegall, the lover of Britomart, the virtuous female warrior. In an extension of what Spenser portrays as gender chaos, Radigund's city is ruled by women and she dresses all her male prisoners in women's clothes to further demean them.[27] On an allegorical level, justice, the order of society itself, is held hostage by lust and can be freed only through the triumph of chastity. A man as the captive prize is the similar plot of Ludovico

Ariosto's sixteenth-century poem *Orlando Furioso*. Bradamant, the niece of Charlemagne, lovely and the bravest of female knights, successfully battles Atlantes, a powerful magician, to claim the foretold love of his imprisoned adopted son, Rogero, who eventually becomes the king of Bulgaria.[28] The theme is also adopted in "A Love Fight" in the "Battles with Humans" section of the Almanac tales. Here Crockett's seagoing sidekick, Ben Harding, is the prize in a knockdown, drag-out brawl between two Cuban women in a story that is liberally ornamented with nautical metaphors. Operating a bit further down the social scale than female knights, these women cumulatively lose clothes, one nipple, one eye, and half a nose in the fray.(178–79)

Another now-famous woman warrior, due to the Walt Disney Studio's production of the film *Mulan*, Hua Mu Lan is one in a long literal tradition of "clothes make the man" stories. As recorded in a Chinese poem (ca. 960–1279), Hua Mu Lan's story is one of family honor, disguise, and heroism. She goes to fight an enemy invasion to fulfill the edict of the emperor that each family send a male into battle. Dressing like a man, Hua Mu Lan goes to war to save her elderly father from certain death. Over the next ten years, she helps win many battles and returns home to great acclaim with the rank of a general.[29] From India comes the tale of Ajít, a Paul Bunyan–like young woman of gargantuan appetite who is strong enough to sweep a dead elephant out the door without effort, carry her house upon her head, and toss three tied-together elephants on the roof of the Raja's palace. When the Raja attempts to kill her out of fear, she simply stuffs him, his troops, and their weapons under her arm, imprisons them, and makes herself the rani, or woman ruler, of his kingdom.[30]

Also worthy of note are the women warriors in disguise who appear with reasonable regularity in Anglo-American balladry in the seventeenth and eighteenth centuries. This character is often a male-female double and garnishes the best of both gender worlds. She is further significant in that the ballads' point of view is that she not only can but should play the role of a man. The ballad "Mary Ambree" illustrates all these points. Possibly written by one "Elderton," and related in part to events in the 1580s, "Mary Ambree" was a "hit" for two hundred years and is still occasionally collected today.[31]

When Mary's "own true love," her "brave Serjeant Major," is killed in line nine of a two-hundred-line version of the ballad, she swears revenge upon the enemies of England, dons a man's clothes, and arms herself for battle. The verse before she is betrayed by one of her own men and dispatches him for his villainy ("she slasht him in three") encapsulates her prowess:

> The skie she then filled with smoak of her shot
> And her enimies bodies with bullets most hot
> For one of her owne men a score killed she
> Was not this a brave bonny Lasse, Mary Ambree?

Clearly related to the Crockett Almanac shemales by activity and class, Mary Ambree likewise plays with gender roles. Like the historical Catalina de Erauso in disguise and adventures, when she finally has no hope of escaping capture, Mary also does not hesitate to reveal her womanhood now that it is to her advantage and becomes "a poore bonny Lasse" to escape her fate as a man. Far from rebuking her, her enemies praise her manly valor, and love reemerges as a theme when the prince of Parma seeks to marry her. She spurns him for his impudence, an act that intensifies the original theme of true love with which the ballad begins.[32] In some ways these ballad heroines revisit the merging of heroic and romantic strains in Brynhild but escape her tragic end.

While all these general parallels document the existence of a long and varied tradition of shemales, one of the most important precursors and influences upon the depiction of women in the Crockett Almanacs may come from Indian captivity narratives. Many of the stories within this genre are told by or are about women, deal with their adventures in the wilderness, and are particularly popular in the first half of the nineteenth century, though the dates of their publication range from the late seventeenth through the beginning of the twentieth century. They tend to yield up several categories of women, two of which—the suffering victim and the woman turned warrior—are of particular interest. Both are well established and quite popular before the publication of the Almanacs begins, and each gives voice to respective traits that the women in Crockett's stories also evince—endurance and violence.[33]

Mary Rowlandson's *The Sovereignty and Goodness of God, Together with the Faithfulness of His Promises Displayed, Being a Narrative of the Captivity and Restoration of Mrs. Mary Rowlandson* (1682) is the first Puritan Indian captivity narrative and establishes the archetype of the suffering female as victim. Extraordinarily popular, going through four editions in 1682 alone, it was intended originally to explain why God chose her, the minister's wife and most prominent woman in her community of Lancaster, Massachusetts, to undergo such an ordeal, to present her as a moral model and touchstone whom others could use in their times of trial, and to use her as a warning to the community not to stray from the Puritan faith. All this is made clear through the "Preface" by the unknown "Per Amicum" (By a Friend) and the sermon "The Possibility of God's Forsaking a People . . . ," by her husband Joseph, which bracket the narrative proper. When these framing pieces are discarded by Revolutionary-era publishers, the sufferings and harrowing experiences of Mary Rowlandson are further highlighted and audiences likely more titillated than religiously enlightened. The tendency to popularize the text began, in fact, with a London edition of 1682, which changed the title to *A True History of the Captivity and Restoration of Mrs. Mary Rowlandson. . . .*[34]

Hers is one of the best personal accounts of Metacom's (or King Philip's) War of 1675–76, a savage conflict in which approximately five thousand Native Americans and five hundred English were killed, or 40 and 5 percent of their respective populations.[35] Rowlandson's captivity began February 20, 1676, when her garrison house was attacked in part of a larger raid upon the town of Lancaster. Bringing flax and hemp from Rowlandson's own barn, the war party set the house on fire. Given Rowlandson's vivid descriptions of the grisly scene, her narrative was destined for best-seller status:

> Some in our House were fighting for their Lives, others wallowing in their blood; the House on fire over our heads, and the bloody Heathen ready to knock us on the Head if we stirred out. . . . But out we must go, the Fire increasing, and coming along behind us roaring, and the *Indians* gaping before us with their Guns, Spears, and Hatchets, to devour us. . . . There was one who was chopp'd into the Head with a Hatchet, and stripp'd naked, and yet was crawling up and down. It is a solemn Sight to see so many Christians lying in their Blood, some here, and some there, like a company of Sheep torn by Wolves. All of them stript naked by a company of hell-hounds, roaring, singing, ranting and insulting, as if they would have torn our very hearts out. . . .[36]

Twelve of the house were killed, one escaped, and Rowlandson, her three children, and twenty of her relatives and neighbors were taken hostage. During her captivity, she recovered from a bullet wound, watched her infant daughter wounded by the same bullet die in her arms, became a slave, and was regularly abused by her mistress, Weetamoo, the "squaw sachem" of the Pocassets, in part because Rowlandson could not comprehend the idea of a matrilineal society and did not show Weetamoo the proper respect. Rowlandson inhabited the lowest rung of a culture that was completely alien to her as her captors moved her from one village to another for a total of twenty "removes," as she termed them. Sustained by her faith and a tenacious will, this survivor and suffering captive was eventually ransomed for the price of twenty pounds on May 2, 1676, at Princeton, Massachusetts.

The other category of Indian captivity narratives that foregrounds the shemales of the Crockett Almanacs, that of the woman turned warrior, finds its earliest version in Cotton Mather's retelling of the exploits of Hannah Dustan.[37] A further parallel to the shemales exists in that Dustan does not tell her own story and it consequently lacks some of the immediacy of Rowlandson's tale. Deeds, not narrative style, ensure Dustan's fame. Along with thirty-eight other people, she was captured on March 15, 1697, in an attack on Haverill, Massachusetts, that was likely encouraged by the French bounty offered for English prisoners and scalps. Her husband managed to rescue seven of their children, but the forty-year-old Dustan, still recovering from giving birth about one week earlier, her infant, and her nurse were taken. The Abenaki Indians almost immediately "dash'd out the Brains of the *Infant* against a Tree" and began a trek of nearly 150 miles in the next few days. Given to an Indian family of "Two Stout Men, Three Women, and Seven Children," Dustan learned that she, the nurse (Mary Neff), and an earlier captive, an English boy named Samuel Leonardson, would soon "be Stript, and Scourg'd, and Run the *Gantlet* [gauntlet] through the whole Army of *Indians.*" On April 30, while their captors were sleeping, Dustan roused Neff and Leonardson, grabbed some hatchets, and together they murdered ten of the twelve Indians, one boy and a wounded squaw escaping their vengeance. And "cutting off the *Scalps* of the *Ten Wretches*, they came off, and received *Fifty Pounds* from the General Assembly of the Province, as a Recompense of their Action."[38]

As Dustan is transformed from the suffering victim at the outset of her narrative to the avenging warrior and mercenary at its conclusion, her tale echoes, illustrates, and supports the tradition of Indian hating common to the Crockett Almanacs and many other inexpensive popular texts. As distasteful as they prove today, and far older than that of Columbus and Isabella, ethnocentrism and overt racism are norms and a source of much humor for the authors and then-contemporary readers of the Almanacs. Attacking the romantic ideal of the "Noble Savage" in "The Indian and Crockett's Grandmother," for example, the Almanacs' authors have their fictional Davy regale those other authors and people who believe such fanciful notions: "Arter all their boastifferous spoutin, preachin, lecterin an song makin, about the splendifferosity o' the injun character, its all a full blown up bladder o' humbug, for as nigger will be nigger, so injun will be injun, the tar-nal head cutter, blood drinken, rum drinkin, humanity cookin varmints."(164) All nonwhites in the Almanacs are often lumped together as a bestial sub-species whose link to humanity is judged extremely doubtful.[39]

The opposing tradition, the concept of the noble savage, is in the minority in the Almanac tales but championed in the novels of James Fenimore Cooper. In *The Last of the Mohicans* (1826), the nobility of Chingachgook and Uncas dominate the plot; their enemy, Magua, has no nobility because he has adopted the deceitful ways of the white man. In general in the Almanacs, the reverse is true: an Indian's goodness increases proportionally to his whiteness. Interest-ingly in Dustan's case, her reputation is revised in the hands of nineteenth-century authors, who see her "Indian" behavior in the same negative light as Magua's "white" behavior. John Greenleaf Whittier, Nathaniel Hawthorne, and Henry David Thoreau condemn Dustan's murderous act and she, rather than the Indians, is cast as the villain of the incident.[40]

Perhaps one of the finest Almanac examples of the humanity of Indians occurs in "Indian Notions." Crockett begins by condemning the race as "all a pesky set of hethens" in general and says of the "hansum yung injun" brave whom he convinces to tell his story "that if he had had a white skin instead of a red one I might ha' kinder half beleeved what he said." However, after hearing of the death of his wife and two of his three young children and his heartrending trip to the spirit world where he saw them again but could not touch them, Crockett is overcome with emotion and empathy: "Davy Krockitt is none of your whimperers, but if I didn't drop tears as big as a bul-let, I hope I may be shot."(253–55)

No matter what judgment is passed on these fictional views attributed to Crockett or on the historical Hannah Dustan, his notions of Indians and her heroism or heinousness stem from a perceived or actual immersion in the wilderness itself, an experience that is as powerful as it is transforming. Sur-vivors like Rowlandson and especially conquerors like Dustan are significantly changed. So is Mary Jemison (Dehgewanus), who undergoes a complete trans-formation. Her captivity narrative (1824) chronicles both her life among the Senecas and her refusal to return to a white society that places more restric-tions upon women than does her tribe and would ostracize her and her chil-dren.[41] The strength drawn forth from these women by their captivities is the same strength celebrated in the shemale stories of the Almanacs. Such power is derived from the notion of the wilderness as a place of absolute freedom, a place where women can act as the equals of men and do so with impunity. Such actions challenge culturally established gender divisions and generate fear on several levels. There is the fear of the wilderness and its savagery as almost a gravitational force, exerting a pull that represents the dark side of a Romantic return to nature. The wilderness is not just a place for revitalization but possibly also of a consuming conversion that can produce the most subversive of all individuals, the white Indian. Termed racial turncoats, Jemison and, a year earlier in 1823, Daniel Boone were condemned for turning their backs on civilization and preferring the company of savages.[42] The threat of such women in the history and fiction of antebellum America to the cultural status quo far exceeded that of men, because women were the defining factor of civilization itself. On one level, the riproarious shemales of the Crockett Almanacs had to be satirized to undercut the threat that they posed to society by acting as men. The individual power that they and other fictional and historical figures gain from their immersion in the wilderness comes at the expense of their standard gender role; they shed femininity and hence vulnerability to survive in an essentially male environment. To remain free and unrestricted, they become the literal antithesis of civilization.[43]

Given the rise of women's movements in the political, social, and religious arenas during the same time period, the idea of frontier freedom, assertiveness, and even aggression fostered collateral fears that such behavior might not be limited to the confines of the wilderness and could challenge the basic fabric of a male-dominated society. The authors of the Crockett Almanacs often allay such fears and forestall such transboundary identification through a satire that defeminizes the appearance of the shemales while keeping a semblance of the gender roles intact. On a covert level, they thus parody the "New Woman" of the nineteenth century while building on the ancient stereotypes of shrew or savior to produce humor that far exceeds the contemporary situational set pieces of the nagging wife and daughter-as-mother whom Washington Irving uses to begin and resolve the story of Rip Van Winkle. They are closer to Tom Walker's strong wife, in Irving's "The Devil and Tom Walker," who lost her life by putting the lie to the old saying that "a female scold is generally considered a match for the devil." But after viewing the mayhem of the battleground, Tom exclaimed "'Egad . . . Old Scratch must have had a tough time of it!'"[44] Still, Mrs. Walker is strictly typecast and is a secondary character; shemales are far more than bit players or stereotypes in the imaginary world of the Almanacs. Ferocious and domestic, religious and sensual, in their outlandish adventures they break traditional boundaries with gleeful abandon. That they often wreak havoc with attempts at categorization is fitting, given the course of history and the emerging role of women in the antebellum era.

## CONTEMPORARIES

The Age of Jackson is both chronologically and intellectually central to the understanding of the place of nineteenth-century women in American history and popular culture before the Civil War. The period itself, even before the spotlight turns to women as a focus, is complex, varied, and at times tumultuous. Debate over the nature of the great political experiment of the United States, the rise of the power and influence of the West in the wake of Jefferson's Louisiana Purchase of 1803 and consequent elevation of the common man as the democratic ideal, the contention between the federal government and those of the states, reform movements, profound changes in the economy through increasing industrialization, a revolution in transportation, an emphasis upon internal development and isolationism versus the idea of the country as the highpoint of Western civilization and a model for the world, and a general optimistic feeling that progress is inevitable given the enterprising "go-ahead-itiveness" of the American people are the often-heralded developments that are cited as fundamental to the present-day configuration of America. The era has also been more recently examined as the seedbed of the ills of modern society and held up to illustrate the polarization of society by race, class, and gender; the exploitation and the institutionalization of inequality; the breakdown of traditional family and community values; and lurking behind all aspects of a newly emerging national character, an unbridled, ravenous, entrepreneurial capitalism.

Examining the role of women during these times and within these valid themes does nothing to reconcile such divergent perceptions, but does also underscore the need for prudence and caution in making judgments. Historically, hindsight may not be twenty-twenty, especially given the radically different lenses that researchers adopt. The lack of agreement may tell as much about the cultural fragmentation of the world of today's specialized scholars and their search for its sources as it does about the Age of Jackson. The transition from a home/farm-based economy to an industrialized society is a case in point. Are women its victims or beneficiaries? Are sturdy colonial dames transformed to frail housewives as factories draw their husbands away from home, or does their new separate sphere provide greater chance for education, advancement, and power?[45] Examining the shemales of the Crockett Almanacs will not resolve the dispute, but does throw into similar high relief the core issue of independence and its relation to traditional roles and values that are of great topical interest to the authors and readers of the Almanac stories.

It does seem reasonably sure that by about 1820, the concept of separate spheres for men and women begins to approach an established norm. As man's work moves away from the home and as he becomes immersed in the "harshness and greed" of the marketplace, woman's work likewise becomes stereotyped. Centered in the home, it is concerned with the protection and guardianship of a nurturing social environment, a retreat from a wicked world, and matters of the "heart." In a variant of life imitating art, her role reenacts that of the heroines of eighteenth- and early-nineteenth-century literature, in which women, the supposed intellectual inferior of men, are essentially emotional creatures who respond spontaneously to suffering, cry easily, depend upon men to solve their problems, are smaller of stature, weak, frail, sickly, and often the victims of unknown fatal diseases.[46] These heroines could feel love but never passion, could not show anger (even though as an irrational being one might expect a flare-up or two), and could rule the home, at least indirectly through moral vision and example, but never participate in the public sphere. This sentimental, Romantic ideal grows to dominate women's popular literature in America from 1820 to 1860 and reinforces the ideal of the "saint upon a pedestal," the "true" woman who is domestic, pious, pure, and submissive.[47]

The Almanacs, Sarah Josepha Hale's *Godey's Lady's Book,* other magazines, etiquette and behavior manuals, books of regional interest and humor, and a host of sentimental novels[48] that provide substantial comment on these issues are also part of a huge upsurge in the availability of popular materials made possible by the invention of inexpensive printing machinery and processes about 1830. Technology had a wide impact upon print culture. In general, those works that upheld the ideal of a true woman and those that sought to attack or replace it were written and printed in the Northeast, often within the major printing axis of Boston–New York–Philadelphia. These works in turn reached other regions more quickly because improvements in internal transportation made nationwide circulation of printed materials a reality, and the same ease of transportation also encouraged the spread of presses to the West and South. All brought topics such as the proper role of women in American society to the foreground emphatically and quickly.

The actual sphere of women in the Age of Jackson is far more diverse and complex in terms of interests, goals, and activities than is conveyed by the idea of true womanhood. No single concept could eliminate the boundaries of class, wealth, religion, and race to unite women under one banner. How can anyone, for example, who knows the story of "Houston's Defeat" place Pamela Mann within a sentimental tradition? In 1836, Mann's team of oxen was commandeered by Houston's troops to pull cannon to Nacogdoches. She agreed, but when they changed course to Harrisburg, she believed they voided the bargain. Gathering a brace of pistols and a long knife, she overtook Houston and dressed him down in front of his troops: "'General, you told me a damn lie, you said that you was going on the Nacogdoches road. Sir, I want my oxen.'" When Houston said that he could not move the cannon without them, Mann snapped back, "'I don't care a damn for your cannon, I want my oxen.'" Another version has Mann pulling a pistol, jumping down from her horse, and using her long knife to cut her oxen loose, and according to an eyewitness, she then "'jumpt on her horse with whip in hand, & way she went in a lope with her oxen.'"[49] The brief incident was given relatively little attention in the eastern press, and even today Mann's story is little known outside of Texas.

Stereotypes of women reinforced by the popular press of the day generally tended to ignore the effect of the antebellum western experience as a formative influence on female character. These stereotypes, which are derived mainly from and for middle- and upper-middle-class white women, serve to hide from popular knowledge the actual diversity of women's experience at the time and allow writers who are so inclined to represent women in the abstract as a single entity. As Sarah Josepha Hale firmly states:

> WOMAN is God's appointed agent of *morality*, the teacher and inspirer of those feelings and sentiments which are termed the virtues of humanity; and that the progress of these virtues, and the permanent improvement of our race, depend on the manner in which her mission is treated by man. . . . Obedience, Temperance, Truth, Love, Piety,—these she must build up in the character of her children. . . . The *moral sense* is the highest natural faculty or element of the human soul; woman has this moral sense, the intuitive feeling of disgust for sensuality, vice, and falsehood; the intuitive feeling of love for the innocent, beautiful, and true, better developed and more active than is found in the other sex.[50]

Stereotypes like Hale's do reveal or reflect some "truths," or they could not exert and maintain a significant influence over the views of the public. The general role of a woman in the Jacksonian era, for example, is strictly limited. The bulk of her education is designed to allow her to master domestic skills and to make her the best possible wife and mother, and perhaps a teacher of children. Science and pseudoscience, medicine and phrenology, judge her brain smaller and her cerebral system less developed than man's and restrict her gifts to the instinctive, intuitive, and emotional sphere. Her innocence reinforces the notion of her moral superiority and allows her to rule in the home, but politically and legally she is subjugated into near nonexistence as a person, as state after state from New York in 1778 to New Jersey in 1844 officially eliminate her right to vote. Her property rights are restricted as well, with the legislature of Tennessee going so far in the spring of 1849 as to declare that women had no souls and therefore had no right to own property.[51]

As noted at the outset, it is the West itself that helps to modify somewhat the role and depiction of women. Viewed predominantly through Eastern eyes, the West is uncivilized, seen both as a new Eden without an Eve, a place of boundless future wealth within the grasp of those men strong enough to take it, and also as a region that must yield under the domesticating influences of civilization if the country as a whole is to survive and prosper. In 1835, Lyman Beecher spoke eloquently for both the primacy of the West and the need to temper its opportunistic primitivism: "the religious and political destiny of our nation is to be decided in the West. . . . It is equally clear, that the conflict which is to decide the destiny of the West, will be a conflict of institutions for the education of her sons, for purposes of superstition, or evangelical light; of despotism, or liberty." Beecher demands that the East educate the West: "We must educate! We must educate! or we must perish by our prosperity. . . . If in our haste to be rich and mighty, we outrun our literary and religious institutions, they will never overtake us. . . . Her destiny is our destiny; and the day that her gallant ship goes down, our little boat sinks in the vortex!"[52]

Although Beecher was specifically seeking support for the Cincinnati Lane Seminary on his Atlantic tour, his ostensible comments on converting the Jacksonian wilderness to at least the pastoral middle landscape of Jefferson applied to women as well. According to the article "The Pioneer Mothers," published that same year in the *Western Literary Journal and Monthly Review*, these women went forth "as volunteers to act as hand-maids in rearing a nation in the wilds of the West."[53]

Historically, Daniel Boone (1734–1820) and David Crockett (1786–1836) both exemplified the materialistic pull of the West that Beecher addressed. Among their many enterprises were commercial hunting and land speculation. After their initial forays into the "unknown" wilderness, however, rather than participating in the great American myth of the solitary hunter eventually established by Cooper in the person of Natty Bumppo in the *Leatherstocking Tales*, they were usually accompanied by their wives. No woman was featured prominently in the "autobiographies" of these American icons, but certainly the portrayal of Rebecca Boone, rather than any of Crockett's wives, came closest to that of one of the "hand-maids in rearing a nation in the wilds of the West."[54] Boone felt that the presence of his wife and daughter, "the first white women that ever stood on the banks of Kentucke river," civilized his settlement, and indeed Kentucky. Judge James Hall added bravery, self-sufficiency, and fortitude to Rebecca Boone's assumed and usually unstated feminine accomplishments and, in describing Boone's heroism, noted, "Nor did he suffer and conquer alone; his wife accompanied him to the wilderness, and shared his danger." She was in many ways the prototype for the women of the West described in "The Pioneer Mothers," women more suited for life on the frontier than in the East: "they were not so refined, so deeply schooled in that which is delicate and beautiful," but "they had those [qualities] which were the developments of their nature's purity, uninfluenced by the fashion and artifice of society. We admit they were masculine, if you term that masculine, which prompted them to defend, aye die, for their husbands, their children."[55]

Even in the male-dominated *Leatherstocking Tales*, Cooper occasionally builds on the image of the woman of the West as protectress, echoing the role of Athena and that of the biblical Esther, in his character Esther Bush in *The Prairie* (1827). Esther is willing to risk her life to find her missing son Asa: "'I will shoulder a rifle myself, and woe betide, the red-skin, that crosses my path! I have pulled a trigger before to day, ay, and heard an Indian yell, too, to my sorrow. . . . I am leader to day, and I *will* be followed—who so proper, let me know, as a mother to head a search for her own lost child!'" Thus Cooper creates Esther as more of a shemale than his other women characters, but still one that adds the masculinity necessitated by the West to her traditional role as mother, following the same line of thought expressed in "The Pioneer Mothers." Cooper sees her as a shemale, a "person, who, attired in a dress half-masculine, and bearing a weapon like the rest, seem'd no unfit leader for the groupe of wildly clad frontier-men, that followed in her rear."[56]

Not all the fictional portraits of western women focused upon the heroic. In *A New Home—Who'll Follow? Or, Glimpses of Western Life* (1839), Carolyn Kirkland filters her own experiences into a realistic fiction that serves as the base for her satire of many of the conventional portrayals of women, true womanhood, and of the West through an acerbic examination of her new Michigan neighbors. "Mrs. Mary Clavers, an Actual Settler" is Kirkland's pseudonym for the author-narrator of the book, who promises the reader "very nearly—a veritable history, an unimpeachable transcript of reality" and, after confessing to some slight colorings, notes "however, that whatever is quite unnatural, or absolutely incredible, in the few incidents which diversify the following pages, is to be received as literally true."[57] The statement is not meant to set the stage for tall tales or for a possible hoax, but to give dramatic notice to eastern readers about the unbelievable aspects of lower-class society on the frontier. Kirkland is, for the most part, even-handed in her abuse and praise. *A New Home* is not merely a savaging of lowly western democrats by a superior from the East, for Kirkland turns a withering gaze on many subjects, including her own foibles and pretensions and, perhaps in a process of acculturation, adopts or sometime switches readily between both cultures and classes. As a realist, Kirkland critiques the glowing descriptions of travel guides, exposes the edenic West as a figment of the imagination of Romantic writers, and mocks the crude versions of the sentimental tradition and fashions upheld by western women as the epitome of their "high" society. She does so directly to reinforce the idea that only a true eastern lady, one such as herself, can bring proper refinement and civilization to the frontier.[58] Thus there are obvious parallels in the satiric targets of *A New Home* and the Almanac stories, particularly in the overt incongruity of transplanting rough versions of delicate eastern ways into the western wilderness. Just as her hostesses at the "hotel" (essentially a one-room log cabin with a sleeping loft) announce that they will "'slick up'" for dinner by changing dresses behind quilts that serve as screens, so too do the shemales in preparation for a "tea squall" (tea party) or going to church.[59] But Kirkland's Mary Clavers is, at bottom, an outsider, an observer rather than a full participant in the world she describes, while exuberant shemales revel in the riotous contradictions of their tall-tale universe.

The folklore of the times of the Crockett Almanacs does provide examples that may have influenced the depiction of the riproarious shemales. One of the most likely is the story of Bess Call, the sister of Joe Call (d. 1834), the "Lewis Giant." Joe lived in Essex County, New York, and was thought to be the strongest man in the country. Famed as a wrestler, and accommodating challengers even after his retirement, Joe often had Bess do the wrestling when he was away. Like her brother, Bess could lift a plow or an ox with one hand, so her defeat of an English champion who trains and trains to wrestle Joe is no great surprise. Other heroines include "Sweet Betsey from Pike," who, according to the ballad made popular in the gold rush of 1849, had the gumption to survive the grueling journey from Missouri to California, crossing the desert on foot.[60]

This combination of literature, history, and folklore, of stereotypes and general roles of women, are but part of the gender profile of these turbulent times. They do establish, however, a norm of sorts, that the authors of the Almanac tales seem to use as both a touchstone and a whipping post. In many ways, the shemales whom they create and satirize have more in common with the strident reformers who dedicate themselves to fighting the oppressive nature of a patriarchal world, because as wilderness women they are distinctly outside the limits of civilized society. These tall-tale women also reflect the reality of pioneer life for women (and of many lower-class laboring women), whose work was physical, hard, and interdependent with and sometimes independent of men. Although the authors maintain a type of frontier domesticity for these women, the implicit satirization of shemales in the Crockett Almanacs lies in their dramatic divergence from sentimental ideals in behavior and looks and their usurping of traditional male roles, characterizations that parallel the attacks upon militant women reformers.

There are many such contemporary female lightning rods. Frances (Fanny) Wright (1795–1852), actress, editor, and author, is now generally regarded as a pioneer in the women's movement. This English woman spoke in favor of women's education, advocated and put into practice the idea of the gradual emancipation of slaves by having them earn their freedom in colonies like the one she established in Tennessee in 1825 and named Nashoba, and determinedly followed her strong sense of social justice into arenas of public life deemed appropriate only for men.[61] Due to her attempt to eliminate gender roles, Wright was accused of so far demeaning her sex that she had abandoned all the noble characteristics of femininity, retaining only the physical "shape of a woman." Near the start of the publication of the Crockett Almanacs, large controversies swirled as well around the Grimké sisters and their ardent abolitionism. Angelina (1805–79) and Sarah's (1792–1873) anti-slavery publications and lectures, beginning in 1836, earned them unexpected censure from the Congregational clergy of Massachusetts, not for their cause but for abandoning the proper role of women to pursue it publicly. Soon, as the parallels between the groups became increasingly apparent, the Grimkés' sense of injustice was extended from slavery to the lot of women in a free, democratic society,[62] a shift that foreshadowed a similar transference as the civil-rights movement of the 1950s reinspired the second wave of the women's movement in the 1960s and 1970s.

Even as the ideas and causes of crusading women gained support, the attack upon women who stepped outside their expected role and into the public sphere increased in intensity. In another version of life imitating art, the tragic fate of women who violated expected patterns of behavior in popular fiction was also now a curse laid at the feet of actual women who spoke out or were otherwise involved in "unseemly" public debate. In 1838, the article "Hints to Young Ladies—No. 2" in *The Mother's Magazine* voiced the common condemnation of "female orators and public teachers": "These Amazonians are their own executioners. They have unsexed themselves in public estimation, and there is no fear that they will perpetuate their race. We treat insanity in all its forms, with allowance. This should save them from contempt, and, if need be, assign them a house at the public expense."[63]

The quote brilliantly reprises in capsule form the attacks previously noted in individual cases. Women who act like men are Amazons, oddities, self-destructive grotesques fit for derision. Further, in publicly breaking the norms of society, they are judged insane, just as personally their actions and mindset conspire to keep them unmarried or sterile, much to the benefit of the race, since they could not conceivably function as mothers and wives. Margaret Fuller was seen as such an Amazon when, after appropriating Ralph Waldo Emerson's idea of true manhood for women, she argued for a return to original freedom and attacked gender roles, particularly those that limited women to home and hearth. Such a viewpoint was the opposite of the norm of woman's inferiority to man and the subjection of a wife to her husband. The author of "Hints to Young Ladies" stated the case unequivocally—"to preserve her influence, woman must adhere to her appropriate sphere of duty"—and further gave biblical analogies:

> She must be in subjection to her own husband. When she leaves this sphere, she loses a principal bond on his affections, and must rule by power. This she has not, and therefore is soon degraded. The angels lost all by attempting too much. So did Eve. Let her daughters be careful to cherish and protect what has been preserved to them by the provisions of the gospel. She may still rule by love, but if she attempts to wield a rod of iron, she will be crushed under its weight.[64]

Yet redemption for transgressors was possible. Even Fuller, one of the most strident voices for and examples of the intellectual achievements of women in the 1840s, was judged a person transfigured through marriage and motherhood by those who supported the point of view noted in *The Mother's Magazine*. That her formidable intellect was tamed by or purified into domesticity was an interpretation made all the easier by her untimely death and that of her new family in a shipwreck off Fire Island on her return to America from Rome on July 19, 1850. Many traditionalists such as Nathaniel Hawthorne felt more kindly toward her, assuming that her heart, that "rude old potency," had finally won its battle with her mind, resulting in marriage and motherhood. His concluding observation on Fuller's supposed return to the norm of domesticity patly reinforces the sentimental strictures of the times: "On the whole, I do not know but I like her the better for it;—the better, because she proved herself a very woman, after all, and fell as the weakest of her sisters might." Reflecting on Fuller in his autobiography, Horace Greeley concurred with Hawthorne's chauvinism: "noble and great though she was, a good husband and two or three bouncing babies would have emancipated her from a deal of cant and nonsense."[65]

Emma Willard and Catherine Beecher were among those other reformers who, unlike Wright, the Grimkés, and Fuller, embraced the idea of separate spheres and used distinction as the base argument from which to improve women's lot through education. Their seminaries of higher education, founded in 1819 in Troy, New York, and in 1821 in Hartford, Connecticut, offered academic preparation in mathematics, philosophy, history, morality, and home economics to develop the minds of young women so they could teach well, both as mothers and, for some, as part of a core of professional teachers whose feminine influence would "elevate the whole character of the community" and ultimately have a profound positive effect upon the entire country.[66] In 1841, Catherine Beecher summed up her idea of the profound importance of women's role as the teacher and moral instructor of man in her work A Treatise on Domestic Economy for the Use of Young Ladies at Home and at School by noting:

> The mother writes the character of the future man; the sister bends the fibres that hereafter are the forest tree; the wife sways the heart, whose energies may turn for good or for evil the destinies of a nation. Let the women of a country be made virtuous and intelligent, and the men will certainly be the same. The proper education of a man decides the welfare of an individual; but educate a woman, and the interests of a whole family are secured.
>
> If this be so, as none will deny, then to American women, more so than to any others on earth, is committed the exalted privilege of extending over the world those blessed influences, that are to renovate degraded man, and "clothe all climes with beauty."[67]

Reformers like Beecher sought to empower women within their domestic sphere, and then to extend the impact of that sphere as well by proving that the greater public good would thus be served. Viewing this new domesticity as of paramount importance to the prosperity of the country enhanced the status of women, and because it worked within an accepted, existing societal framework, it began without suffering the same censure as those movements whose activists immediately attacked or violated gender role boundaries. Beecher addressed "those who are bewailing themselves over the fancied wrongs and injuries of women in this Nation" and told them flatly "that it is in America, alone, that women are raised to an equality with the other sex. . . . They are made subordinate in station, only where a regard to their best interests demands it, while, as if in compensation for this, by custom and courtesy, they are always treated as superiors." If they take no interest in "civil and political affairs," they have superior influence in education, religion, "all benevolent enterprises, and in all questions relating to morals or manners."[68] The link between women and children's education succeeded. The 1870 federal census, the first to count gainfully employed women, noted that two-thirds of public and private school teachers were women.[69]

The progress of women toward complete equality is neither linear nor unambiguous. Audiences who tolerated Fanny Wright's radical proposals for overhauling society in the 1820s shouted her down in 1836 as she lectured not against slavery or inequality but the Bank of the United States.[70] As with the Grimkés, who now nearly shared Wright's position on the equality of women, the fact that Wright was lecturing was more inflammatory than her views. Willard and Beecher's plan for an educated female citizenry as one bulwark of the new republic was also a two-edged sword. Not all women were content to eschew "civil and political affairs." The stress on education in the new domesticity also encouraged some women to move toward greater gender reforms such as those promulgated by women's rights conventions, commencing with that of Seneca Falls, New York, in 1848, whose manifesto drafted by Elizabeth Cady Stanton argued the direct applicability of the words and ideas of the Declaration of Independence to women. Stanton, other women, and Frederick Douglass, who was in attendance at the convention, flatly disagreed with Beecher's views and proclaimed "civil and political affairs" as the most important for women. The fear of such a step was underscored by the fact that the only resolution not unanimously adopted at the convention was the one supporting women's suffrage, but through Stanton and Douglass's persistence, it did carry by a small majority.[71] Without such rights, Stanton believed that women were not, as Beecher said, "treated as superiors," but as slaves. For her, as she later expressed in 1854 in a comment bracketed by analogous references to the evils of slavery, "woman falsifies herself and blasphemes her God, when in view of her present social, legal and political position, she declares she has all the rights she wants." That same year, Antoinette Brown, again hearkening back to the founding fathers, challenged America to efface "the stigma resting on this republic, that while it theoretically proclaims that all men are created equal, deprives one-half of its members of the enjoyment of the rights and privileges possessed by the other."[72]

While the women's rights conventions at Seneca Falls and Rochester in New York, Worcester, Massachusetts, and other locations served to intensify the demand for equality, the abolitionist movement had already both paralleled the lot of women and slaves, as noted in the case of the Grimkés, and was explicitly restated by Douglass in the lead editorial of his paper, *The North Star*, the week following the Seneca Falls Convention: "Many who have at last made the discovery that the negroes have some rights as well as other members of the human family, have yet to be convinced that women are entitled to any." The intertwining of reform movements allowed other early female abolitionists in addition to the Grimkés to attack the new domesticity in 1836. In *Right and Wrong in Boston*, abolitionist Maria Weston Chapman stated that male domination had destroyed the real "true womanhood" and that the only woman who would object to another woman speaking out publicly against slavery was the "sort of woman who is dead while she lives, or to be pitied as the victim of domestic tyranny. The woman who makes it [such an objection] is generally one who has struggled from childhood up to womanhood through a process of spiritual suffocation."[73] For Chapman, society's "true woman" had become a dead woman, a woman afraid to exercise her voice in a cause whose moral nature demanded a woman's participation.

But for women for whom Catherine Beecher's words and ideas rang true, the debate further entrenched the concept of separate spheres and led to a greater cleavage between those who were leaders and followers in women's movements and the general population of women whose lives were bounded by domestic functions linked to the home. In the second half of *Democracy in America*, published in 1840, that astute foreign commentator upon American affairs, Alexis de Tocqueville, remarked, "Thus in the United States the inexorable opinion of the public carefully constrains woman within the narrow circle of domestic interests and duties and forbids her to step beyond it."[74]

In satirizing contemporary notions of womanhood in the Crockett Almanacs, the authors often try to have it both ways by replicating independence as well as a wild frontier brand of domesticity in their characters. Their illustrators similarly provide the reader with both grotesque and romantic woodcut depictions of the heroines of the tales, though there is no overt correlation between behavior and looks. For example, the most romantic and beautifully executed woodcut of a shemale accompanies "A Bundling Match" in "Courting Stories and Amorous Adventures," but this pretty shemale in a flowing dress says, "I am a she steamboat and have doubled up a crocodile in my day." Although she looks like a saint, she refuses to marry Davy until she has tried him out bundling first. Increasingly delighted at his prospects as she agrees to take off nearly all her clothes, Davy soon finds that she is not quite as eager a sexual partner as he thought: "Her under petticoat was made of briar bushes woven together, and I could not come near her without getting stung most ridiculous. I would as soon have embraced a hedgehog."(193–94)

Independent shemales, despite their level of domesticity, can be beautiful or hideous. It is also clear that just as the authors directly play upon the cultural norm of the attributes of the "true" woman as a given as they construct the tales, they seem purposely to exclude direct attacks upon the women's movement. The only direct reference, in fact, is a one-line dig that occurs in the 1855 Almanac, in which Davy expresses "My Idee of a Bloomer Kuss-Tume": "A Female with bishop sleeves on her legs, and a *corn-cake* on her head."(321) This critique of women's fashion, a feature present in American satiric literature since Nathaniel Ward's *The Simple Cobbler of Aggawam* (1647), is astoundingly mild, given the furor generated elsewhere by the implications of women wearing pants.[75] The illustrators of the Almanacs further distance themselves from such controversy by having all their shemales appear in dresses to set them apart both from reformers and also from those women who throughout history have disguised their sex to gain the freedom of action of men.[76]

The overreaching satire of the four general qualities of a true woman is a factor that unites the eight sections into which the Almanac tales in this volume are grouped. The inversions and absurdities of these qualities are the means by which the authors create much of the humor of the Almanacs, but such "true woman" satire does generally receive stronger emphasis in particular categories. Domesticity, although bridging many categories in the portrayal of shemales, expectedly also occupies center stage in the brief "Recipes and Household Hints" section. Piety tends to dominate the "Sentimental and Religious Stories," as purity, in a broad sense, does in the "Courting Stories and Amorous Adventures." Submissiveness is a virtue that receives the most radical of tall-tale revisions for shemales in "Wild and Grotesque Description," "Battles with Animals," "Battles with Humans," and occasionally in the "True Adventure Stories."

Shemale domesticity rampages through the tales in outrageous fashion. "Battles with Animals" offers up numerous examples of how shemales rule the home. Sappina Wing killed a big crocodile that invaded her cabin, after "her dander riz, an she lifted the mop an pointed rite at his infarnal tongue, an rammed it down his throat." (134) In "A Dangerous Situation," a big bear who walked in the front door is fended off by Davy's wife, who drew "out her two nitting needles, and while the bear war looking up at her she stuck 'em both into his eyes." (135–36) Nance Bowers, interrupted by "the great king bear" in her kitchen, began taming him for a dog and a horse as follows: "she had jist taken hot dumplings out of the pot, for dinner, an she turned her head suddenaciously round, smacked a big red hot smoking one into the critter's throat." (148–49) These amazing feats are "domesticated" both by their protection of the sanctity of the home and by the shemales' choices of weapons—a mop, knitting needles, and a dumpling. The authors satirically evolve their own standards for backwoods femininity that are a far cry from anything that Catherine Beecher ever envisioned in her emphasis upon the sanctity of motherhood or that Sarah Josepha Hale ever allowed to grace the pages of Godey's Lady's Book. This most influential publication of the time of the Almanacs celebrated the wholesomeness of service to family in hyperbolic prose and enshrined Queen Victoria as the ideal, "the representative of the moral and the intellectual influence which woman by her nature is formed to exercise."[77]

Davy's ideal was Katy Whippoween. In "A Good Wife," he tells us that she "war the gratest wife that ever lived in our cleering." She would sew all the clothes for her children, cutting down garments to fit the next in line, and when she ran out of cloth, she smeared her son with melted glue and rolled him in a torn-open featherbed for his winter clothes. But even the best woman cannot guarantee her children's future through her Victoria-like "moral and intellectual influence." Both turned out bad: One became a Yankee peddler and the other a minister. Davy pronounced the verdict: "They knowed nothin of life in the woods, and is a living disgrace to old Kaintuck."(248)

Considering the growth of voluntary women's associations during the time of the Almanacs, as well as their alliance to and growth from various churches,[78] Katy's sketch provides both a dig (at the calling of a minister as a failure) and also a prime example of how the virtue of piety is revised for the wilderness. Although shemales are independent agents rather than members of associations, they too rarely imbibe alcohol, preferring instead the social aspects of numerous "tea-squalls" (tea parties). Despite any possible unstated sympathy with the temperance movement, however, Katy is willing to provide for her husband's needs. By acting as a "wet nuss" for another family's pet bear, she "arned enuff to keep her husband in whiskey, and that is saying a good deal, for he was a ripsnorter over the keg." Mr. Whippoween knew the treasure he had and "war as proud of her as he war of his dog."(248) Could there be higher praise?

Moving from satire to tall tale in the area of piety brings Davy's sister Comfort to the foreground as "one of the finest samples of Christianity, an womananity," for

> she swallowed religion hull, an fed on that an do good-a-tiveness all the days of her life, till she war a parfect model of a natural saint; she could preach a few too; her pulpit was the rock, an her sacrament the pure nat'ral element of Adam; her words would make the coldest individuals heart open up like a clam in dog dogs [dog days of summer], an a reprobates hair stand straight up, an bow to her, an when she sung a psalm you'd a thought all the trees in creation war organ pipes, an a harrycane blowin the bellows; she has put her tracks an her tracts all the way from the Alleghany to the Rocky mountains.(260–61)

As the title "Davy's Sister. Rescuing Adventurers in the Rocky Mountains" indicates, later in the tale, Comfort also serves as a one-woman traveler's aid society for the entire Northwest. The author of the story may have also had historical women missionaries to the West in mind in this sketch. Narcissa Whitman's arrival with her husband, Marcus, at the annual hunters' and trappers' hell-raising rendezvous on the Green River as these missionaries were on their way to the Oregon Territory in 1836 signaled the end of an era and raised the prospect of settlement, even though that was not her intent. Her calling was as a missionary to the Indians, to bring the word of God to the "heathen savage" in the West and convert them, just as others were doing in the Sandwich Islands (Hawaii), Africa, and other similar wild and exotic locations. Ultimately unsuccessful in her mission, Narcissa Whitman was killed in 1847 by the Cayuse Indians she had tried to convert.[79]

Comfort Crockett is one of the liveliest exaggerations of both women's missionary work and of female orators, the "Amazons" so roundly condemned in *The Mother's Magazine*, yet her religious activism is generic and unthreatening. No specific cause such as demon rum, abolition, or conversion to a particular sect is mentioned. She explodes the bounds of the most liberal interpretation of true womanhood, but the story gives little offense, since she simultaneously upholds accepted norms, the virtuousness of piety and of a life of service. The propriety of Comfort's path was argued in 1834 by William A. Alcott as a fit unpaid career for "those females who despise domestic life and its duties." In "Female Attendance on the Sick," he presented neighborhood nursing not only as a way of doing a needed good, but of saving such aberrant nondomestic women from misanthropy, ennui, and sometimes from "speedy or more protracted suicide" by utilizing their feminine gifts.[80] Comfort Crockett does so, but in a way that may have made Alcott reconsider his views.

Since the church is nearly as important a force in the life of women as the home, it is no surprise that church going is part of shemales' lives as well. In "A Thief of an Alligator," Davy's "wife was getting ready to go to a meeting, that was to be held about fifteen miles from our clearing by old Lorenzo Dowe [sic]."(130) Mention of Dow (1777–1834), one of the great horseback itinerant preachers of the day, grounds the tale firmly within the revivalist tradition that brought many women into church-based social and political activities. Shemales, however, have their own reasons for attendance. Florinda Fury was a regular member and would set off for the "Deer Meetin' House, every Sunday morning," but "sometimes she carried a rooster in her pocket, as they used to have a cock-fight in the meetin' house arter sarvice war over."(108) Perhaps Sal Waterman's behavior at meeting was a bit more in line with the sentimental norms for impressionable young girls of the day, as she "shed a grate lot of teers at the preaching." But when her mother found out that all that flow was induced by an onion Sal kept in her pocket for that purpose, she put an end to it: "if it takes onions to practiss godliness, it is too expensive. So if she wants to go to heaven that road, she must find onions for herself."(256) Feeding another long-standing stereotype of behavior, Sunday was the time to display one's finery, and Lottie Ritchers, "The Flower of Gum Swamp," was no exception: "she carried twenty eyes in her work bag, at one time, that she had picked out of the heads of certain gals of her acquaintance. She always made them into a string of beads, when she went to church, and wore 'em round her neck."(113)

Purity is likewise remolded in the wilderness. The authors again begin by accepting some norms as givens. Women of the Almanacs will resist all improper advances, particularly by an unworthy beau. The same Florinda Fury who loved cockfighting in the meetinghouse "war a very varchus gal, too; for when a Yankee pedlar undertook to come the soft soap over her, she kotched him by the heels and poked him up the chimbly till his head come out the top."(108) Deserved fate awaits both man and beast. Davy's six-year-old daughter was attacked by "a thunderin great hungry he barr" who "was jist about bitin a regular buss ont [out] on her cheek, when the child resentin her insulted wartue, gin him a kick with her south fist, in his digestion, that made him buss the arth instanterly." Still indignant, when the bear tries to pounce on her again, she draws deep into the Crockett gene pool, and "the little gal grinned sich a double streak o' blue lightnin into his month [mouth], that it cooked the critter to death as quick as think, an she brought him home for dinner." Rightly proud of his chip off the old block, Davy concludes that "She'll be a thunderin fine gal when she gets her natteral growth, if her stock o' Crockett lightnin don't burst her biler, and blow her up."(141)

The tales also at times reinforce the "die for true love" theme of sentimental literature, particularly the romances, whose success made Nathaniel Hawthorne so jealous in 1855 that he gave it as one reason for his wish to remain in England for an additional two years: "America is now wholly given over to a d——d [damned] mob of scribbling women, and I should have no chance of success while the public taste is occupied with their trash."[81] While Hawthorne retreated from the battle, the authors of the Almanac tales also had surveyed popular taste and attacked it through their satire. In "A Single Combat," Sal Fungus is so in love with Davy that "her heart growed too big; and when I left her to go to Texas, it burst like an airthquake, and poor Sal died. She died with a bursted heart—it war too big with love for me, and it's case war not big enough to hold it."(170) Men are more fortunate. When Davy suffers his first disappointment in love at the hands of Sal Tuig, he says that "At fust I konkluded to p[u]t an end to myself; but finally I wauked down to the Mississippi and drunk out of the stream. I spose I swallowed a gallon or two. Then I took a swett under seven bear skins, and ett a crocodile's tale roasted. Arter that I keered nothin' about Sal."(106) Davy prefers drastic cures for love, particularly illicit love. In another tale, as a married man, he stifles his yearnings for a gal by swallowing a thunderbolt, which "tore the trowsers cleen off as it cum out. I had a sore gizzard for two weeks arterward, and my inwards war so hot that I use to eat raw vitals for a month arterward, and it would be cooked befour it got farely down my throte. I have never felt love since." (1842, p. [13], "The Colonel Swallows a Thunderbolt")

This adept mockery of conventional sentiment is most evident in the section of tales grouped under "Courting Stories and Amorous Adventures." Often a degree of role reversal also occurs, since some shemales are unabashedly forward in pursuing the opposite sex, even to the point of physically fighting other women to secure their intended choice of mates, as is the case in "A Love Fight—by Ben Harding."(178) More frequently, men initiate the seduction or the rituals of courtship. In "A Love Adventure and Uproarious Fight with a Stage Driver," Davy discovers that the driver stops the delivery of "the great Southern Mail . . . half an hour every day or two" to "see his doxy." Davy gets off at the next stop, doubles back to her cabin, and "quickly got into her good graces, as she was 'nothing loth,' as the poets say. I kept her company for two days." When the driver catches them together, a ferocious fight ensues. Crockett masters the driver and takes his leave, noting, "This adventure I never told to Mrs. Crockett."(189–90) The last line is in some ways a slap at the type of male reformation that Catherine Beecher sought by making women the teachers of young boys and that in 1834 was one of the founding premises of the New York Female Moral Reform Society. The society's attempt to limit male sexual license was linked to the elimination of houses of prostitution and double standards in sexual mores,[82] ideas that find an unexpected and unwanted kind of sympathy in the Almanacs as shemales enjoy their liaisons and suffer no stigma or ill effects from them. They also control their encounters, even through the unexpected protection of briar-bush petticoats, as noted in "A Bundling Match." The wilderness gives she-males far more power than their historical counterparts could hope to obtain in civilization in the nineteenth century. A life in untamed nature lifts sexual restrictions to allow these fictional frontier women to function with nearly the same impunity as men.[83]

"Colonel Coon's Wife Judy" is a fine sample of a courting tale between near equals. Indeed, in first identifying Judy as Colonel Coon's wife, the title of the story implies a traditional subservience that her description as a prime shemale who could outscream a catamount quickly sets aside. At fourteen, "she wrung off a snapping turtle's neck and made a comb of its shell." At sixteen, she "chased a bear three mile through the snow, because she wanted his hair to make a tooth brush." And to complete her toilet on her wedding night, she "sucked forty rattlesnake's eggs to g[i]ve her a sweet breath." With these accomplishments, it was no wonder that a "Tennessee roarer" named Tom Coon "tarmined to try his flint agin her steel." Tom won Judy with a grand, gallant gesture that would not likely find its way into the etiquette manuals or sentimental literature of the period: "He pulled half a dozen eyes out his pocket, and flinging 'em down on the floor, swore with a round oath he'd place any man's eyes by the side of them that dared to say a word agin Judy! Judy than jumped up like a frog and said, 'Tom Coon, I'm yours for life—I know what you've come for, and I'll be your wedded wife without any more fustification about it.'"(245–46) Just as Judy actually raises and decides the issue of their apparently common-law marriage, so too do her adventures before and after her marriage serve to dominate the tale and reveal her true grit.

The flip side of such a successful frontier union is satirized in "A Scienterifical Courtship." Wicket Finney and Meg Wadlow's "match" was ill-fated from the start, not so much because he was the epitome of the sexual predator (Wicket as wicked?) that the Female Moral Reform Society hoped to eliminate, but because Meg thought herself too good for her Kentucky surroundings after going "to bording skool for to finish her eddication." This is enough to make Wicket set his cap for her; he even buys a suit of clothes from a store to increase his odds. Through Meg, "educated" women become the butt of satire. Her "wonderful accomplifications," such as playing the "piny forty [piano forte]," and haughty manners make her ripe for a fall. Her language also pokes fun at her veneer of refinement when she acknowledges that she likes Wicket ("my hart is deceptible to your honors") but is already engaged: "'Oh, sir!' sez she, 'my trough is invocably plagued to another.'" He persists, but as soon as his fervent pleas win a kiss and her consent, Wicket calls her "too fast" and leaves. Davy concludes with the immediate moral of the story: "So when Meg seed he didn't want her arter all the fuss, she went into the high sterricks and the rumytiz, and the fainting fits, and all that sort o'thing, wich she had larnt at the boarding skools."(242–44)

In demeaning Meg's education and her civilized virtues, the authors point up the traits of true womanhood that receive probably the most revision in the Crockett Almanacs: passivity and submissiveness. Kitty Cookins, in "Larned Courting," provides another example of a woman completely out of her element in the backwoods.(196) The premier assault, however, on the uselessness of civilization's trappings and the superiority of a life in nature occurs in high style in "Crockett's Account of the Concerts in Kansas." The initial target is "One of our extremely sentimental and musical ladies of New York . . . who had long run mad after the Italian opera" and who had emigrated to Kansas "merely for the romance of the thing, and for some new sort of excitement." The tale is all the more biting because the satire has the twofold targets of an overly emotional woman and the frivolous ever-changing fashions of civilized life. When Crockett takes her out into the woods at night to experience a "consart" and an opera given by "Signorina Screech-Owl-ine," "the two great *Bassos*, Signors Wolfini and Bearini," and "the great *tenore*, Signor Painterini," she responds expectedly: "The lady screamed, and fell into convulsions."(288) In "[The Corruption of Frontier Ways]," Davy is also "afeered" that these curses of civilization, particularly a slavish adherence to the trends in backwoods fashion, may be infectious and "that old Kaintuck will be ruined by them ar gals that can't keep up the old ways of thar four-fathers."(114)

Nearly every characterization of a riproarious shemale is active and assertive and stands in direct contrast to the ideals of passivity and submissiveness that are associated with the sentimental norms of the day and with the occasional sentimental sisters of the tales. These women are far fewer in number in the Almanacs, perhaps because such depictions were the standard in other literature, whether they were as simple as the cheering notion in "The Rag Fair" to "keep up your hearts gals, every Jack has his Jill"(304) or as involved as the repeated rescuing of a "damsel in distress" in "A Terrible Fight with a Snake and Panther, and a Young Lady Rescued."(270) The shemale stories, both because of their number and the interest that they attract by outrageously reversing these norms, bulk large in the Almanac stories involving women and serve to undercut the stereotypical portrayals of the day.

Part of the uniqueness of the riproarious shemales of the Almanacs comes from their ties to the untamed West and to the then still relatively new political experiment of the United States. The intertwined concepts of wilderness and democracy conveniently support the traditional limiting of comedy to the lower, nonaristocratic class. In many ways, the shemales are involved in a new version of a comedy of manners in which the incongruous contrast between the characters representing the different classes is implied or at best offstage. Rarely does a shemale confront a lady in the tales. The reader simply makes the contrast between their outlandish behavior and the understood and generally unstated cultural norm.

If Meg Wadlow's, Kitty Cookins's, and the lady from New York's pretensions to cultivation and citified manners have a certain dramatic flair, they may well be acquired from an earlier staple of the Crockett canon, James Kirke Paulding's melodrama, *The Lion of the West*. The combination of Paulding's dialog, the abilities of actor James Hackett, and the legend of Crockett make the play's lead character, Nimrod Wildfire, a hilarious and memorable American original who is superimposed on an otherwise rather standard comedy of manners. First staged in New York in April 1831 and seen by Congressman Crockett in Washington, D.C., in December 1833, the play focuses in part on the interesting relationship of Wildfire and Mrs. Amelia Wallope, a transparent version of Mrs. Frances Trollope, the British traveler so famed for her dislike of Americans and their uncivilized behavior. Wallope's intended book, *Domestic Manners of the Americans*, bears the same title as Trollope's, and like her, as well as Catherine Beecher and many others for that matter, Mrs. Wallope hopes to make over American character. Amelia will, she says, "ameliorate the barbarism of manners in America," cultivate their sensibilities, and train uncouth Americans, particularly males, to observe the proprieties: "Now my system is to raise my own sex to its proper dignity, to give them the command and so refine the men." But Wildfire mistakes her attempt to control him and enlist his help in establishing "a national social academy for refinement of manners" as a proposal of marriage, and overjoyed, he sends for a preacher and a wagon to tote her back "to old Kaintuck." After a series of twists and turns in the plot, which include the unmasking of a false English lord (Amelia's brother), the American rejection of her plan so offends her that she vows to return to England and expose the loutish manners of Americans by publishing her book of observations, in which the uncivilized "Alligator Colonel" plays a prominent role.[84]

While Colonel Wildfire's uninhibited behavior is the first and foremost offender of propriety, his language draws the most attention:

> "there's no mistake in me; of all the fellers on this side the Alleghany mountains, I can jump higher—squat lower—dive deeper—stay longer under and come out drier! There's no back out in my breed—I go the whole hog. I've got the priettiest sister, fastest horse, and ugliest dog in the deestrict—in short, to sum up all in one word . . . —I'm a horse!"[85]

His bravado and exaggeration are in part the model for traits later expanded in the fictional Crockett and also in the riproarious shemales of the Almanacs, just as Mrs. Wallope/Trollope is a model for the false and useless refinement of Meg, Kitty, and the lady from New York. Shemales are much like Wildfire in their straightforward, if somewhat crude, honesty, and their comedy, like his, is generated from and magnifies the incongruity between the staid manners and conventional actions of European-like easterners and the "true" American spirit of westerners reveling in their near absolute freedom.

The language of the Crockett Almanacs has ancient roots. It is grounded in part in the flyting, the contest of roaring boasts that regularly precedes combat between epic and mythic figures. The verbal duel between Medb and Ailill in their "pillow talk" in *The Tain* is one such historical antecedent. It is more pronounced in the Almanacs than in many other instances of frontier tall talk because it draws upon ancient myth and itself operates within a heroic framework. Frontier boasts are, for example, a staple of the humor of the Old Southwest of which the Crockett Almanacs are a part, but even a work such as Augustus Baldwin Longstreet's "The Fight" from his *Georgia Scenes* (1835) pales before the verbal barrages of the Almanacs and does not provide the reader with the larger "epic" context for its warriors. They are the "best" men of their county in a fight, but nothing of their deeds before or after their battle is presented. Crockett is the only figure in Southwestern humor whose language and heroism are so fully developed as to mimic that of Cuchulainn or other figures of the Heroic Age like Siegfried, Antar, and Roland. James Kirke Paulding's *Letters from the South* provides an early, albeit limited, version of both the boasts and the battle between an unnamed wagoner and batteauxman in a short vignette that foreshadows Longstreet's "The Fight" and the contests between Crockett and Ben Harding in the Almanacs. Other major protagonists in Southwestern humor are of a slightly different stripe. George Washington Harris's Sut Lovingood is fully drawn, as is Johnson Jones Hooper's Simon Suggs, but as tricksters and con men rather than heroes. Sut lives to create chaos, just as Suggs, whose motto is "'It is good to be shifty in a new country,'" lives "as merrily and as comfortably as possible at the expense of others." Neither rogue measures up to Crockett. Sut would rather run, and Suggs would rather bluff or talk his way out of a confrontation than fight. Since the participants in battles in the Crockett Almanacs are normally male rather than shemale, women seldom are as active in boasting as Davy himself. But as the narrator of the bulk of the shemale tales, he describes them, particularly in the "Wild and Grotesque Description" section, using the same language of exuberant boasts that introduces epic battle.[86] Crockett says that his daughters, for example, are "the tallest and fattest, and sassyest gals in all America. They can out run, out jump, out fight, and out scream any crittur in creation; an for scratchin, thar's not a hungry painter, or a patent horse-rake can hold a claw to 'em." (140) Sut and Suggs would not have a chance in a fair fight with a shemale.

The Crockett Almanacs are nearly unique in terms of shemales as characters. Most Southwestern humor was written by men for men and was often published in sporting gazettes, newspapers like William T. Porter's *Spirit of the Times* that were geared toward the interests of men. The fact that the riproarious shemales appeared in the Almanacs, a more gender-neutral form, make them more likely to have secured a female readership for the tales as well. The female characters who appear occasionally in other works of Southwestern humor, however, are often straightforward stereotypes with no redeeming uniqueness or eccentricity, set pieces displayed as humorless moral examples or geared for a cheap, easy laugh. Longstreet's "The 'Charming Creature,' as a Wife," which appeared first in three installments in his *Augusta State Rights' Sentinel* in 1834 before its reprinting the next year in *Georgia Scenes*, is an extended treatise that contrasts the practical qualities of a good wife—stressing economical household management (a common theme upon which Catherine Beecher later expanded)—with the frivolous, flirtatious "Charming Creature" who bankrupts her husband, George. Ruined, he "now surrendered himself to drink and to despair, and died the drunkard's death." In the last sentence of the story, the blame for this tragedy is ultimately laid at the feet of mothers, who are warned "against bringing up their daughters to be 'Charming Creatures.'"[87] The other pole of depiction, the cheap, easy laugh, is evident in Joseph G. Baldwin's *The Flush Times of Alabama and Mississippi* (1853). In "The Earthquake Story," the main satire is directed against the long-winded narrator, Cave himself. Along the way, however, we meet "old Miss Julia Pritcher, a *girl* who was lank, hysterical, and . . . had just got about five thousand dollars from her aunt." Courted successfully by a lawyer whose profession was marrying for money, she arrives at the ceremony "painted up like a doll: her withered old face streaked like a June apple. She needn't have put herself to the trouble for Girard; he would have married her in her winding-sheet, if she had been as ugly as original sin, and only had enough breath in her to say yes to the preacher." The cry of "'fire!'" rings out, and the ceremony dissolves before it begins, as a fire engine's hose dislodges the groom's wig and then drives Julia's "curls through the window opposite, and which washed all the complexion off that cheek, and the paint ran down the gullies and seams like blood; the other side was still rosy." Girard's wig is brought back later in the story for a laugh, but the reader hears no more of Miss Julia.[88]

The shemale tales of the Crockett Almanacs seldom echo the "Charming Creature" or pitiable spinster stereotypes. One has to examine the category of

"Stereotypes, Stock Figures, and Jokes" to find anything quite comparable, and there only the "Young Lady's Diary" displays a mindless young woman devoid of practicality, but with no consequences for any of the characters.(298) There is also no tale in which a woman without pretensions is victimized by humor. "The Rag Fair" includes a disparaging remark about "Old Sal Sparks" as "kinder shop worn," but she wins the heart of "a dreadful nice young man."(304) Even the wicked-tongued husband of "[Why the Groom Avoids the Church]" never subjects his mate to the public ridicule Julia will face.(321) None of these Almanac tales involves shemales at all; not one takes place in the wilderness; and not one incorporates the audacious deeds or the colloquial and manufactured language of the majority of the tales.

The New England, or "Down East," humor of the antebellum period offers up no shemales, but does provide two examples of independent Yankee women who bear some superficial resemblance to the women of the Almanacs. Frances M. Whitcher's (1814–52) Widow Bedott and Benjamin P. Shillaber's (1814–92) Mrs. Partington were the first fully developed American female comic characters, first appearing in newspapers in the mid-1840s and later gathered into extremely popular books, *The Widow Bedott Papers* (1855) and the *Life and Sayings of Mrs. Partington* (1854). Like the many women of the Almanacs, part of the humor of these vernacular characters develops from dialect and a flaunting of sentimentality and gentility. They also share a general lack of concern over politics. Both, however, do more to reinforce the traditional stereotypes of humor directed at women than to overturn them or break new ground. The Widow, in fact, makes fun of women like the Grimkés who dare to give public lectures and of anyone who violates or questions the established norms of proper behavior for women. Indirectly, Mrs. Partington likewise supports the status quo, as Shillaber follows a standard satiric technique of the day and puts sentiments favorable to women's rights and suffrage in the mouth of an unsympathetic or ridiculous character. Both Bedott and Partington are also consistently targeted for their conspicuous vices—the widow's obsessive quest for a new husband, together with her penchant for unending circumlocution and for producing uncommonly bad "poitry," and Mrs. Partington's inability to complete even the briefest story without falling into a malapropism or other hilarious error of speech. Whitcher uses the Widow as well to expose the pettiness that can breed in a small town, especially among women who struggle for social status. The Widow's determination to remarry to raise her position in the community exemplifies this theme. After the remarriage, Whitcher has the Widow fall victim in even a greater sense to the same pretentious malaise of class boundaries by showing her thoroughgoing intolerance toward her "lessers" in a way that throws her foolishness into higher relief. Shillaber's Mrs. Partington is cast as a type of wise fool, one who is often unaware of her wisdom. She is an uneducated, good-natured, rural worthy born in Dog's Bondage, Massachusetts, who as a widow eventually moves to Boston, a center of high culture, and is completely uninhibited about offering her advice or opinions to anyone on any subject from religion to home remedies. She has no sense at all of inferiority.[89] Neither character, however, attempts to cross gender role barriers to usurp the role or actions of a man in the way that the riproarious shemales do, but all do use humor to attempt to navigate the antebellum crosscurrents of domesticity and women's rights.

The only major humorist during the age of the Crockett Almanacs to produce an actual shemale character was George Washington Harris, in his *Yarns* of Sut Lovingood. As the most sexual, sensual, and subversive character in the humor of the Old Southwest, Sut has his own version of the doctrine of separate spheres, which survives even Harris's accurate but difficult rendering of East Tennessee mountain dialect (reading aloud helps comprehension): "Men wer made a-purpus jis' tu eat, drink, an' fur stayin awake in the yearly part ove the nites: an' wimen wer made tu cook the vittils, mix the sperits, an' help the men du the stayin awake. That's all, an' nuthin more, onless hits fur the wimen tu raise the devil atwix meals, an' knit socks atwix drams, an' the men tu play short kerds, swap hosses wif fools, an' fite fur exersise, at odd spells."[90]

This quotation, taken from "Sicily Burns' Wedding," is the second of two stories that deal with Sicily, the true shemale of the *Yarns*. Sut is smitten with Sicily's beauty: "She shows among wimen like a sunflower amung dorg fennil, ur a hollyhawk in a patch ove smartweed. Sich a buzzim! Jis' think ove two snow balls wif a strawberry stuck but-ainded [butt-ended] intu bof on em." Harris takes the comparatively veiled sensuality of the Almanacs and escalates it more than any other humorist of the period to capitalize fully on the wild in wilderness. Besides being the object of Sut's sexual desires, Sicily has all the attributes of a Crockett shemale. Sut says:

> I've seed her jump over a split-bottim cheer wifout showin her ankils, ur ketchin her dress ontu the knobs. She cud cry an' larf et the same time, an' either lov'd ur hated yu all over. Ef her hate fell ontu yu, yu'd feel like yu'd been whipp'd wif a pizen vine. . . . Three ove her smiles when she wer a tryin ove herself, taken keerfully ten minutes apart, wud make the gran' captin ove a temprunce s'iety so

durn'd drunk, he wudn't no his britches frum a par ove bellowses, ur a pledge frum a—a—warter-pot. . . . Sich an 'oman cud du more devilmint nur a loose stud hoss et a muster groun', ef she only know'd what tools she totes, an' I'se sorter beginin to think she no's the use ove the las' durnd wun, tu a dot.[91]

Harris certainly ups the ante in his satire of many of the same targets that fell to the pens of the Almanac authors, and he gives the reader a trickster-temptress in Sicily, who parades promises of pleasure before Sut to beguile him into swallowing a "love potion" made up of ten doses of soda powder, saying "'Sutty, luv, I'se got sumthin fur yu, *a new sensashun.*'" He downs the mixture, but soon "felt sumthin cumin up my swaller, monstrus like a hi pressur steamboat. I cud hear hit a-snortin, and scizzin." In eruption, and leaving a "road ove foam frum the hous' tu the hoss two foot wide," Sut mounts his horse to escape and sees "Sicily, flat ove her back in the porch, clapin her hans, screamin wif laughin, her feet up in the air, a-kickin em a-pas' each uther like she wer tryin tu kick her slippers off." For the final humiliation, Sut hears "Sicily call, es clar es a bugle: 'Hole hit down, Mister Lovingood! hole hit down! hits a cure fur puppy luv; hole hit *down!*'"[92] Unwilling to be outtricked by anyone, Sut later takes his revenge by ruining Sicily's wedding. He secures a basket over the head of a bull, which blindly upsets a dozen beehives and runs amok through the dinner while the bees attack the bull and all the guests. Finding Sicily squatting in a cold spring with a milk crock over her head and trying to drown all the bees that had gotten under her petticoats, Sut fires both verbal barrels: "'Yu hes got anuther new sensashun haint yu?'" and, in reply to her telling him "'Oh, lordy, lordy, Sut, these yere 'bominabil insex is jis' burnin me up!,'" he says "'Gin 'em a mess ove SODY,' sez I, 'that'll cool 'em off.'"[93] While Sut may or may not come out ahead in his contest with Sicily, he has at least managed to even the score.

## INHERITORS

There are a huge number of inheritors of the characteristics of the riproarious shemales of the Crockett Almanacs. Harris's Sicily Burns stories, first available in book form in 1867, point to only one of the directions in which such depictions continue. Sicily is also, however, one of the very few characters to continue the triple-threat attack of the Almanac writers that combines man-like deeds, outrageous language and physical descriptions, and the sentimental stereotype of the true woman into a single rollicking satire. Historically, the entrance of women into the public sphere entangles the notion of gender with public policy and politics, religion, moral reforms, and antagonisms of class, race, and ethnicity. In literature, popular fiction continues to earn a large readership using female stereotypes. These evil, angelic, and more human characters who mediate between these extremes generally affirm a Christian model and often assert the secondary status of women, perhaps also paralleling the rise in popularity of social Darwinism after the Civil War, but seldom involve humor.[94] There are also authors, however, who still cast women as the equal of men but make them heroic, dropping the grotesque descriptions that make them the object of satire. Many other authors continue to work with physical, behavioral, and sentimental stereotypes of women to produce satire, although with far less frequency in and after the late 1980s, given either the political correctness deflation of such humor or, from another perspective, the increased sensitivity toward other than a white male point of view. In-group written satiric humor survives and prospers, but the safe universal targets across race and gender lines open to a white male author in the nineteenth century may be limited, as one female wag suggests, to WASP male lawyers at the beginning of the twenty-first. Similarly, the satire of domesticity has become the purview of women, authors like Erma Bombeck or performers like Roseanne Barr, who transform the "duties" of a television housewife to the prerogatives of a "domestic goddess." All this is merely to say that the culture of America has changed significantly since the Civil War, continues to evolve, and humor and its boundaries reflect those changes.

While it is impossible to track all the evolutionary strands that have been spun out of the Jacksonian era that produced the shemales of the Crockett Almanacs, even if the trail is mainly limited to print rather than extended to visual culture and to fictional characters rather than historical women, it is possible to trace forward a few examples of the depiction of fictional women as man's near equal or equal that may well find their origin in the mighty or manlike deeds of Davy's female protagonists. All these portrayals, of course, still depend in some way upon the popular assumption that women are not generally capable of such behavior. Dime novel heroines are the first link in this chain. An extraordinarily prolific form of popular literature that prospered after the demise in 1856 of the Crockett Almanacs from the start of the Civil War through World War I, many early dime novels inherited the West as a subject from the Almanacs. These adventures still sold well as settlement gradually civilized the trans-Mississippi region, and they helped establish both a mythic past for the United States as a frontier country as well as a nostalgia for that past. The dime novels helped Buffalo

Bill Cody, the subject of more than five hundred novels, push Crockett to a secondary position in the pantheon of American folk heroes of the frontier before the turn of the twentieth century.

Like the Almanacs, dime novels were mainly male-generated litera-ture for a male, in this case often adolescent male, audience, and like the Almanacs, a number of them featured the exploits of women. Their combi-nation of deed and sentiment, however, usually banished even the hint of satire and humor, particularly the sometimes low comedy of the Almanacs.[95] The reason for this shift becomes clear in the rules that one of the most pro-lific early publishers of the dime novels, Beadle and Adams, set down for their authors. Reacting to and agreeing with the criticism of much of the popular literature of the day, they clearly instructed their authors to observe propriety and moral sensibility, perhaps in hopes of pleasing an eastern audi-ence, since it was by far the largest market. Beadle's first four commandments were prohibitions: "We prohibit all things offensive to good taste in expres-sion and incident—We prohibit subjects of characters that carry an immoral *taint*—We prohibit the repetition of any occurrence which though true, is yet better untold—We prohibit what cannot be read with satisfaction by every right-minded person—old and young alike—." The firm also required an author's "best work," "unquestioned originality," strong plot and high drama, graceful, correct composition, and intimate familiarity with the subjects and places that they incorporate in their stories. Although their large output of novels precluded a thorough policing of their policies, these standards did have an appreciable effect, albeit one that diminished as the firm approached the new century.[96]

In the main, the women of the dime novels are heroines that grow from the earlier sentimental fiction of the day, rather than shemales. They are generally young, beautiful, and more self-sufficient than their forebears; their manlike behavior is often the result of a horrendous act of violence that eliminates their entire family or selected loved ones, for which they swear undying vengeance, or may result from their uneducated rearing in the depths of the wilderness or as captives of an Indian tribe; their language is usually proper; and those who are not consumed by their personal passion for vendetta are normally saved through true love and marriage. Very few female grotesques are in evidence; indeed, nearly every heroine is curiously given the ladylike quality of "dainty feet."

The reader is introduced to Joseph E. Badger's title character, Mountain Kate, the child of an outlaw, as she battles and helps kill a ferocious wolver-ine in the Rockies. She later saves her rescuer, Frank Yates, by killing three of his attackers and wounding another, reenacting the ancient role of protectress, and the adventure ends in their marriage and happy return to civilization: "They still reside in St. Louis, happy and contented, surrounded by a goodly family."[97] After the "Wild Huntress," Marian Holt, is deceived into a sham marriage with the villain Stebbins, who hopes to marry her and her sister to "the Mormon Prophet," she escapes and is adopted by a friendly tribe. She makes the wilderness her home, and with her prowess as a huntress earns the respect of all, but longs to go back to civilization. Both sisters are rescued, marry their deliverers, and return to build plantations in Tennessee.[98] The moral of these stories seems to be that no matter how free or wild a woman may be in the wilderness, all she really wants or needs is a good man and a house.

Hurricane Nell has much more of the wild activity of a shemale in her, although she begins as a victim at the hands of Bob Woolf and his band of marauders, who torch her house with her dying parents inside. Dime novels are as sensational as they are sentimental. She swears the customary dire oath of vengeance: "'Girl though I am, and young and feeble, I will sweep into the robbers' ranks and take a life for every word that the desperado chief uttered ten hours ago! I *swear it!* before high heaven I *swear it!*'" Nell perfects her manly skills until she can "outrun, out-ride, out-shoot, out-lasso, [and] out-yell" all comers in true Crockett-like fashion, but then unleashes a string of murders that would make Davy blanch and a serial killer proud. A third of the way through the novel, she has executed and placed her "death-mark" upon half of the "two-score of ruffians." As she and the romantic lead hero, Cecil, flee on horseback from Woolf and his brigands, Cecil's mount tires. Bracing herself in the saddle, Nell *"seized him about the waist, raised him high over her head by the power of her wonderful arms, and deposited him upon the back of the wild stallion"* that she rode. She later escapes from a slow death-by-barbecue by thrusting herself into the fire to burn off the entrapping ropes to free herself. Still later, when both Nell (in disguise) and Cecil are captured, she gains a stay of execution for them both by shooting a pea from the tip of her love's nose that Woolf had attached with a bit of pitch. Her sarcasm about Woolf's kindness ups the ante for achieving their freedom. He nails Cecil's ears to the wall and commands her to put "a head" on each "needle" with her rifle or die. Nell fires, the gang rushes unarmed to view the result, and the hideout is stormed by a band of Pawnees led by Nell's disfigured but very much alive father. Rescued again. With all but one of the villains dead, and that one turned over to the law, Nell and her father now "had by God's kind beneficence been permitted to emerge from the cloud of wrong, hatred and vengeance, into the pure freedom and peace of reunion and a better existence." Not too unexpectedly in this piece of formula fiction, Nell marries Cecil and lives happily ever after. Her shot, by the way, did put "a head" on that "needle."[99] Significantly, what motivates Nell's hurricane of action is the literal destruction of her home, her domestic sphere, and she returns to it as soon as possible. In contrast, the riproarious shemales of the Crockett Almanacs remain wild; the end of their adventures never sees them "domesticated."

Hurricane Nell's story is also notable for the use of sensational, graphic descriptions that find an antecedent in the captivity narratives and for its almost Dickensian number of subplots, at least for a dime novel. Herein lies another major difference between the Crockett Almanacs and the dime novels. Shemale stories are generally short, quick, and to the point. The length of the dime novels, often one hundred times that of the tales, fosters intertwined adventures, multiple revelations, and reversals, all usually advanced through chapters that alternate subjects, to reach a level of complexity never attempted in the shemale stories.

There is also a long list of women characters like Nell in the dime novels who are transformed by love and saved by marriage from their roles as avenging angels: "Tiger-Lily, The Vulture Queen," "Wild Edna, the Girl Brigand," "The Girl Avenger," and "Silver Rifle, the Girl Trailer" are among that noteworthy group.[100] Not all end well. "Wild Nell," the "Western Amazon" who terms herself "the wildest she-devil on the plains," loses the man she loved (who wronged her) to the gun of Buffalo Bill and becomes a shattered hermit "dwelling in a humble cabin, where none dare intrude upon her grief-stricken life."[101] In *The Girl Captain*, Maria Shelby, her gang, and their rival gang are all annihilated by rangers; "Queen Helen, the Avenger," an unrepentant outlaw who leads her band in robbing stage coaches, dies a "wicked woman" and is buried without a prayer.[102] Sad and bad endings are not the fare of the Crockett Almanac tales, but serve as a reminder of the moral base or at least frame for the values that are an integral part of the chronologically increasing sensationalism of the dime novels. Authors can shock and titillate in the sentimental tradition as long as they educate as well. Part of this education is the reaffirmation of the status quo, the confirmation of the domestic sphere as the rightful realm of women.

Three characters that seem to inherit traits of the riproarious shemales in mastery of wild beasts, woodcraft, and language are also published by Beadle and Adams. Katrina Hartstein, the Jaguar Queen, travels with a whole posse of terrible creatures—"seven full-grown jaguars, with two grizzly bears, and several jaguar kittens"—but dies to save the life of her rival for her one true love. Lucinda "Cindy" Steele, although a minor character, breaks the dime novel mold by being an older woman. Searching for her husband, she is "'as good on the trail or in a fight as most of the men'" and "too good a scout to smoke [her pipe] in the presence of the enemy, and she is hunting Shawnees and her 'old man.'" The description of another subordinate character, California Kate Savage, by her intended, Beautiful Bill the giant, rivals those that Davy Crockett pronounces about his relatives and female friends: "'Oh! she's a reg'lar war-horse, is my Kate, pilgrims—a two-storied complex catapultian comet.'" But Kate's actions place her beyond shemales into the camp of the Amazons; she is a comic-aggressive who delivers verbal abuse for the challenge. To win Bill's hand in marriage, she calls the mayor out to a duel: "'meet me in ther street, wi' ther broadsword or dueling blade, an' fight me till I or you ar' licked, ter our full satisfaction. By admitting yourself ter be an unmitigated coward an' nincompoop, ye can honorably refuse this challenge, but ef ye aspire ter be a gentleman, ye're bound ter cum an' face me.'" Kate is a master with a sword and Bill taunts the mayor with her skill: "'she will lam it to you beautiful, will my gal Kate—she'll cut ye up inter sirloin stakes afore ye can spit a stream o' terbaccy-juice over yer under jaw, an' I'll bet two ter one on't.'" The duel to the death is child's play for Kate, who toys with the mayor by alternately slapping him on each cheek with the flat of her blade so rapidly that he drops his weapon from the pain and runs away from "the girl gladiator."[103]

From about the last quarter of the nineteenth century, the dime novel authors apply new categories to these western women of the wilderness. The "sport" and the "pard" (partner) would normally designate men and a man-to-man relationship and attaching these labels to women is meant to startle and, as in the shemale tales, to challenge traditional roles. As "sports" and "pards," women characters are not simply aligned with bad and good, the single and the soon to be attached, those who die and those who marry, although all those characteristics can at times apply. The authors vary the formula for interest. Both types of women also do mighty deeds that equal those of men, with the "sport" more likely to surpass her male competition. The "sport" is distinguished as the equal of the male dandy in dress; often adopts men's clothing, complete with a swagger and attitude to match; is more of a loner; and, with the exception of her sex, could be a man for all intents and purposes. The "pard" is generally just what the name implies, more of an equal partner to the hero, a trusty, skilled sidekick who shares adventures and risks, is generally more feminine, and has a better chance of permanent male company when she rides into the sunset at the end of the novel.

A fine early example of the "sport," and perhaps the most recognizable female protagonist of the dime novel is Calamity Jane:

> Her dress was buckskin trowsers, met at the knee by fancifully beaded leggings, with slippers of dainty pattern upon the feet; a velvet vest, and one of those luxuries of the mines, a boiled shirt, open at the throat, partially revealing a breast of alabaster purity; a short velvet jacket, and a Spanish broad-brimmed hat, slouched upon one side of a regally beautiful head. There were diamond rings upon her hands, a diamond pin in her shirt-bosom, a massive gold chain strung across her vest front.

"Trowsers" are a necessity for a "sport" like Calamity. Like the more civilized bloomers favored by some women's rights activists, they simultaneously provide freedom of movement and assert equality with men. Later in the novel, Calamity explains why she dresses this way: "'I don't allow ye can beat men's togs much fer handy locomotion an' so forth, an' then, ye see, I'm as big a gun among the men as any of 'em.'" Calamity is described as quite the dandy, and her horse is decked out to match, "richly decorated and bespangled, after lavish Mexican taste." Her skills are legendary in the town of "Whoop-Up." This "dare-devil" can light her "cigar at full motion" on her horse and let out "a ringing whoop, which was creditable in imitation if not in volume and force to that of a full-blown Comanche warrior." Calamity is described as quite the man: "'She ar the most reckless buchario in ther Hills, kin drink whisky, shute, play keerds, or sw'ar, ef et comes to et.'" But she, like the vast majority of "sports" in the dime novels, has been driven to such behavior: "'I reckon ther gal's got honor left wi' her grit, out o' ther wreck o' a young life.'" Calamity is still a physical beauty, but on her pretty face "were lines drawn by the unmistakable hand of dissipation and hard usage." At the conclusion of the tale, the narrator teases the reader with the rumor that "Calamity will soon start East on a bridal tour" but undercuts her prospects immediately: "As to the truth of this, I cannot say; I doubt much if Calamity will ever marry."[104]

"Sports" and "pards" share the frontier-derived independence of the riproarious shemales of the Almanacs, but if the "sports" echo more of the dialect and manufactured language of the wilderness, the "pards" emphasize a bit more of the sentiment through their emotional responses.[105] The example of Reta Grant in T. C. Harbaugh's *Cool Sam's Girl Pard; Or, Captain Dick and His Texans* should suffice. While Cool Sam is occupied with Captain Dick and his band of desperadoes, Reta sets off on her own to find young Roy Robsart, who, taken captive as an infant, is now the Apache war chief Panther Robe. As best friends, their fathers pledged Reta and Roy as "best pards" over their cradles. When both men die, Cool Sam, the witness to their oath, takes and raises Reta and eventually commences a search for "the Infant," as he calls him. Impulsively slipping away from Sam and successfully tracking the Apaches, Reta marches right into their camp despite the sentry's warning that they would take no prisoners. She fends them off with the same pistol used to keep the sentry cooperative and bursts through the band to grab Panther Robe's arm, saying: "'Roy! Roy! my long hunt has ended at last! Years have separated us; but now we are united. The vow over the two cradles—.'" But interrupted by the boy chief's wild cry, she hears his oath never to look on the face of a white woman, as he strides away. Disarmed, pinioned, and true to the sentry's word, given a death sentence by the braves who remain, Reta is freed by Panther Robe, who breaks his Indian oath to save her and is forced to leave his adopted tribe. Reta soon shows her true grit as a protectress when they are captured by Captain Dick and his gang and they threaten to kill Roy: "'Harm him to-night and I will take vengeance. Laugh at me. Call me a girl, but recollect that under Cool Sam's eye I have learned to kill!'" She later wounds Captain Dick and even kills an Apache to defend and rescue Sam. She is not as lethal as Cool Sam, however, whose blazing guns exterminate Dick, his gang of thieves, and nearly all of Panther Robe's former raiding party of Apaches. This swirl of events allows Reta and Roy to settle down on adjacent farms in Texas and, the narrator announces in the last sentence of the novel, they are soon to marry.[106] The author adds a level of complexity to the novel by having Reta apprentice and serve as Cool Sam's "pard" until she is reunited with Roy. Only then, after fulfilling his vow, can Cool Sam honestly relinquish his role as the guardian of Reta as a "pard" to Roy. Unstated but understood is Reta's future role after her marriage to Roy. Single "pards" retain their independent spirit; dime novel wives generally do not.

"Sports" and pards" seem generally to divide and extend the characteristics of the shemales of the Crockett Almanacs. Shemales often act out their adventures individually, as do "sports," but never dress like a male dandy or "swell," or act with such bravado. Like the "pards," shemales are sometimes paired with a backwoods beau, but their "romances" and marriages, if they occur, are treated satirically rather than sentimentally. And most important, shemales are liberated to the full extent of the authors' imaginations, not bound by the demands of convention or of realism that constrain the dime novel heroines of the West. In defiance of convention, shemales remain free in the Almanacs, and no matter how implausible, contrived, coincidental, or contorted the plots of the dime novels may be, the "tall" has fallen away from most of those tales.

Other changes are also apparent. The West, which served as the cornerstone of the success of the publishing house of Beadle and Adams, eventually gave way before even more sensational stories and before the new blockbuster that was certainly all the rage by about 1890, the detective novel. A harbinger of this trend perhaps lay in the fact that rumor about Calamity Jane's "bridal tour" in the East pairs her with a detective; recall as well that the primary title of her tale is *Deadwood Dick as Detective* and that Dick himself progresses from bandit to reformed criminal to detective in his dime novel careers. The most famous of these detectives are male—Old Sleuth, Cap Collier, and Nick Carter. Of the few that are female, even fewer have ties to the West, as the labyrinthian maze of the growing metropolises seems the more natural base for their exploits.[107]

Outside the dime novels, the West continued to draw readers in huge numbers to the popular literature of Bret Harte, Zane Grey, Luke Short, Max Brand, and Louis L'Amour, among others. But the unique era and combination of genres and traits that so marked the riproarious shemale of the Crockett Almanacs had passed. Gender stereotypes and the tradition of the sentimental are extraordinarily strong in much western popular fiction. The environment still usually demands self-sufficiency, physical skill, and ingenuity of women characters, but the constraints of the genre and perhaps the marketplace reinforce the oldest polarity in stereotypes—woman as passive civilizer, the moral and emotional center, and the wellspring of all domestic good versus woman as independent, active, and assertive, a sometime seducer and sexual being who lives to ensnare, bedevil, or otherwise lead man to an ignominious fall. At times for this literature, overt generalizations seem like truisms. If the West is the place where a man can truly be a man, the corollary stereotype is that then a woman must be a woman.

Most twentieth-century versions of the shemales have left the frontier. Looking briefly outside the West into the worlds of other fictional women in print culture yields an intriguing and diverse catch. Again, like the dime novels, the net contains some interesting inheritors of the actions and descriptions of the Crockett Almanacs' shemales, inheritors whose creators twist and remake their behavior to match their culture through different settings, times, occupations, and media. Although television and the movies are generally beyond the scope of this essay, it is mainly in these media that the idea of a frontier and the power of an unexplored wilderness to affect character survives. Here too, however, even when the women have or exceed the prowess of men in their exploits, one or more of the comic, satiric, and wildly imaginative elements of the shemale stories is usually lacking.

A very eclectic tour of print sources could begin with Tugboat Annie Brennan, whose exploits for the Deep-Sea Towing and Salvage Company based on Puget Sound delighted readers of *The Saturday Evening Post* throughout the 1930s. When Norman Reilly Raine introduced readers to his character on July 11, 1931, his description of Annie resonated with some of the more memorable shemales of the Crockett Almanacs:

> She was large-framed, solidly built, with rugged masculine features, and shrewd, quick, blue eyes, and her movements had an elephantine energy that galvanized everyone with whom she came in contact. When she passed through a room, dust and odd bits of paper danced in her wake. And when she stood, as now, with beetling brows and sturdy legs apart, the feather in her antiquated bonnet nodding raffish defiance, she looked not unlike a blowzy but exceedingly combative bulldog.

So too do her actions, which have her besting nearly every man whom she meets, most of whom initially judge her unfit for skippering a tug. The ultimately heroic nature of Annie's character overshadows her description, which borders on that of the grotesques of the Crockett Almanacs, and places her in a different category than Shillaber's Mrs. Partington to espouse her rights as a woman, because Annie is neither unsympathetic nor ridiculous as a character. A penetrating realist, she states her views directly, without a sugar-coating, and occasionally with such sarcasm and boisterous wit that she bears a striking similarity to Marietta Holley's Samantha Allen.[108]

Beyond description, another common thread between Tugboat Annie and the shemales of the Almanacs is her ability to merge both gender roles. While her salty language, fists, seamanship, and knowledge of maritime law convince her male doubters of her abilities one way or another, she is still a woman. Her voice grows husky and she nearly cries gazing at the picture of her dead husband, needing to turn it to the wall, saying, "'Sentimental old fool I'm growin' to be!'" In this first episode, she saves the company she works for from a "modern" businessman, who seeks to buy a controlling interest and to fire her because she is a woman and because "'Her influence, in what essentially is a man's sphere, is bound to have undesirable results.'" Annie deftly turns the tables on this "'lallapaloosa,'" whom she also calls "'Mr. Great Thinker'" and "'Frog-Face,'" and on the captain of the "Barracuda," who thinks he has succeeded in chiseling down her fee for towing his vessel off a reef to an absurdly low level, when she says that she knew that the skipper had lied about the damage to his ship when they made their bargain. So, she announces triumphantly:

> Because he concealed from me the fact that the Barracuda had stripped her propeller in among the rocks, our towing agreement didn't mean a thing, and we've got an unbeatable claim for salvage. If I'd left him piled up on the rocks, the Barracuda would have been pounded to pieces in the gale. But bein' just a stupid, mutton-hearted female, I yanked her home. So instead of a lousy towin' fee of two hundred and forty dollars, we'll get a salvage award of about a third the value of the ship and cargo.

Annie saves the company, harangues the captain and the businessman out of the office, and the story ends with her voice growing husky again at the sight of another picture of her late husband.[109] Like the riproarious shemales, Annie always displays a bit of her feminine side. In a 1939 episode, for example, after again filling the company's coffers, she asks her employer for "'the loan o' six bits'" to go to the stevedores union's "'shenanigan'" with Big Sam so she can "'l'arn to be a glitterbug.'"[110]

The most popular and most imitated of the twentieth-century inheritors of the abilities of the shemales is clearly Wonder Woman. Not only is there a direct line of descent from almanac to dime novel to comic book as popular inexpensive print media, but with Wonder Woman, the actual lineage comes full circle back to the Amazons. She is Princess Diana, daughter of Queen Hippolyte, the ruler of Paradise Island, the refuge granted the Amazons by Aphrodite after their defeat at the hands of Hercules. More than a simple female clone of Superman, Wonder Woman was created by William Moulton Marston, writing as Charles Moulton, and first appeared in December 1941. Both the author and the date are significant. Marston was a well-known psychologist and the inventor of the polygraph, who used these comics to explore his ideas about male-female relationships, which, if his superhero's comments are indicative, hearken back to the issue of sovereignty so dear to Chaucer's Wife of Bath. In Wonder Woman's world, the spirits of Aphrodite and Mars contend for control of the Earth, and the battle of the sexes is linked directly to the struggle between good and evil, between the goddess of love and the god of war. When Wonder Woman's companion cannot understand why former slave girls refuse their newfound freedom, Wonder Woman attributes it to their subjugation by a "man-ruled world," saying: "'They want to be slaves because they're afraid to be free and compete with men!'"(February–March 1943). The archvillain Dr. Psycho's goal is "to change the independent status of modern American women back to the days of the sultans and slave markets, clanking chains and abject captivity" (June–July 1943). Three years later, Wonder Woman exacts revenge by transporting Dr. Psycho's wife, Marva, to Reform Island, where her mind will receive "Amazon training" so that "no one man'll ever be able to dominate her again!" (July–August 1946). In winter 1943, when Queen Hippolyte gazes into her magic sphere and sees the utopian world of 3700 A.D., she finds that "Men and women will be equal. But woman's influence will control most governments because women are more ready to serve others unselfishly!" Not only does the civilizing influence of women endure well into the future, but it also becomes apparent that marriage, even to a good man, like Wonder Woman's true love, army pilot Steve Trevor, will mean a life of relative submission to his will.[111]

The date for launching this superhero's career, December 1941, rather naturally enlists Wonder Woman in the American cause on two fronts, one personal and one idealistic or nationalistic. The personal cause results from her falling in love with the injured Steve Trevor, the first man whom she has ever seen, who crash lands on Paradise Island while in pursuit of a Nazi spy plane. Princess Diana (soon to be Wonder Woman) wants to help Steve complete his mission, but her mother decides to consult their goddesses first. Aphrodite warns Queen Hippolyte that "'Danger threatens the entire world'" and she must deliver Steve "'back to America—to help fight the forces of hate and oppression.'" Athena concurs: "'American liberty and freedom must be preserved! You must send him with your strongest and wisest Amazon—the finest of your wonder women!—For America, the last citadel of democracy, and of equal rights for women, needs your help!'"[112] Thus Wonder Woman dons her star-spangled costume of red, white, blue, and yellow to become one of the many superheroes gladly mustered into duty to fight for the United States in World War II, but one of the few who openly fights under the banner of preserving equal rights for women. Although some today would call her subsequent beliefs and actions in the comics patriotic (and

nearly all those then immersed in post–Pearl Harbor America would certainly do so), these stories can as well echo the racism and sometimes the jin-
goism of manifest destiny, held so high in the Crockett Almanacs of the
1840s and likewise popular in their time. In this line, it is also interesting to
note that the utopian vision of Queen Hippolyte for 3700 A.D. reveals that
"the whole world will be one nation called the United States of Earth."[113]

For the most part, the shemales of the Almanacs have no cause beyond
the personal, no issue or motive greater than themselves or their individual
affairs that would shift the focus away from their primary independence and
pursuit of backwoods adventures. Almanac women are cultural reflectors, in
a fun-house mirror fashion, not direct commentors on or shapers of culture.
They are not, like Wonder Woman, able to bring or interested in bringing
"the invincible power of perfect womanhood to the supreme task of defend-
ing democracy and transforming evil to justice and happiness!" (September
1942).[114] Nor, with the lack of some overt cause for their behavior, do they
somehow parallel the more realistic depictions of the premier World War II
shemale, Rosie the Riveter.[115] Shemales are not "perfect womanhood," but a
comic inversion of nineteenth-century "true womanhood"; their tales produce humor through the incongruity and displacement that results when the
tenets of "true womanhood" meet the wilderness.

Wonder Woman is extreme. Since she is "as lovely as Aphrodite—as
wise as Athena—with the speed of Mercury and the strength of Hercules"
(February 1942), her powers far exceed those of the riproarious shemales, and
given her magic lasso, her invisible robot plane, and her bullet-deflecting
bracelets, among other gadgets, her powers outdo those of Davy Crockett
himself as the superhero of the Almanacs. The key ingredient lacking is
again comedy and satire. Amazons like Wonder Woman are serious. After
Marston's death in 1947, the "psychology" in the series is preempted by more
straightforward adventure narratives, though probably not to the comic's
overall advantage.[116] But Wonder Woman eventually encouraged a host of
imitators, some of which survive to the present day.

At first glance, outer space as a setting seems to offer fertile ground for
flourishing modern versions of the shemales of the Crockett Almanacs. Historically and imaginatively, it is a frontier—John F. Kennedy's "New Frontier" and William Shatner's "final frontier" for "Star Trek." If the "pard"
whimpers to a saccharine end in the person of Dale Evans on television's
"The Roy Rogers Show," moving from its 6:30 to 7:00 P.M. family slot on
Sunday night (1951–57) to that of a Saturday morning kids' show in reruns
(1961–64), it is more than restored on the big screen with Princess Leia

(Carrie Fisher) in the *Star Wars* trilogy (1977, 1980, 1983). After Wonder Woman, the "sport" blasts off as well. Television's Kathryn Janeway (Kate Mulgrew) is a captain on "Star Trek: Voyager," and in the movies, Ellen Ripley (Sigourney Weaver) demands attention for her portrayal in the *Aliens* trilogy. Both are smart, tough, and effective heroes but are separated from the Crockett shemales by class and by the lack of comedy. Match and solve these problems with Granny and Elly May Clampett of "The Beverly Hillbillies" or Mammy Yokum of *Li'l Abner,* and the adventures are lost.[117] Without reassembling all the various strains that spin out of the shemales of the Almanacs in a precarious balance, it seems harder and harder to find them replicated in today's culture.

The daughters of Wonder Woman explore the dark as well as the good side of shemale behavior, a journey that never appears in the Crockett Almanacs. The "bad girl" fad in comics of the mid-1990s, for example, has no forebear in the Almanacs; there, "bad" is linked predominantly to those wilderness women who are too citified or incomplete in their adoption of frontier ways. Given the Romantic movement's overlay of the Age of Jackson, which promotes the "noble" in the Noble Savage and holds untrammeled nature up as the source of inspiration and goodness, one should indeed be hard pressed to find an evil woman in the Almanac world. The authors do tinker quite a bit to make savagery a virtue in these backwoods, but never incorporate evil in the form of venomous women or true femme fatales.

The female villains and heroes of the comic books that appear after Wonder Woman, although still in the minority when compared to male superheroes, present a dizzying array of characters involved in adventure, violence, and sex. Even a partial composite list is formidable, with their names occasionally betraying their predilections: Bat Woman, Spider Woman, Supergirl, She-Hulk, and Ms. Marvel, some of whom echo the "pard," as well as Banshee, Dagger, Darkstar, Dazzler, Bloody Mary, Sersi, Shadowcat, Medusa, Namorita, Quicksilver, the Scarlet Witch, Silver Sable, Feral, Psylocke, Husk, Moondragon, Black Widow, Phoenix, Stryke, Razor, Jazz, Rogue, Witchblade, Martha Washington, Storm, Elektra, Lady Death, and Tank Woman.[118]

Almost universally bold, beautiful, and brassy, these scantily clad curvaceous women are meant primarily to target young male readers, since women make up less than 3 percent of the audience for comics. The most successful character at capturing a female audience began in a comic book but made the jump to greater distribution in mass culture through television as "Xena: Warrior Princess."[119] No bolt out of the blue in terms of behavior, Xena is perhaps the most popular and extreme of the recent reincarnations of the "sport." She also derives much of her character from the television shows and films of the 1960s and 1970s that parallel the emergence of the women's movement. Examine the James Bond phenomenon and uncover a sample of corollary female spy–detective shows and movies such as "Honey West" (1965–66), whose title character's shemale credentials include a pet ocelot, the French secret agent *Modesty Blaise* (1966), *Fathom* (1967), starring Raquel Welch as a sky-diving spy, or the more successful "The Avengers" (1966–69) and "Charlie's Angels" (1976–81), and see that these women all demonstrate independence and exhibit varying degrees of a male hero's abilities, but a good deal of the focus on their characters highlights their femininity and sex appeal. While Xena is far more the aggressive warrior than anyone else in this group and does not play up to the male characters, she is also arguably one of the most sensual, a holdover from the comic book tradition.

Xena began her television career as an evil warrior princess and warlord on the show "Hercules: The Legendary Journeys" before beginning her own series in September 1995 and undergoing a reformation of sorts. She attacks evil, defends the powerless, and makes victimizers her victims in a way that puts Rambo to shame. Campy, melodramatic, and a bit New Age, the series draws women and men as viewers, particularly those from eighteen to thirty-five, who cannot get enough of Xena's mayhem-laden adventures with her "pard," Gabrielle, of Xena's ambiguous sexuality, and of the writers' unwillingness to cast main characters as simply good or bad.[120] Satire even plays a minor role in the series, as the punning names of episodes like "A Fistful of Dinars" or "Here She Comes . . . Miss Amphipolis" and a revisionist feminist ending for *The Iliad* broadly hint. "Xena to Helen of Troy: 'What do you want to do?' Helen: 'No one's ever asked me that before!'"[121]

Although few would initially link Xena to the shemales of the Crockett Almanacs simply because the visual media and culture of the 1990s is hard to connect to the print culture of the Age of Jackson, Xena's sense of adventure and her wild environment provide a prime connection to the shemales, as do the shared aspects of comedy, satire, and violence. Like most of the shemales, Xena's tale of adventure never ends, because she never marries and settles down. Both venues have also given free range to the imagination of their writers. Perhaps the most substantial difference is that Xena tells her own story and is never the butt of the humor or satire.

The print culture of the 1990s does bear some evidence of the continued popularity of the tales of the riproarious shemales. It occurs, appropriately enough, in a genre where imagination holds grand sway over authors and readers alike, that of children's literature, and where much of what is written is initially meant to captivate the parents, who buy and first read these often sumptuously illustrated volumes to their children. In *Sally Ann Thunder Ann Whirlwind Crockett* (1995), Steven Kellogg combines, modifies, and expands the Almanac tales about Davy's wife into a rollicking legendary biography.[122]

Of the children's books that deal with the American frontier and the wilderness experience, one in particular captures the tall-tale spirit of the shemales and reinvents them for today's audience. Ann Isaacs's *Swamp Angel* (1994) records the fictional adventures of Angelica Longrider, born August 1, 1815, and destined to "become the greatest woodswoman in Tennessee." At age two she builds a cabin, as a young woman she rescues a mired wagon train by lifting all the wagons to high ground (after the fashion of Bess Call lifting her ox and plow), and for the main event, she outdoes a passel of male "Tennessee daredevils" to take on "Thundering Tarnation," a bear that, like Angelica, is of epic proportions. Swamp Angel throws Tarnation so high that she has to lasso him with a tornado just to bring him down. Their wrestling raises up the Great Smoky Mountains. They even wrestle in their sleep until Swamp Angel snores down a tree that flattens Thundering Tarnation. The celebration feast fills all the empty storehouses in Tennessee with meat and so enlarges the citizens' stomachs that "You could hear waistcoat buttons popping as far away as Kentucky." Tarnation's pelt is so large that Swamp Angel has to move to Montana to spread it out: "Nowadays, folks call it the Shortgrass Prairie."[123] Part Crockett, part Paul Bunyan, and all shemale, Swamp Angel creates an indelible impression as a flamboyant tall-tale heroine who does true justice to her forebears.

So what, after all, would be Davy Crockett's "receipt" for concocting a modern shemale? Take the setting and tall-tale nature of a Swamp Angel, tenderize it with Tugboat Annie's heroic "grotesque" femininity and rugged sentimentality, season with the nobility of Wonder Woman and the sensuality and satire of Xena, and simmer on a lightnin' bolt for violence and adventure until ready to serve.

Taken as part of a historical continuum of thousands of years and as a seedbed for a range of modern fictional depictions of women who adopt the roles traditionally associated with or limited to men, the uniqueness of the riproarious shemales of the Crockett Almanacs is clear. Whether they are as obviously linked as Swamp Angel through multiple features or a more distant relative like Xena, in whom one can make out various traces of family resemblance, is ultimately beyond the point. These shemales open up worlds— both the wondrous and sometimes cankered world of the tales as stories in themselves and open as well the world of the authors and the culture that produced and relished them. When readers knock at their door, shemales greet visitors with a smirk, perhaps knowing that a good deal of present-day cultural baggage is yet to be unpacked and that such satire, even in its own time, suffers equivocal interpretation at best. Are the tales simply the riotous fun that results from injecting "true womanhood" into the stereotypically male wilderness? Or is this satire as a more complex social corrective? Do the authors develop the anarchy of the fictional situation and the disruption of norms to its maximum outlandish potential to warn society of the dangers of the women's movement and thus try to chart a course away from extremes back to the center? Why do Davy Crockett and Ben Harding narrate so many of the women's tales, and why are these shemales nearly always described rather than given their own voice? Are these male hack writers simply in the normal rush of getting out a "cheap" publication, or do they somehow seek to affirm the power of men over women by making men the narrators, keeping the shemales as only almost the equal of male ring-tailed roarers, and having them keep a foothold, however ironic, in a nonetheless reassuring backwoods femininity? And if so, does the satire eventually back-fire on itself to open the vision of alternative paths for women through the challenges that the stories issue to the conventional views of gender, social-ization, and roles using characters so attractively subversive?

Yes.

All these views are sound, informative, and supportable, but are never mutually exclusive. Like gender itself in the Almanacs, these views blend into one another. While at bottom one cannot realistically analyze the con-scious or unconscious motivation of anonymous authors or offer their depic-tions as completely representative of their society, their stories provide the tantalizing hints and clues for investigation that only simple imaginative tales can do. As indicators, even oblique ones, they rightly claim a special place in the historical sweep of the literary treatments of women. By bringing the belief of Margaret Fuller that begins the headnote of this essay to a wide swath of the American public in an almanac, one of the most popular forms of publication of its day, they underscore both her idea of the fluidity of gen-der and especially that of gender roles: "There is no wholly masculine man, no purely feminine woman." Davy shows his feminine side by providing wild "recipes" and at times responding sentimentally to emotional situations in the tales. He also takes great care to emphasize and appreciate the masculin-ity of the riproarious shemales, who zestfully fulfill traditional male roles due to the inherent freedom of the wilderness and the inherent potential for comedy in redefining the stereotype of true womanhood.

Davy makes this combination of traits clear in "Sal Fink, the Mississippi Screamer" through repetition and emphasis in a passage that both liberates and satirizes the nature of women. Just before he outlines Sal's true grit and manlike achievements and adventures, such as her duel with a thunderbolt, her clearing the Mississippi River for navigation, her riding "down the river on an alligator's back, standen upright, an' dancing *Yankee Doodle*," and her roasting of Indians, Davy hammers home the point that this is exactly what a backwoods woman should do:

> I dar say you've all on you, if not more, frequently heerd this great she human crittur boasted of, an' pointed out as *"one o' the gals"*—but I tell you what, stranger, you have never really set your eyes on *"one of the gals,"* till you have seen Sal Fink, the Mississippi screamer . . . —an' if thar ever was a gal that desarved to be christened *"one o' the gals,"* then this gal was that gal—and no mistake.(171–72)

Riproarious shemales are a breed apart.

## NOTES

1. Margaret Fuller, *Woman in the Nineteenth Century* (New York: Greeley & McElrath, 1845), p. 109; Dr. Charles D. Meigs, *Lecture on Some of the Distinctive Characteristics of the Female* (Philadelphia: T. K. and P. G. Collins, 1847), pp. 16–17. Note that this oft-quoted statement is a description of a statue of the Venus de Medici as compared with that of the Apollo of the Belvidere as representatives of the female and male physical form rather than a direct description of a woman. Meigs's intent, however, to allow it to stand for the women of his day is clear. "Crockett's Mother [age 148]," 1845, p. 5; "Crockett's Disappointment," 1843, p. 8; "Col. Crockett Beat at a Shooting Match," 1840 Nashville, p. 11. Walter Blair and Franklin J. Meine mistakenly list this tale as appearing in the 1839 Nashville Almanac in their *Half Horse Half Alligator: The Growth of the Mike Fink Legend* (Chicago: University of Chicago Press, 1956), pp. 63, 65.

   Consult the Appendix for full bibliographic descriptions of the Crockett Almanacs. References to Almanac stories not included in this volume are cited parenthetically, but by year and page numbers if the Almanac appears in Appendix I; otherwise, the full citation is recorded in the note.

   For a brief history of the Crockett Almanacs in the context of other almanacs, a biography of the historical David Crockett, and an overview of the folk and tall-tale elements of the stories told by the fictional Davy Crockett, see Michael A. Lofaro, "Davy Crockett, Tall Tale Humor, and the Second Nashville Series of Crockett Almanacs," in *The Tall Tales of Davy Crockett: The Second Nashville Series of Crockett Almanacs, 1838–1841*, ed. Michael A. Lofaro (Knoxville: University of Tennessee Press, 1987), pp. xv–xxxviii. This facsimile edition of three of the Almanacs also provides the reader with the only readily available text of the tales in the format in which they originally appeared.

2. There is, however, a subgenre of antebellum "female fiend" popular literature. See Dawn Keetley, "Victim and Victimizer: Female Fiends and Unease over Marriage in Antebellum Sensational Fiction," *American Quarterly* 51 (June 1999): 344–84. No such women appear in the Crockett Almanacs.

3. For a fine discussion of this issue, see Robert Kimbrough, "Androgyny, Old and New," *Western Humanities Review* 35 (1981): [197]–215.

4. Robert Eisler, *Man into Wolf: An Anthropological Interpretation of Sadism, Masochism, and Lycanthropy* (1951; reprint, New York: Greenwood Press, 1969), p. 177.

5. E. G. Suhr, "The Daughter of the Dragon," *Folklore* 80 (Spring, 1969): 1–11; David Leeming and Jake Page, *Goddess: Myths of the Female Divine* (New York: Oxford University Press, 1994), pp. 133–38; "Athena," in Robert E. Bell, *Women of Classical Mythology: A Biographical Dictionary*, (Santa Barbara, CA: ABC-CLIO, 1991) pp. 84–88; and "Athene, Athena" in Patricia Monaghan, *The Book of Goddesses and Heroines*, (New York: E. P. Dutton, 1981), pp. 34–35.

6. The role of protectress holds true for sentimental sisters as well as riproarious shemales. See, for example, "A Gold-Ruminating upon Ruination." (251–52)

7. Mary Lefkowitz, "Classical Mythology and the Role of Women in Modern Literature," in *A Sampler of Women's Studies*, ed. Dorothy G. McGuigan (Ann Arbor: University of Michigan Center for Continuing Education of Women, 1973), pp. 77–84; Karl Kerényi, "A Mythological Image of Girlhood: Artemis," in *Facing the Gods*, ed. James Hillman (Irving, TX: Spring Publications, 1980), pp. 39–45; Leeming and Page, 138–39; "Artemis," in Bell, p. 7074, and in Monaghan, pp. 27–28.

8. Alexis de Tocqueville, *Democracy in America* (New York: Alfred A. Knopf, 1948), II, 201.

9. Donald J. Sobol, *The Amazons of Greek Mythology* (South Brunswick, Great Britain: A. S. Barnes and Company, 1972), pp. 115–16ff.; René Malamud, "The Amazon Problem," in Hillman, *Facing the Gods*, pp. 47–66; "Amazons," in Bell, pp. 29–32; and Martha Wiegel, *Spiders & Spinsters: Women and Mythology* (Albuquerque: University of New Mexico Press, 1982), pp. 269–75. The first chapter of this work provides some mythological examples from Native American culture. See also G. M. Mullett, *Legends of the Hopi Indians: Spider Woman Stories* (Tucson: University of Arizona Press, 1979), and for a broader selection of such tales encompassing the continental United States and Alaska, see Susan Hazen-Hammond, *Spider Woman's Web: Traditional Native American Tales about Women's Power* (New York: Penguin Putnam, 1999).

10. Dietrich von Bothmer, *Amazons in Greek Art* (Oxford: Claredon Press, 1957), pp. 30–69; Bell, p. 31.

11. Page duBois, *Centaurs and Amazons: Women and the Pre-History of the Great Chain of Being* (Ann Arbor: University of Michigan Press, 1982), pp. 33–41; Sobol, pp. 33–38. Phyllis Chesler, "The Amazon Legacy: An Interpretive Essay," in *Wonder Woman*, ed. Gloria Steinem (New York: Holt, Rinehart and Winston and Warner Books, 1972), pp. [10–19].

12. Sobol, p. 36.

13. Richard M. Dorson, "Davy Crockett and the Heroic Age," *Southern Folklore Quarterly* 6 (June 1942): 95–102; Crockett appears as Prometheus in "Crockett's Morning Hunt," 1854, p. [25]. Samuel L. Knapp, *Female Biography; Containing Notices of Distinguished Women in Different Nations and Ages* (1833; reprint, Philadelphia: Thomas Wardle, 1842). "Hannah Duston" (her name is also spelled Dustan and Dustin), treated later in this introduction, is also treated in Knapp's book. For a more readily available source for this and other selected tales about Crockett from the Almanacs, see Richard M. Dorson, *Davy Crockett: American Comic Legend* (New York: Rockland Editions, 1939); Franklin J. Meine, ed., *The Crockett Almanacs: Nashville Series, 1835–1838* (Chicago: Caxton Club, 1955); and Michael A. Lofaro, ed., *The Tall Tales of Davy Crockett: The Second Nashville Series of Crockett Almanacs, 1839–1841*. Dorson's sampler is far from a complete collection of the tales and does make some changes to the texts. See, for example, Michael A. Lofaro, "The Hidden 'Hero' of the Nashville Crockett Almanacs," in Michael A. Lofaro, ed., *Davy Crockett: The Man, The Legend, The Legacy, 1786–1986* (Knoxville: University of Tennessee Press, 1985), pp. 46–79.

14. For more information on Esther and these other famous queens and crusaders, the interested reader can also refer to the numerous biographies and biographical dictionaries. The frequent retelling of these stories and how they are modified over time to suit a particular author's view or culture is another interesting avenue of investigation. See, for example, for the purposes of this study, Mary De Jong, "God's Women: Victorian American Readings of Old Testament Heroines," in *Old Testament Women in Western Literature*, ed. Raymond-Jean Frontain and Jan Wojcik (Conway, AR: UCA Press, 1991), especially pp. 252–54 on Esther. Similarly, one can examine the recent portrayals of heroic women in today's children's literature as a cultural influence and reflector in such works as Gail Meyer Rolka, *100 Women Who Shaped the World* (San Mateo, CA: Bluewood Books, 1994), Rebecca Hazell, *Heroines: Great Women through the Ages* (New York: Abbeville Press, 1996), Richard Dungworth and Philippa Wingate, *The Usborne Book of Famous Women: From Nefertiti to Diana* (New York: Scholastic, 1998), and one of the best of these works and more focused on our particular study, Milton Meltzer, *Ten Queens: Portraits of Women of Power* (New York: Dutton Children's Books, 1998), which contains a sound beginning bibliography, pp. 127–29. For an interesting view of Cleopatra and Eleanor of Aquitaine, see Tristram Potter Coffin, *The Female Hero in Folklore and Legend* (New York: Simon

and Schuster, 1975), pp. 15–36 and 63–75, respectively. Perhaps the best single source, although one that does not make as fine a distinction between queens and warrior queens as the present study, is Antonia Fraser, *The Warrior Queens* (New York: Alfred A. Knopf, 1989). Other helpful single-subject works include Michael Grant, *Cleopatra* (London: Weidenfeld and Nicolson, 1972); Marion Meade, *Eleanor of Aquitaine: A Biography* (New York: Hawthorn Books, 1977); Peggy K. Liss, *Isabel the Queen* (New York: Oxford University Press, 1992); Jasper Ridley, *Elizabeth I: The Shrewdness of Virtue* (New York: Viking, 1988); Edward Crankshaw, *Maria Theresa* (New York: Viking Press, 1970); and John T. Alexander, *Catherine the Great: Life and Legend* (Cambridge: Oxford University Press, 1989). Information is relatively meager on Queen Tamara. See Ronald Grigor Suny, *Making of the Georgian Nation* (Bloomington: Indiana University Press, 1994), pp. 39–40, Kevin Tuite, *An Anthology of Georgian Folk Poetry* (Cranbury, New Jersey: Associated University Presses, 1994), pp. 68, 133, and Rolka, p. 20.

15. Thomas Kinsella, trans., *The Tain* (Philadelphia: University of Pennsylvania Press, 1985), pp. 52–253; Miles Dillon, *Early Irish Literature* (Chicago: University of Chicago Press, 1948), pp. 3–13; Eleanor Knott and Gerard Murphy, *Early Irish Literature* (London: Routledge & Kegan Paul, 1966), pp. 116–31; Fraser, pp. 15–17; Norma Lorre Goodrich, *Heroines: Demigoddess, Prima Donna, Movie Star* (New York: Harper Collins, 1993), pp. 197–202.

16. Fraser, pp. 58–106ff.

17. Ibid., pp. 107–28.

18. Goodrich, pp. 209–15.

19. Catalina de Erauso, *Lieutenant Nun: Memoir of a Basque Transvestite in the New World*, trans. Michele and Gabriel Stepto (Boston: Beacon Press, 1996), pp. 64–79, xxvi.

20. David Birmingham, *Trade and Conflict in Angola: The Mbundu and Their Neighbours under the Influence of the Portuguese, 1483–1790* (Oxford: Claredon Press, 1966), pp. 88–123; C. R. Boxer, *Race Relations in the Portuguese Colonial Empire: 1415–1825* (Oxford: Claredon Press, 1963), pp. 22–30; Fraser, pp. 226–46.

21. Lydia Maria Child, *An Appeal in Favor of That Class of Americans Called Africans* (1833; reprint, Amherst: University of Massachusetts Press, 1996), p. 145 (see also pp. 146–48). Native American matrilineal societies also provide examples of tribal queens and warriors. See Carolyn T. Foreman, *Indian Woman Chiefs* (Muskogee, OK: Hoffman Printing Com-

pany, 1954). Interestingly, Child uses the intelligence of Native Americans to argue that of the Africans, an argument that in part refers to Jinga: "And where will you find an Indian Chieftain, whose pride, intellect, and valor, are more than a match for Zhinga's?" (p. 161).

22. Frank B. Goodrich, *World-Famous Women. Types of Female Heroism, Beauty, and Influence, from the Earliest Ages to the Present Time* (Philadelphia: P. W. Ziegler & Co., 1880), pp. 335–41; A. R. Hope Moncrieff, *Heroines of European History* (New York: Dodge Publishing Company, [1913]), pp. 228–32; Rolka, p. 40. Byron's point is both her heroism and how unusual it is for a woman to be so "unsexed." For to him "are Spain's maids no race of Amazons,/ But form'd for all the witching arts of love." "Childe Harold's Pilgrimage," canto I, verses 54–58, ll. 560, 585–86, in *Lord Byron: The Complete Poetical Works,* ed. Jerome J. McGann (Oxford: Claredon Press, 1980), II, 29–30.

23. The general folk antecedents to "The Wife of Bath's Tale" point also to a rich tradition of stories that portray women who step outside of gender roles. These stories are serious, in that their characters are not the objects or perpetrators of humor, are less complex in narrative form, and often shy away from the bawdy, at least in printed versions. Sigmund Eisner, *A Tale of Wonder: A Source Study of The Wife of Bath's Tale* (1957; reprint, New York: Burt Franklin, 1969); G. H. Maynadier, *The Wife of Bath's Tale: Its Sources and Analogues* (1901; reprint, New York: AMS Press, 1972); Peter G. Beidler and Elizabeth M. Biebel, eds., *Chaucer's "Wife of Bath's Prologue" and "Tale": An Annotated Bibliography, 1900 to 1995* (Toronto: University of Toronto Press, 1998), pp. 29–54. For examples of the complexity of the tale, see Ruth Evans and Lesley Johnson, eds., *Feminist Readings in Middle English Literature: The Wife of Bath and All Her Sect* (London: Routledge, 1994). For other literary examples, see Simon Shepard, *Amazons and Warrior Women: Varieties of Feminism in Seventeenth-Century Drama* (Brighton, Great Britain: Harvester Press, 1981), and Carol Pearson and Katherine Pope, *The Female Hero in American and British Literature* (New York: R. R. Bowker, 1981).

24. Paul Varley, *Warriors of Japan as Portrayed in the War Tales* (Honolulu: University of Hawaii Press, 1994), pp. 82–85, 103–4; Ellis Amdur, "Women Warriors of Japan: The Role of Arms-Bearing Women in Japanese History," *Journal of Asian Martial Arts* 5 (1996): 12 (also online at www.koryubooks.com/Library/wwj1.html).

25. Jerome W. Clinton, trans., *The Tragedy of Sohrab and Rostam* (Seattle: University of Washington Press, 1996), pp. 31–53. I retain the name

Gurdafrid, while Clinton renders her name as Gordafarid. The events narrated in the *Shahname*, or *Book of Kings*, date from the mid-third century B.C. to the mid-seventh century A.D.

26. Theodore M. Andersson, *The Legend of Brynhild* (Ithaca, NY: Cornell University Press, 1980), pp. 5, 15–16, 236–49.

27. Edmund Spenser, *The Fairie Queene*, ed. Thomas P. Roche, Jr. (New Haven: Yale University Press, 1981), book V, but especially cantos v, vi, vii (pp. 773–810).

28. Ludovico Ariosto, *Orlando Furioso*, trans. William S. Rose, ed. Stewart A. Baker and A. Bartlett Giamatti (org. 1516; Indianapolis: Bobbs-Merrill Company, 1968), pp. 28–34 (IV, I–L).

29. "The Ballad of Mulan," in *The Columbia Anthology of Traditional Chinese Literature*, ed. Victor H. Mare (New York: Columbia University Press, 1994), pp. 474–76. For modern children's versions of the tale, see *China's Bravest Girl: The Legend of Hua Mu Lan*, told by Charlie Chin, trans. Wang Xing Chu (Emeryville, CA: Children's Book Press, 1993); Robert D. San Souci, *Fa Mulan: The Story of a Woman Warrior* (New York: Hyperion Books, 1998); Jiang, Wei and Gen Xing, *The Legend of Mu Lan: A Heroine of Ancient China* (Monterey, CA: Victory Press, 1992); Song Nan Zhang, *The Ballad of Mulan* (Union City, CA: Pan Asian Publications, 1998).

30. "A Wonderful Story," in *Indian Fairy Tales*, ed. Mave Stokes (London: Ellis & White, 1880), pp. 108–13. This and similar stories can be found in *Fearless Girls, Wise Women, and Beloved Sisters: Heroines in Folktales from around the World*, ed. Kathleen Ragan (New York: W. W. Norton & Company, 1998), pp. 184–88. For a brief sample of Native American shemales, see Margaret Lantis, "The Mythology of Kodiak Island, Alaska," *Journal of American Folklore* 51 (April–June 1938), 157–59 for what she terms "Amazon Tales" of the Koniag Eskimos. See also note 9 for other Native American shemale tales.

31. Diane Dugaw, *Warrior Women and Popular Balladry, 1650–1850* (Cambridge: Cambridge University Press, 1989), pp. 1–7.

32. Ibid., pp. 32–45, with the text of the ballad on pp. 37–39. The ballad, "The Female Warrior," has a similar theme but takes place at sea. Noted in William Main Doerflinger, *Shantymen and Shantyboys: Songs of the Sailor and Lumberman* (New York: Macmillan, 1951), pp. 143–44.

33. Earlier male captivity narratives exist (Cabeza de Vaca, Juan Ortiz, Hans Staden, Job Hortop, Captain John Smith, and Jesuit missionary martyrs Isaac Jogues and Christophe Regnaut) and often illustrate similar cate-

gories. For a handy selection of women's narratives, including those of Rowlandson and Dustan, see Kathryn Z. Derounian-Stodola, ed., *Women's Indian Captivity Narratives* (New York: Penguin Books, 1998). A broader selection can be found in Gordon M. Sayre, ed., *Olaudah Equiano, Mary Rowlandson, and Others: American Captivity Narratives* (Boston: Houghton Mifflin Co., 2000).

34. Neal Salisbury, ed., *The Sovereignty and Goodness of God, Together with the Faithfulness of His Promises Displayed, Being a Narrative of the Captivity and Restoration of Mrs. Mary Rowlandson and Related Documents* (Boston: Bedford Books, 1997), pp. 1–7, 21–35; June Namias, *White Captives: Gender and Ethnicity on the American Frontier* (Chapel Hill: University of North Carolina Press, 1993), pp. 21–36. For a concise critical overview of the narratives, see Richard VanDerBeets, *The Indian Captivity Narrative: An American Genre* (Lanham, MD: University Press of America, 1984). For one view of the extension of the genre, see Christopher Castiglia, *Bound and Determined: Captivity, Culture-Crossing, and White Womanhood from Mary Rowlandson to Patty Hearst* (Chicago: University of Chicago Press, 1996).

35. Salisbury, p. 1.

36. Rowlandson, in Derounian-Stodola, pp. 13–14.

37. The movement from captive to conqueror in the Almanacs was noted earlier in the tale "Sal Fink, the Mississippi Screamer, How She Cooked Injuns." (171–72)

38. Dustan, in Derounian-Stodola, pp. 58–60. See Namias, pp. 30–36ff., for other examples. The Massachusetts Bay Colony had repealed its bounty on Indian scalps, but Dustan's husband successfully petitioned them for a reward. Dustan received twenty-five pounds; Neff and Leonardson split the other twenty-five pounds.

39. See also, for example, "Indian Barbarity" (276–79) and "The Wife Swallowed." (295–96) The racism of the day was the subject of Ann Stephens's very popular "Malaeska." Appearing first in three issues of the *Ladies' Companion* (February–April 1839), "Malaeska" allows Stephens to explore racism through the tragedy of the title character, who possessed all the virtues of a proper white woman but was an Indian princess married to a white trapper. Reissued in 1860 as the first Beadle dime novel, its eventual sales were estimated at more than a half million copies. See Madeline B. Stern, "Ann Sophia (Winterbotham) Stephens," in *Antebellum Writers in New York and the South*, ed. Joel Myerson, in the *Dictionary of Literary Biography* (Detroit: Gale Research Company, 1979),

pp. 3, 318–21. For a historical example of racism involving women, see Dorothy Gray, *Women of the West* (Millbrae, CA: Les Femmes, 1976), pp. 61–62. White women were revered, but a "Mexican" woman could be hanged.

40. Robert D. Arner, "The Story of Hannah Duston: Cotton Mather to Thoreau," *American Transcendental Quarterly* 18 (Spring 1973): 19–23.

41. Jemison in Derounian-Stodola, pp. 122–210.

42. Daniel Boone, *Life and Adventures of Colonel Daniel Boone . . .* (Brooklyn: C. Wilder, 1823). See also Michael A. Lofaro, "Tracking Daniel Boone: The Changing Frontier in American Life," *Register of the Kentucky Historical Society* 82 (Autumn 1984): 321–22, and Richard Slotkin, *Regeneration through Violence: The Mythology of the American Frontier, 1600–1860* (Middletown, CT: Wesleyan University Press, 1973), p. 400ff.

43. While I explore land-bound shemales, a similar tradition exits for women and the sea. For a fine sampler of these women that goes beyond pirates like Anne Bonny and Mary Read, see Joan Druett, *She Captains: Heroines and Hellions of the Sea* (New York: Simon & Schuster, 2000). Other non-traditional occupations of women have likewise attracted attention. See Sally Zanjani, *A Mine of Her Own: Women Prospectors in the American West, 1850–1950* (Lincoln: University of Nebraska Press, 1997).

44. Washington Irving, *Tales of a Traveller by Geoffrey Crayon, Gent.*, ed. Judith Giblin Haig, in *The Complete Works of Washington Irving* (Boston: Twayne Publishers, 1987), X, 222.

45. Carroll Smith-Rosenberg, *Disorderly Conduct: Visions of Gender in Victorian America* (New York: Alfred A. Knopf, 1985), pp. 14–22; Gerda Lerner, "The Lady and the Mill Girl: Changes in the Status of Women in the Age of Jackson," *Midcontinent American Studies Journal* 10 (Autumn–Winter 1971): 5–15. Industrialization does surface as a minor theme in some of the Almanac tales. At one point in "Ben Hardin in a Dancing Match," Crockett says, "I had a hemlock fiddle made to play by steam, and some new tunes that went so fast that a humming birds wing couldn't keep time with it."(181).

46. Barbara Welter, "Anti-Intellectualism and the American Women: 1800–1860," *Mid-America* 48 (1966): 258–70; Carl Degler, *At Odds: Women and the Family in America from the Revolution to the Present* (New York: Oxford University Press, 1980), pp. 180–82; Cynthia Griffin-Wolff, "A Mirror for Men: Stereotypes of Women in Literature," *Massachusetts Review* 13 (Winter–Spring 1972): 210–12; Julie Roy Jeffrey, *Frontier Women: The Trans-Mississippi West, 1840–1880* (New York: Hill

and Wang, 1979), pp. 4–7; and, as a general source, Ann Douglas, *The Feminization of American Culture* (New York: Alfred A. Knopf, 1977).

47. Barbara Welter, "The Cult of True Womanhood: 1820–1860," *American Quarterly* 18 (Summer 1966): 151–74. Although some critics take issue with the historical accuracy of submissiveness as one of these cardinal virtues, the concept remained a central part of the stereotype of the true woman insofar as most men were concerned. For two examples of this qualifying view, see Mary P. Ryan, *The Empire of the Mother: American Writing about Domesticity, 1830–1860* (New York: Haworth Press, 1982), p. 2ff., and Lerner, "The Lady and the Mill Girl": 11–14. One extremely popular book of the period, Sara Willis Parton's *Fern Leaves from Fanny's Port-Folio* (Auburn, NY: Derby and Miller, 1853), provides a sampler of sentimental vignettes, a good number of which center upon the proper role and conduct of women in various situations and stages and states of life. In the second part of the volume, Parton dramatically shifts gears to produce acerbic commentary on vain women, helpless men, and sentimental authors. See Nancy Walker, "Wit, Sentimentality and the Image of Women in the Nineteenth Century," *American Studies* 22 (Fall 1981): 7–9. For men, as Bertram Wyatt-Brown notes, "Passionate chest-thumping was highly self-conscious in these decades. . . . The age required assertions of warrior-spirit and 'forthright' denunciations of an adversary's 'cowardice and servility' from its young men." See his "The Abolitionist Controversy: Men of Blood, Men of God," in *Men, Women, and Issues in American History*, ed. Howard H. Quint and Milton Cantor (Homewood, IL: Dorsey Press, 1975), I, 216.

48. See the still-useful Frank Luther Mott's *A History of American Magazines, 1741–1850* (New York: D. Appleton and Company, 1930), pp. 482–87, 524–25, and 580–92, and James D. Hart's *The Popular Book: A History of America's Literary Taste* (New York: Oxford University Press, 1950), pp. 85–113, 140–47.

49. William Ransom Hogan, "Pamela Mann: Texas Frontierswoman," *Southwest Review* 20 (July 1935): 360–62; Gray, p. 115.

50. Jeanne Boydston, Mary Kelley, and Anne Margolis, ed., *The Limits of Sisterhood: The Beecher Sisters on Women's Rights and Woman's Sphere* (Chapel Hill: University of North Carolina Press, 1988), pp. 4–8; Lori D. Ginsberg, *Women and the Work of Benevolence: Morality, Politics, and Class in the Nineteenth-Century United States* (New Haven, CT: Yale University Press, 1990), pp. 6–8. Sarah Josepha Hale, *Woman's Record; or, Sketches of all Distinguished Women from the Creation to A.D. 1868* (New

York: Harper & Brothers, Publishers, 1868), pp. xxxv, xlvi, and xlviii. This third edition of her work makes no significant changes from the second edition of 1855 except "to add a *Synopsis* for 'Woman's Record' . . . from 1855 to 1868," and the second edition added only a few names (p. vii). The first edition was published in 1853.

51. Carroll Smith Rosenberg, "Beauty, the Beast and the Militant Woman: A Case Study in Sex Roles and Social Stress in Jacksonian America," *American Quarterly* 23 (October 1971): 563–64; Edward Pessen, *Jacksonian America: Society, Personality, and Politics* (Homewood, IL: Dorsey Press, 1969), pp. 84–90; Welter, "Anti-Intellectualism and the American Woman: 1800–1860," 258–63; Charles Neilson Gattey, *The Bloomer Girls* (New York: Coward-McCann, 1968), pp. 39–41.

52. Lyman Beecher, *A Plea for the West* (1835; reprint, New York: Arno Press, 1977), pp. 11–12, 30–31; Charles A. Barker, "Moral Man and Moral Society: Lyman Beecher, Brigham Young, Henry D. Thoreau," in Quint and Cantor, I, 176–78.

53. "The Pioneer Mothers," quoted in Jeffrey, p. 19.

54. The characterizations of pioneer women were perhaps most captive to the point of view of the writer. Boone's autobiography was ghost written by John Filson, an eighteenth-century schoolteacher. Crockett's *A Narrative of the Life of Col. David Crockett of West Tennessee* was mainly his own offering, but was also a presidential campaign autobiography. See Michael A. Lofaro, "The Eighteenth-Century 'Autobiographies' of Daniel Boone," *Register of the Kentucky Historical Society* 76 (April 1978): 85–97, and Michael A. Lofaro, Introduction to James A. Shackford, *David Crockett: The Man and the Legend*, ed. John B. Shackford (1956; Chapel Hill: University of North Carolina Press, 1986), pp. ix–xx.

55. John Filson, *The Discovery, Settlement and present State of Kentucke* (Wilmington, DE: James Adams, 1784), p. 60; James Hall, *Letters from the West* (London: Henry Colburn, 1828), p. 259 (see Filson, p. 72, for the original passage); "The Pioneer Mothers," quoted in Jeffrey, p. 19.

56. James Fenimore Cooper, *The Prairie: A Tale*, ed. James P. Elliott (Albany: State University of New York Press, 1985), pp. 130, 132, 131. Cooper's women are kept in their sphere in different ways. Active women in Cooper are often somehow burdened or tainted: Esther by her class and Cora Munro, in *The Last of the Mohicans*, by her mixed blood. Cooper also uses the shemale at sea, but in the tradition of a woman masquerading as a man, as the title character in *Jack Tier; Or, The Florida Reef* (1848; reprint, New York: James G. Gregory, 1864).

57. Caroline M. Kirkland, *A New Home—Who'll Follow? Or, Glimpses of Western Life* (1839; 3rd ed., New-York: Charles S. Francis, 1841), pp. iii–iv. See also Sandra A. Zagarell's introduction to Caroline M. Kirkland, *A New Home—Who'll Follow? Or, Glimpses of Western Life* (New Brunswick: Rutgers University Press, 1990), pp. xi–xlvi, and David Leverenz, *Manhood and the American Renaissance* (Ithaca, NY: Cornell University Press, 1989), pp.151–64.

58. Refinement comes in many varieties and is the arena of all women, according to Kirkland; any woman can tame the frontier unless her husband be "a Caliban" (pp. 230–31). Kirkland also mocks city dwellers for their world of high fashion and affectation and feels that a good dose of Michigan would serve as a spring tonic for "the Sybarites, the puny exquisites, the world-worn and sated Epicureans of our cities" (p. 288). The realities of mud holes and a log "hotel" of the first two chapters have faded somewhat before nature's beauty, which clearly exerts a Romantic tug on her prose in chapter 36 (pp. 5–13, 231–33). Kirkland never achieves a full synthesis of her dual cultures, but wends her way forward in a continuing balancing act.

59. Kirkland, *A New Home*, pp. 13–15, 20–23.

60. Bess, Betsey, and the shemales live on in twentieth-century creations, who were probably also influenced by the popularity of Paul Bunyan. Two of the best known are African-Americans. Annie Christmas is six feet, eight inches tall, weighs 250 pounds, and, combining parts of the tales of Mike Fink and John Henry, uses her keelboat and her own great strength to save the passengers of a sinking steamboat; but her heart gives out after she tows the passengers on her keelboat to New Orleans in record time. Old Sally Cato makes up for her lack of size by her ingenuity. She saves her sons from a giant by running into his mouth, sliding down his gullet, jabbing him with knitting needles (shades of Davy's wife and the bear, 135), working her way to his heart, stabbing him to death, and nonchalantly cutting herself free to go back to spinning. The most convenient collection of these stories is Robert D. San Souci, *Cut from the Same Cloth: American Women of Myth, Legend, and Tall Tale* (New York: Philomel Books, 1993). Some of the Crockett Almanac stories about Sal Fink are also included in the volume. See also Tristam Potter Coffin and Hennig Cohen, eds., *The Parade of Heroes: Legendary Figures in American Lore* (Garden City, NY: Anchor Press/Doubleday, 1978).

61. Celia Morris Eckhardt, *Fanny Wright: Rebel in America* (Cambridge: Harvard University Press, 1984). Native-born Americans, in addition to

those activists from abroad like Wright, found the country the best hope of the world for social justice and spoke out well before Wright on their own ideas about equality between the sexes. See, for example, the "Gleaner" essays of Judith Sargent Murray (1751–1820), published first in the *Massachusetts Magazine* (February 1792–August 1794) and then collected as *The Gleaner. A Miscellaneous Production. In Three Volumes. By Constantia.* (Boston: J. Thomas and E. T. Andrews, 1798).

62. Angelina E. Grimké, *Appeal to the Christian Women of the South* (1836; reprint, New York: Arno Press, 1969); Sarah M. Grimké, *An Epistle to the Clergy of the Southern States* (1836) is reprinted (as are *Appeal* and *Letters*) in *The Public Years of Sarah and Angelina Grimké: Selected Writings, 1835–1839*, ed. Larry Ceplair (New York: Columbia University Press, 1989), pp. 90–115; Sarah M. Grimké, *Letters on the Equality of the Sexes and the Condition of Woman* (1838; reprint, New York: Burt Franklin, 1970); Gerda Lerner, *The Grimké Sisters from South Carolina: Pioneers for Woman's Rights and Abolition* (New York: Schocken Books, 1967); Eleanor Flexnor and Ellen Fitzpatrick, *Century of Struggle: The Woman's Rights Movement in the United States* (Cambridge: Harvard University Press, 1996), pp. 41–50; Daniel Feller, *The Jacksonian Promise: America, 1815–1840* (Baltimore: Johns Hopkins University Press, 1995), pp. 155–59; Mary P. Ryan, *Womanhood in America: From Colonial Times to the Present* (New York: New Viewpoints, 1975), pp. 183–84.

63. "Hints to Young Ladies—No. 2," *The Mother's Magazine* 6 (February 1838): 27. Also quoted along with several other disparaging excerpts about women in Welter, "Anti-Intellectualism and the American Woman: 1800–1860," 264–66. The first installment of "Hints" in the January issue makes clear that the discussion is not one-sided, but deals with woman "as the *superior,* the *inferior,* and the *companion* of man," and all of the first category is dealt with in this issue. Her superiority lies in organization, quick sensibilities, morality, and harmony with the social system, and she forms "the sanctuary of his domestic affection, purity, and peace." (22–23). The balance that the author achieves is all in keeping with the stereotype of the "true woman."

64. "Hints to Young Ladies—No. 2": 25–26.

65. For biographical information on Fuller, see Joan von Mehren, *Minerva and the Muse* (Amherst: University of Massachusetts Press, 1994), and Madeleine B. Stern, *The Life of Margaret Fuller* (Westport, CT: Greenwood Press, 1991). A fine condensed biography is contained in Barbara Welter's "Patterns and Mentors: American Women before the Civil War,"

in Quint and Cantor, I, 194–201. For Hawthorne's notorious comments on Fuller, see Nathaniel Hawthorne, *The French and Italian Notebooks*, in *The Centenary Edition of the Works of Nathaniel Hawthorne*, ed. Thomas Woodson (Columbus, OH: Ohio State University Press, 1980), XIV, 155–57 and also 766–72. Horace Greeley, *Recollections of a Busy Life* (New York: J. B. Ford and Company, 1868), p. 178. See also Judith Fryer, *The Faces of Eve: Women in the Nineteenth Century American Novel* (New York: Oxford University Press, 1976), pp. 8–19; Welter, "Anti-Intellectualism and the American Women," 267–69.

66. Feller, pp. 156–57; Boydston, Kelley, and Margolis, pp. 116–22, 130–42. See also in this volume pp. 125–29 for Catherine Beecher's response to Angelina Grimké's *Appeal to the Christian Women of the South*, in which Beecher attacks abolitionism as inappropriate for women. Elizabeth Peabody also sought to transform the feminine gift of mother love into the science of education (Ryan, *The Empire of the Mother*, p. 99).

67. Catherine E. Beecher, *A Treatise on Domestic Economy for the Use of Young Ladies at Home and at School* (Boston: Marsh, Capen, Lyon, and Webb, 1841), p. 13.

68. Ibid., p. 9. See also Kathryn Kish Sklar, *Catherine Beecher: A Study in American Domesticity* (New Haven, CT: Yale University Press, 1973), pp. 151–67. For a brief overview of the issue of the education of women, see Flexnor and Fitzpatrick, pp. 22–37.

69. G. J. Barker-Benfield, *The Horrors of the Half-Known Life: Male Attitudes toward Women and Sexuality in Nineteenth-Century America* (New York: Harper & Row, 1976), p. 21.

70. Never one to shy from controversial issues, here Wright sides with the Democrats rather than the Whigs on this key bone of political contention. While my approach in this essay focuses on tales depicting women, and thus generally deemphasizes politics, many of the tales featuring Crockett himself are more overtly political. While not within the scope of this study, it is interesting to note that the publication of the Crockett Almanacs (1835–56) coincides nearly exactly with the existence of the Whig party from its rise to its demise (1834–56), that the historical Crockett became a puppet of sorts for Whig interests as he tested the waters in 1835 for a run for the presidency, and that Turner & Fisher, the dominant publisher of Crockett Almanacs in the 1840s, also published Whig almanacs and documents. But the most constant political refrain that these Crockett Almanacs sound is the Democratic anthem of Manifest Destiny rather than the internal improvement theme of the

Whigs. As John Seelye suggests, expansionism sold well. In the case of the Almanacs, it may be profit first, politics second. For a few of these political tales in a more readily accessible form than the original Almanacs, see Dorson, *Davy Crockett*, pp. 93–96, 138–39, 150–51, 157–58. See John Seelye, "A Well-Wrought Crockett: Or, How the Fakelorists Passed through the Credibility Gap and Discovered Kentucky," in Lofaro, *Davy Crockett*, pp. 28–29. Some works that background the Whig party are Michael F. Holt, *The Rise and Fall of the American Whig Party: Jacksonian Politics and the Onset of the Civil War* (New York: Oxford University Press, 1999), Daniel Walker Howe, *The Political Culture of the American Whigs* (Chicago: University of Chicago Press, 1979), and Rush Welter, *The Mind of America, 1820–1860* (New York: Columbia University Press, 1975).

71. Flexnor and Fitzpatrick, pp. 69–72; Welter, "Patterns and Mentors," in Quint and Cantor, I, 191–93; Feller, pp. 198–99. For the "Declaration of Sentiments," resolutions, and a very brief history of the Seneca Falls Conventions, see Elizabeth Cady Stanton, Susan B. Anthony, and Matilda Joslyn Gage, eds., *History of Woman Suffrage* (New York: Fowler & Wells, 1881), I, 67–75.

72. Stanton, Anthony, and Gage, *History of Woman Suffrage*, I, 859 (Stanton), 595 (Brown).

73. Ibid., I, 75 (Douglass); Maria Weston Chapman, *Right and Wrong in Boston* (Boston: Issac Knapp, 1836), in Harriet Martineau, *The Martyr Age of the United States* (1839; reprint, New York: Arno Press, 1969), p. 29. This treatment is based in part on Susan P. Conrad, *Perish the Thought: Intellectual Women in Romantic America, 1830–1860* (New York: Oxford University Press, 1976), pp. 150–52.

74. How humor is one way in which men and women deal with the double-edged nature of domesticity and ambivalence over gender roles is the subject of Gregg Camfield's *Necessary Madness: The Humor of Domesticity in Nineteenth-Century American Literature* (New York: Oxford University Press, 1997). De Tocqueville, II, 201. By 1850, however, the demand of growing industrialization for labor, particularly for work in textile and clothing mills, led to the employment of over 225,000 women in manufacturing, nearly 24 percent of that workforce (Flexnor and Fitzpatrick, p. 73). For how this change is reflected in the popular literature of the day, see David S. Reynolds, *Beneath the American Renaissance: The Subversive Imagination in the Age of Emerson and Melville* (New York: Alfred A. Knopf, 1988), pp. 351–57.

75. Efrat Tseelon, *The Masque of Femininity: The Presentation of Woman in Everyday Life* (London: SAGE Publications, 1995), pp. 15–17. After the Seneca Falls Convention, the women's movement was perhaps one of the most fertile areas for caricature as well as satire in other almanacs and illustrated periodicals. See Gary L. Bunker, "Antebellum Caricature and Women's Sphere," *Journal of Woman's History* 3 (Winter 1992): 6–43. In his fine study focusing mainly on 1848–60 materials, Bunker was obviously unaware of the Crockett Almanacs. He also states as a premise what the tales in this volume disprove: "Caricature of the departure from women's sphere through 1850 was sparse" (7). That said, very little work has been done on the illustrations of the Crockett Almanacs. See, Meine, p. xviii, and Seelye, pp. 38–41. For more information on Amelia Bloomer, see the note on p. 321.

76. In addition to those noted in this essay, see Julie Wheelwright, *Amazons and Military Maids: Women Who Dressed as Men in the Pursuit of Life, Liberty and Happiness* (London: Pandora, 1989).

77. Ryan, *Womanhood in America*, pp. 143–44. Carroll Smith-Rosenberg rightly points out that the bourgeois family was the institution most frequently lampooned and subverted in the Almanacs (*Disorderly Conduct*, pp. 103–5).

78. Anne Firor Scott, *Natural Allies: Women's Associations in American History* (Urbana: University of Illinois Press, 1991), pp. 11–57ff.; Jeffrey, pp. 10–11; Ryan, *The Empire of the Mother*, pp. 71–72.

79. Gray, pp. 21–35.

80. William A. Alcott, "Female Attendance on the Sick," *American Ladies' Magazine* 7 (July 1834): 301–2. Alcott also argues for the scientific education of nurses and nursing as a profession for women, in part because "they can be employed much cheaper," but also fears his entire project is too visionary to succeed (304–6).

81. This famous quote is from Hawthorne's letter of January 19, 1855, to William D. Ticknor. See *The Letters, 1853–1856*, in *The Centenary Edition of the Works of Nathaniel Hawthorne*, ed. Thomas Woodson, et al. (Columbus: Ohio State University Press, 1987), XVII, 304. Hawthorne's negative view of women authors was a long-standing one. In his 1830 biographical sketch of Anne Hutchinson, the assertive religious leader expelled from the Massachusetts Bay Colony to Rhode Island for heresy, he decries in the body of his text the qualities now generally used to support the view of Hutchinson as a strident early advocate of women's rights and uses his introductory remarks to lash out at women writers. Those who feel the

"impulse of genius," he warns, face virtually the same fate as Hutchinson—exile from society and loss of femininity. He also prefigures his "scribbling women" comment by noting that if encouraged by the public, "the ink-stained Amazons will expel their rivals by actual pressure, and petticoats wave triumphant over all the field." See Hawthorne's "Mrs. Hutchinson," in *Miscellaneous Prose and Verse*, in *The Centenary Edition of the Works of Nathaniel Hawthorne*, ed. Thomas Woodson, et al. (Columbus: Ohio State University Press, 1994), XXIII, 66–67.

82. Rosenberg, "Beauty, the Beast and the Militant Woman," 562–84. For an early American example of satire on the double standards applied to prostitution, see the now heavily anthologized "The Speech of Polly Baker," by Benjamin Franklin.

83. Nineteenth-century sexual theory encouraged women to cool rather than kindle man's passions by equating loss of semen with loss of vital energy, a problem with obvious national ramifications. Marriage manuals concurred. Husband and wife should limit sexual intercourse to once a month, up to a lifetime limit of no more than ninety times, and should abstain for twenty-one months. Cited in Ryan, *Womanhood in America*, pp. 158–59.

84. James Kirke Paulding, *The Lion of the West* (Stanford, CA: Stanford University Press, 1954), pp. 31, 41, 45, 61–62; Pessen, pp. 8–9; Feller, pp. 198–99; Richard Boyd Hauck, "Making It All Up: Davy Crockett in the Theater," in Lofaro, *Davy Crockett*, pp. 103–11. For previous versions of wild backwoodsmen on the stage, see V. L. O. Chittick, *Ring-Tailed Roarers: Tall Tales of the American Frontier* (Caldwell, ID: Caxton Printers, 1943), pp. 15–16.

85. Paulding, *The Lion of the West*, p. 27.

86. Dorson, "Davy Crockett and the Heroic Age," 95–102; Dorson, *Davy Crockett*, pp. xv–xxvi; Harry J. Owens, ". . . And Laugh Out Loud!," in Meine, pp. xxvii–xxxvi; Dorothy Dondore, "Big! The Flyting, the Gabe, and the Frontier Boast," *American Speech* 6 (October 1930): 45–55; Augustus Baldwin Longstreet, *Georgia Scenes, Characters, Incidents, &c., in the First Half Century of the Republic* (1835; reprint of the second edition of 1847, Atlanta: Cherokee Publishing Company, 1971), pp. 53–64 ("The Fight" was first published in the *Milledgeville Southern Recorder* on November 27, 1833); James Kirke Paulding, "Letter XXIX," *Letters from the South, Written during an Excursion in the Summer of 1816* (New York: James Eastburn & Co., 1817), II, 89–96; John Joseph Arpad, "The Fight Story: Quotation and Originality in Native American Humor," *Journal of*

the *Folklore Institute* 10 (1973): 141–72; George Washington Harris, *Sut Lovingood. Yarns Spun by a "Nat'ral Born Durn'd Fool." Warped and Wove for Public Wear.* (New York: Dick & Fitzgerald, 1867); and Johnson Jones Hooper, *Adventures of Captain Simon Suggs, Late of the Tallapoosa Volunteers* (1845; reprint, Chapel Hill: University of North Carolina Press, 1969), p. 8. Karen Halttunen views the Yankee as the "superior" national character in dealing with confidence men in her *Confidence Men and Painted Women: A Study of Middle-Class Culture in America, 1830–1870* (New Haven, CT: Yale University Press, 1982), pp. 30–31. A fine overview and brief sampler of Southwestern Humor is in Walter Blair's *Native American Humor* (1937; reprint, New York: Harper & Row, 1960), pp. 62–101. See also Hennig Cohen and William Dillingham, eds., *Humor of the Old Southwest* (Boston: Houghton Mifflin, 1964).

87. Longstreet, pp. 82–110. Quoted sections appear on pp. 109–10. David Rachels, ed., *Augustus Baldwin Longstreet's "Georgia Scenes" Completed* (Athens: University of Georgia Press, 1998), p. 268.

88. Joseph G. Baldwin, *The Flush Times of Alabama and Mississippi. A Series of Sketches.* (New-York: D. Appleton and Company, 1853), pp. 171–73. Another, albeit milder, case of this type of satire is in "How Sally Hooter Got Snake-Bit: A Yazoo Sketch," (by William Hall?), in Chittick's collection (pp. 69–75). In the introductory scene, "ole Missus Lemay" is bitten by a huge poisonous snake, but the snake dies rather than she. In the main sketch, Sally Hooter is about to be bitten, but the snake under her dress turns out to be the sausage she was using for a bustle. There are thus certainly more than two "types" of female characters in Southwestern humor, but the riproarious shemale is rather rare. William E. Lenz also notes a range of women in the sketches by various authors that William T. Porter, the editor of the *Spirit of the Times*, collected and published in 1845 and 1847, but none, even those who demonstrate independence or best a man, approach the category of shemale. They gain control or mastery through more "feminine" methods rather than following the lead of the Almanacs, where women often adopt or usurp the roles of men. See William E. Lenz, "The Function of Women in Old Southwestern Humor: Re-reading Porter's *Big Bear* and *Quarter Race* Collections," *Mississippi Quarterly* 46 (Fall 1993): 589–600.

89. Frances M. Witcher, *The Widow Bedott Papers* (1855; reprint, New York: J. C. Derby, 1856); Benjamin P. Shillaber, *Sayings of Mrs. Partington, and Others of the Family* (New York: J. C. Derby, 1854); Linda A. Morris, *Women's Humor in the Age of Gentility: The Life and Works of Frances*

*Miriam Witcher* (Syracuse, NY: Syracuse University Press, 1992), pp. 1–17; Linda A. Morris, *Women Vernacular Humorists in Nineteenth-Century America: Ann Stephens, Francis Whitcher, and Marietta Holley* (New York: Garland Publishing, 1988), pp. 91–107, 139–40; John Q. Reed, *Benjamin Penhallow Shillaber* (New York: Twayne Publishers, 1972), pp. 32–54.

90. Harris, "Sicily Burns' Wedding," in *Sut Lovingood,* p. 88. Harris's work is actually a bridge chronologically between the "Contemporaries" and "Inheritors" of the Crockett Almanacs. His first work, "Sporting Epistle from East Tennessee," appeared in the *New York Spirit of the Times* on February 11, 1843. Ten other stories appeared while the Almanacs were being published. The two sketches dealing with Sicily Burns appeared just after the publication of the Almanacs ceased with the issue for 1856. "Sut Lovengood [*sic*] Blown up," was reprinted in the *Nashville Daily Gazette* on July 21, 1857 (it was first published in the *Savannah Morning News,* probably in 1857, but no date can be determined), and "Sut Lovengood [*sic*] at Sicily Burns's Wedding" appeared in the *Nashville Union & American* on April 15, 1858. This information is taken from M. Thomas Inge's bibliography of Harris's works, in *Sut Lovingood's Nat'ral Born Yarnspinner: Essays on George Washington Harris,* ed. James E. Caron and M. Thomas Inge (Tuscaloosa: University of Alabama Press, 1996), p. 315. There are a few other women in the *Yarns,* but none the equal of Sicily. See William E. Lenz, "Sensuality, Revenge, and Freedom: Women in *Sut Lovingood. Yarns Spun by a "Nat'ral Born Durn'd Fool,"* Caron and Inge, pp. 190–99, and Jane Curry, "The Ring-Tailed Roarers Rarely Sang Soprano," *Frontiers* 2 (1977): 129–40.

91. Harris, "Blown Up with Soda" in *Sut Lovingood,* pp. 76–77.

92. Ibid., pp. 80–82.

93. Harris, "Sicily Burns' Wedding," in *Sut Lovingood,* p. 95.

94. Mary P. Ryan, *Women in Public: Between Banners and Ballots, 1825–1880* (Baltimore: Johns Hopkins University Press, 1990), pp. 173–76; Nina Baym, "Portrayal of Women in American Literature, 1790–1870," in *What Manner of Woman: Essays on English and American Life and Literature,* ed. Marlene Springer (New York: New York University Press, 1977), pp. 228–32; David G. Pugh, *Sons of Liberty: The Masculine Mind in Nineteenth-Century America* (Westport, CT: Greenwood Press, 1983), pp. 63–65.

95. Satire, particularly satire geared to both sides of the "women question," continued in its own vigorous tradition. In this venue, however, the fan-

tastical aspects of the tall tales and the wilderness exploits of the Crockett Almanac shemales fell dormant before the reality-based humor used to highlight the disparity in women's role and place in a society that supported the doctrine of separate spheres. Perhaps the master of this genre was Marietta Holley, whose books published about Samantha Allen from 1873 to 1914 rivaled those of Samuel Clemens in sales and wit. Samantha, or, as she first ironically introduces herself to her audience, "Josiah Allen's Wife," is a no-nonsense, practical-minded, hard-working farm wife whose sharp tongue constantly juxtaposes the reality of her life and situation with that of her husband's and her friend Betsey Bobbet's stereotypical views of women as the weaker sex and a group of delicate angels. Holley uses Samantha to expose the often ludicrous inequities produced by the doctrine of separate spheres. Holley's books have unfortunately not been reprinted, but for a fine sample, see *Samantha Rastles the Woman Question*, ed. with an introduction by Jane Curry (Urbana: University of Illinois Press, 1983). Other examples of different traditions among the inheritors are demonstrated in Kathryn B. McKee's doctoral dissertation "Writing in a Different Direction: Woman Authors and the Tradition of Southwestern Humor, 1875–1910" (University of North Carolina at Chapel Hill, 1996), and in Nancy A. Walker's "Sut and His Sisters: Vernacular Humor and Genteel Culture," in Caron and Inge, pp. 261–71.

96. Albert Johannsen, *The House of Beadle and Adams and Its Dime and Nickel Novels: The Story of a Vanished Literature* (Norman: University of Oklahoma Press, 1950), I, 4–5.

97. Joseph E. Badger, Jr., *Mountain Kate; Or, Love in the Trapping-Grounds* (New York: Beadle and Adams, 1872), pp. 17, 94, 102. For comment on some of these dime novel heroines and possible historical parallels for their characters, see Shelley Armitage, "Rawhide Heroines: The Evolution of the Cowgirl and the Myth of America," in *The American Self: Myth, Ideology, and Popular Culture*, ed. Sam B. Girgus (Albuquerque: University of New Mexico Press, 1981), pp. 171–73; and Henry Nash Smith, *Virgin Land: The American West as Symbol and Myth* (1950; Cambridge, MA: Harvard University Press, 1970), pp. 112–20.

98. Captain Mayne Reid, *The Wild Huntress; Or, The Big Squatter's Vengeance* (org. London, 1861; New York: Beadle and Adams, 1882), pp. 19, 21, 22, 25, 28.

99. Edward L. Wheeler, *Bob Woolf, The Border Ruffian; Or, The Girl Dead-Shot* (1877; New York: Beadle and Adams, 1884), pp. 2, 3, 10, 12, 24–25, 29–31.

100. Captain Mark Wilton, *Texas Chick, The Southwest Detective; Or, Tiger-Lily, The Vulture Queen* (New York: Beadle and Adams, 1884); Edward L. Wheeler, *Old Avalanche, The Great Annihilator; Or, Wild Edna, the Girl Brigand* (New York: Beadle and Adams, 1877); Charles W. Short, *The Girl Avenger; Or, The Beautiful Terror of the Maumee* (New York: Beadle and Adams, 1872); Captain Charles Howard, *Silver Rifle, The Girl Trailer; Or, The White Tigers of Lake Superior* (New York: Beadle and Adams, 1873).

101. Major Dangerfield Burr, *Buffalo Bill, The Buckskin King; Or, The Amazon of the West* (org. pub. serially 1879–80; New York: Beadle and Adams, 1880), pp. 4, 5, 8, 23.

102. Joseph E. Badger, Jr., *The Girl Captain; Or, The Reprisal of Blood* (1873; New York: Beadle and Adams, 1878), pp. 101–2; Col. Prentiss Ingraham, *Queen Helen, The Amazon of the Overland; Or, The Ghouls of the Gold Mines* (New York: Beadle and Adams, 1883), pp. 2–4, 6, 23.

103. Frederick Whittaker, *The Jaguar Queen; Or, The Outlaws of the Sierra Madre* (New York: Beadle and Adams, 1872), pp. 17–18, 101–2; Edward Willet, *Abdiel, The Avenger; Or, The Madman of the Miami* (New York: Beadle and Adams, 1873), p. 87; Edward L. Wheeler, *Deadwood Dick As Detective* (1879; Rpt. Cleveland, Ohio: Arthur Westbrook Co., 189[9?], pp. 27, 24, 27–28.

104. Edward L. Wheeler, *Deadwood Dick on Deck; Or, Calamity Jane, The Heroine of Whoop-Up* (1878; New York: Beadle and Adams, 1885), pp. 4, 24, 2, 4, 2, 2, 4, 31. However, in his *Deadwood Dick's Doom; Or, Calamity Jane's Last Adventure* (1881; New York: Beadle and Adams, 1887), Wheeler has Calamity call herself Dick's "truest pard," and the novel ends with a marriage editorially flavored with their pasts and directed by Wheeler's sense that perhaps a "sport" can never totally become a "pard": "They, the two wild spirits who had learned each other's faults and each other's worth in lives branded with commingled shame and honor" (pp. 13, 28). In her *Tough Girls: Women Warriors and Wonder Women in Popular Culture* (Philadelphia: University of Pennsylvania Press, 1999), Sherrie A. Inness sees Calamity in a group with Mattie Ross of Charles Portis's *True Grit* (1968), Idgie Threadgoode of Fannie Flagg's *Fried Green Tomatoes at the Whistle Stop Cafe* (1987), and Aunt Raylene of Dorothy Allison's *Bastard Out of Carolina* (1992). One might also add some detective fiction to this list with Carlotta Carlyle of Linda Barnes's *Coyote* and other novels.

105. Other "sports" include "Cinnamon Chip, right down from the roaring regions of Montana," who, like a male of the Crockett Almanacs,

speaks in backwoods dialect and manufactures words, but shows the flexibility of the division between "sport" and "pard" by getting engaged at the end of Edward L. Wheeler, *Chip, The Girl Sport; Or, The Golden Idol of Mt. Rosa* (New York: Beadle and Adams, 1885). Leadville Lil, in Wheeler's *The Girl Sport; Or, Jumbo Joe's Disguise* (New York: Beadle and Adams, 1888), continues the tradition of rough male language and raises a stake for gambling by wagering a kiss against $100 in gold on a hand of cards. Wheeler's *The Black Hills Jezebel; Or, Deadwood Dick's Ward* (New York: Beadle and Adams, 1881) gives the reader Kentucky Kit Athol, who likewise speaks in dialect, but is killed by a jealous woman after she wins the man they both love.

106. T. C. Harbaugh, *Cool Sam's Girl Pard; Or, Captain Dick and His Texans* (1884; New York: Beadle and Adams, 1890), pp. 22, 7–10, 12, 21–29.

107. Armitage provides a good outline of the continuation and demise of the tradition of the "pard" (pp. 172–77). In Garyn G. Roberts, Gary Hoppenstand, and Ray B. Brown, eds., *"Old Sleuth's" Freaky Female Detectives (from the Dime Novels)* (Bowling Green, KY: Bowling Green State University Popular Press, 1990), they present a sample from the *Old Sleuth* serials. No shemales are among their ranks. Lady Kate has the strength of a man, but her New York adventures show her as polished, even refined, and intelligent (pp. 5–6). Beadle and Adams also pursue this genre. Their La Marmoset centers her investigations in Paris, in Albert W. Aiken's *La Marmoset, The Detective Queen; Or, The Lost Heir of Morel* (org. pub. serially 1881–1882; New York: Beadle and Adams, 1882). Edward L. Wheeler does bring the woman detective west, but such an investigation is beyond our scope here. See, for example, his *Sierra Sam's Double; Or, The Three Female Detectives* (New York: Beadle and Adams, 1888), and his Denver Doll series commencing with *Denver Doll's Device; Or, The Detective Queen* (New York: Beadle and Adams, 1888). For a listing of Denver Doll novels, see Johannsen, II, 360.

108. Norman Reilly Raine, "Tugboat Annie," *Saturday Evening Post* (July 11, 1931): 6. For Holley's Samantha Allen, see note 95.

109. Raine, "Tugboat Annie," 6–7, 67, 70, 72.

110. Norman Reilly Raine, "Tugboat Annie Borrows Six Bits," *Saturday Evening Post* (May 13, 1939): 112. For a view of the treatment of women in the magazine, see Maureen Honey, "Images of Women in *The Saturday Evening Post*, 1931–1936," *Journal of Popular Culture* 10 (Fall 1976): 352–58. The popularity of the character resulted in Annie's very

successful appearance on the silver screen in *Tugboat Annie* (1933), starring Marie Dressler and Wallace Beery; a tepid sequel with different stars, *Tugboat Annie Sails Again* (1940); and a comedy-adventure television series of thirty-nine episodes, *The Adventures of Tugboat Annie* (1956–58).

111. Maurice Horn, ed., *The World Encyclopedia of Comics* (New York: Chelsea House Publishers, 1976), p. 706; Michael L. Fleisher, *The Encyclopedia of Comic Book Heroes*, vol. 2, *Wonder Woman* (New York: Collier Books, 1976), pp. 194, 232–34, 222–32.

112. Fleisher, pp. 195–97.

113. Ibid., p. 233.

114. Ibid., p. 194.

115. Maureen Honey, *Creating Rosie the Riveter: Class, Gender, and Propaganda during World War II* (Amherst: University of Massachusetts Press, 1984); Penny Colman, *Rosie the Riveter: Women Working on the Home Front in World War II* (New York: Crown Publishers, 1995); Judith N. McArthur, "From Rosie the Riveter to the Feminine Mystique: An Historiographical Survey of American Women and World War II," *Bulletin of Bibliography* 44 (1987): 10–18. Rosie's image is still in use. My most recent citing was in a May 30, 2000, advertisement for the Volunteer Women's Medical Clinic in the *Daily Beacon*, the student newspaper of the University of Tennessee.

116. Fleisher, pp. 194–95, 199–217; Horn, p. 706. Lynda Carter brought the character of Wonder Woman to prime-time television (1976–79), right on the heels of Lindsay Wagner's portrayal of the Bionic Woman (1976–78).

117. Inness, pp. 102–20; J. W. Williamson, *Hillbillyland: What the Movies Did to the Mountains and What the Mountains Did to the Movies* (Chapel Hill: University of North Carolina Press, 1995), pp. 225–46. Data concerning these and subsequent television shows and films is taken from Tim Brooks and Earle Marsh, *The Complete Directory to Prime Time Network and Cable TV Shows, 1946–Present*, 6th (rev.) ed.,(New York: Ballantine Books, 1995), and from Leslie Halliwell, *Halliwell's Film & Video Guide*, ed. John Walker (New York: Harper Perennial, 1999).

118. Peter Sanderson, *Marvel Universe* (New York: Harry N. Abrams, 1996); Inness, pp. 138–59; Varla Ventura, *Sheroes: Bold, Brash, and Absolutely Unabashed Superwomen from Susan B. Anthony to Xena* (Berkeley, CA: Conari Press, 1998). The movies also provided a bevy of deadly dolls in

films like *Black Widow* (1987) and *Fatal Attraction* (1987), but *Thelma and Louise* (1991) captures more of the offbeat, wild exhilaration of the Almanacs, even if their title characters' "adventures" are illegal.

119. Guy H. Lawrence, "Sheroes Able to Blast Gender Barriers," in "Weekend!" supplement to *Knoxville News Sentinel*, September 17, 1999, p. 28.

120. Inness, pp. 160–76; Ventura, pp. 313–15; Donna Minkowitz, "Xena: She's Big, Tall, Strong—and Popular," *Ms.* (July–August 1996): 74–77.

121. Inness, pp. 169, 174–75; Minkowitz, p. 77.

122. Steven Kellogg, *Sally Ann Thunder Ann Whirlwind Crockett* (New York: William Morrow and Company, 1995). This focus prevents the treatment of the incredibly popular *Harry Potter* series by J. K. Rowland and of Hermione as Harry's "pard." The audience for Kellogg's book and for *Swamp Angel* (noted below) precludes any incorporation of the earthiness of the Almanacs.

123. Ann Isaacs, *Swamp Angel* (New York: Dutton's Children's Books, 1994), pp. [2, 4, 7, 8, 16, 18, 27–28, 31, 32].

# A Note on Editorial Method

1. Whenever possible, no change is made to the original text.
2. All original illustrations that accompanied the tales are reproduced. Those tales that did not have illustrations are indicated with an asterisk following the title in the table of contents. When necessary, the size of the illustrations has been altered to fit the format of this volume.
3. Brackets always indicate editorial insertions to the text. Since the Almanacs are inexpensive, quick productions, accidental errors occur frequently. Omissions and inversions of letters, questions created by broken or worn fonts, and the obvious omission or repetition of words are some of the matters that are corrected within brackets. Clarifications are also either included in the text of the tale within brackets or explained in a footnote denoted by an asterisk. An obscure or manufactured word or phrase may also be clarified either within brackets or in a note as necessary.
4. The titles of the tales and captions of the illustrations have been regularized. Different typefaces and punctuation occur in different Almanacs and even within the same title in the same Almanac. Captions have been provided for some illustrations from the titles of their respective tales (Figures 3–12, 16, 17, 19, 20, 22–25, 28, 30–35, 37, 39–44, 46, 53, 55, 56, 59, 60, 62, 63, 67, 70, 73, 74, 76, 78–81, 83, 84, and 86).
5. A brief reference follows each tale. The appendix lists the full titles of each of the Almanacs arranged chronologically. Page-only references in the introductory essays to the tales in this volume are noted parenthetically and refer to the pages in this book. References to Almanac stories that do not appear in this volume are also cited parenthetically by year and page if the story appears in an Almanac listed in the appendix; otherwise a full citation is recorded in a note.
6. Many of the stories include multiple themes and could easily be classified in several different sections. They have been placed in categories according to what can best be judged as the tale's major focus.
7. In general, all tales in the Crockett Almanacs that involve women in some substantial way are included in this volume. When in any doubt, I have tried to err on the side of inclusiveness. Tales with only brief mentions of a woman, such as in "A Waking Dream" (1847, p. [32]), where Davy's wife appears only in the first sentence ("me and my wife had been washing, and had jist done ringing out her bearskin petticoat") and is not mentioned again, are not included, as the story bears solely on Crockett's

subsequent adventures. The only exception occurs in the section "Recipes and Household Hints," which includes "To Housewives" and "[Candles]" to give the reader a sample of the normal non-tall-tale, nonhumorous advice that some of the Almanacs occasionally included.

8. Interestingly, there are different types of Crockett Almanacs that focus upon different types of materials. The seven Nashville Almanacs have a certain evolving unity, as do those published after 1839 by the various incarnations of the firm of Turner and Fisher. Both produce legendary tall-tale characters and focus upon wild adventures in the backwoods. However, the popularity of these Almanacs engendered another category of these pamphlets, which I am tempted to name the "non-Crockett Crockett Almanacs," for Davy often appeared in name only, and only on the cover. Among this group are *Crockett's Texas Oldmanick. 1837.* (New York and Philadelphia: Turner and Fisher, 1837), a comic almanac whose main feature is a historical narrative of the Alamo, Crockett's death, and subsequent battles and occurrences in Texas; the *Crockett Awl-Man-Axe for 1839* (New York), Turner and Fisher's first attempt at the genre, which was essentially a straightforward comic almanac with only one story about Crockett; Elton's *Crockett Comic Almanac. 1839* was in the same vein with only one story for which an unnamed Crockett could be considered the narrator; *Crockett's Comic Almanack. '40* (Albany: A. Skinflint), which had nothing to do with Crockett or the backwoods; *Crockett's Harrison Almanac, 1841* (New York: Elton), a presidential campaign almanac with an unnamed narrator, presumably Crockett, who described the heroic life of Old Tippecanoe; and two others that do contribute some of their stories to this volume. *Crockett Comic Almanac Worser 1842* (Gotham [New York]: Doleful Serious [Elton]) contains nothing about Crockett but does provide a baseline for many of the comic depictions of women. It is a major contributor of short items to the section "Stereotypes, Stock Figures, and Jokes." Similarly, the *Crockett Almanac Improved, 1842* omits Crockett but still tries to capitalize on the name recognition of these Almanacs. It is in some ways an anti-Crockett Almanac, for it is "Improved" by its attempt "to elevate its character . . . in the substitution of articles relating to actual adventures in the Western country, for those heretofore published, of a less elevated character." Its stories, "depicted with the pencil of Truth" (p. 2), excluded tall tales and riotous language but provide this volume with one courting, two true adventures, one stereotype, and the two stories noted in point 7 above, which can again serve as a baseline of antebellum culture in the Almanacs. They are the "norm" against which the imaginativeness of the other Almanac adventures can be judged.

# Crockett, Women, and the Age of Jackson: A Chronology, 1786–1856.

*by Steven Harthorn*

1786      David Crockett, son of John and Rebecca Hawkins Crockett, is born on August 17 in Greene County, Tennessee.

1796      Tennessee joins the Union. The Crocketts open a tavern on the road from Knoxville, Tennessee, to Abingdon, Virginia.

1803      Lewis and Clark begin their exploration of the territory comprising the Louisiana Purchase.

1805      David takes out a license to marry Margaret Elder of Dandridge, Tennessee, on October 21, but she decides to marry another.

1806      Crockett courts and marries Mary (Polly) Finley on August 14 in Jefferson County, Tennessee.

1811      David, Polly, and their two sons, John Wesley and William, leave East Tennessee after September 11 and settle on the Mulberry Fork of Elk River in Lincoln County, Tennessee.

1812      War of 1812 begins on June 18. Missouri Territory is established west of the Mississippi.

1813      Crockett leaves Lincoln County to settle on the Rattlesnake Spring Branch of Bean's Creek in Franklin County, Tennessee, near the present Alabama border. Crockett joins a militia and participates in several military campaigns.

1814      War of 1812 ends with the signing of the Treaty of Ghent on December 24.

1815      Polly gives birth to their daughter, Margaret, and dies in the summer. The Battle of New Orleans is fought and won by the Americans on January 8, two weeks after the war has ended. Neither side was aware of the truce.

1816     Crockett marries Elizabeth Patton, a widow with two children, George and Margaret Ann.

1819     Emma Willard founds her female academy in Troy, New York.

1820     Missouri Compromise admits Missouri to the Union as a slave state while admitting Maine as a free state and abolishing slavery in the remainder of the Louisiana Purchase lands. Daniel Boone dies.

1821     Catherine Beecher founds her female academy in Hartford, Connecticut. Crockett is elected a representative to the state legislature.

1822     Catherine Maria Sedgwick, *A New England Tale*.

1823     James Fenimore Cooper, *The Pioneers*.

1824     Lydia Maria Child, *Hobomok*. Mary Jemison's captivity narrative is published.

1825     Erie Canal opens. Frances (Fanny) Wright establishes Nashoba in Tennessee as a "freedom" colony for slaves.

1826     Cooper, *The Last of the Mohicans*.

1827     Crockett is elected to the U.S. House of Representatives. Sedgwick, *Hope Leslie*. Cooper, *The Prairie*.

1828     Andrew Jackson is elected president. Sarah Josepha Hale becomes editor of Boston's *Ladies' Magazine*. James Hall, *Letters from the West*.

1829     Crockett shifts his allegiance from Jacksonian Democrats to the Whigs.

1830     *Godey's Lady's Book* founded by Louis Godey.

1831     William Lloyd Garrison begins publishing *The Liberator*, an abolitionist magazine, in Boston. *The Lion of the West* is performed; "Nimrod Wildfire" is modeled after Crockett.

1832    Supreme Court (in *Worcester v. Georgia*) rules that U.S. government has sole authority over Native Americans and their territories. Mrs. Frances Trollope, *Domestic Manners of the Americans*.

1833    Lydia Maria Child, *An Appeal in Favor of That Class of Americans Called Africans*. Samuel Knapp, *Female Biography*. Lucretia Mott founds Female Anti-Slavery Society.

1834    William A. Alcott, "Female Attendance on the Sick." Crockett, *A Narrative of the Life of David Crockett*. New York Female Moral Reform Society is founded.

1835    First Crockett Almanac is issued. Crockett is defeated in his election to Congress. He sets out for Texas on November 1. Augustees Baldwin Longstreet, *Georgia Scenes*. First half of de Tocqueville's *Democracy in America* is published (second half follows in 1840). Lyman Beecher, *A Plea for the West*.

1836    Defeat of the Americans at the Alamo by General Santa Anna, March 6. Davy Crockett and others are taken prisoner, then executed. Arkansas is admitted to the Union. Angelina E. Grimké, *Appeal to the Christian Women of the Society*. Sarah M. Grimké, *An Epistle to the Clergy of the Southern States*. Martin Van Buren is elected president. Pamela Mann wins "Houston's Defeat." Maria Weston Chapman, *Right and Wrong in Boston*. Narcissa Whitman travels to the Oregon Territory as a missionary to the Cayuse Indians. Louis Godey brings in Sarah Josepha Hale to coedit *Godey's Lady's Book*. It becomes the most popular magazine in America before midcentury.

1837    Queen Victoria ascends the throne of England at age eighteen, after the death of her uncle, William IV. Failure of banks stirs economic depression, the Panic of 1837. Over thirty-nine thousand Americans go bankrupt. Mount Holyoke Female Seminary in South Hadley, Massachusetts, opens as the first U.S. college for women.

1838    Trail of Tears takes over fourteen thousand Cherokees from southeastern United States to Indian territory west of Red River. Over four thousand Cherokees die en route. "Underground railway" organized by abolitionists to transport escaped slaves into Canada. Sarah

M. Grimké, *Letters on the Equality of the Sexes and the Condition of Women*.

1839    Caroline M. Kirkland, *A New Home—Who'll Follow?*

1840    William Henry Harrison, a Whig, wins presidency.

1841    Harrison dies after only a month in office. He is succeeded by John Tyler. Catherine Beecher, *A Treatise on Domestic Economy*.

1842    Elijah White takes first large band of settlers west to Oregon.

1844    James Knox Polk, a "dark horse" Democratic candidate from Tennessee, defeats Henry Clay for the presidency.

1845    Margaret Fuller (Ossoli), *Woman in the Nineteenth Century*. Texas is admitted to the Union. Andrew Jackson dies.

1846    The Mexican War begins. After failing to buy the New Mexico Territory from Mexico, President Polk sends Gen. Zachary Taylor to the Rio Grande, where he builds a fort. The Mexicans order Taylor to retreat, but he does not. Mexican troops cross the Rio Grande and kill some U.S. troops. Polk declares that Mexico "has invaded our territory and shed American blood upon American soil."

1847    Karl Marx, *The Communist Manifesto*.

1848    The Mexican War ends February 2 with the Treaty of Guadalupe Hidalgo, under which Mexico cedes 35 percent of its territory, including California and lands north of the Rio Grande, in return for $15 million. Gold is discovered in California on January 24. Despite attempts to keep the discovery secret, the news is printed in the *New York Herald* on August 19, and thousands rush to California to seek their fortunes. Women's Rights Convention held in Seneca Falls, New York. Organized by Elizabeth Cady Stanton and Lucretia Mott, it is the first convention of its kind. The group passes a resolution in favor of women's suffrage by a narrow margin.

1849    Henry David Thoreau, "Resistance to Civil Government" ("Civil Disobedience").

1850    President Zachary Taylor dies July 9 of acute gastroenteritis. He is replaced by his vice president, Millard Fillmore. Compromise of 1850 admits California to the Union as free state, abolishes slavery in Washington, D.C., enacts a stronger fugitive slave law, and makes no stipulations about slavery in New Mexico territory. Margaret Fuller (Ossoli) dies. Nathaniel Hawthorne, *The Scarlet Letter*. Susan Warner, *The Wide, Wide World* (1851 copyright).

1851    In her magazine, *The Lily*, feminist Amelia Jenks Bloomer urges reform of women's clothing. She is ridiculed for wearing in public a costume designed by Elizabeth Smith Miller, full-cut trousers under a short skirt. The costume, which came to be known as "bloomers," was introduced at the 1848 Women's Rights Convention.

1852    Harriet Beecher Stowe, *Uncle Tom's Cabin*.

1853    Commodore Matthew Perry leads a delegation of U.S. ships to Japan. Sarah Josepha Hale, *Woman's Record*. Joseph G. Baldwin, *The Flush Times of Alabama and Mississippi*. Sara Willis Parton, *Fern Leaves from Fanny's Port-Folio*. Franklin Pierce is elected president.

1854    The Republican party is formed by former Whigs and antislavery Democrats. The Kansas-Nebraska Act repeals the Missouri Compromise of 1820, allowing Nebraska to decide slavery on the basis of popular sovereignty. Benjamin P. Shillaber, *Life and Sayings of Mrs. Partington*.

1855    Frances M. Whitcher, *The Widow Bedott Papers*.

1856    Last Crockett Almanac issued for this year. Demise of the Whig Party.

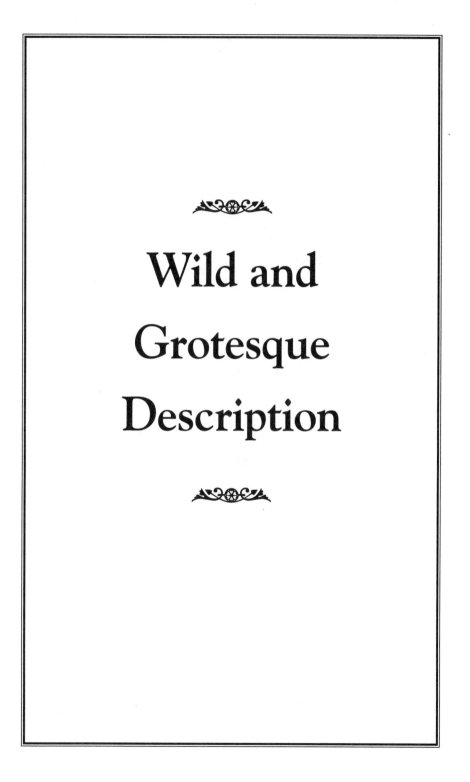

# Wild and
# Grotesque
# Description

# Crockett's Mother

FIGURE 3. *Crockett's Mother*

Now I gin you a genuine portrait of my mammy, in her One-Hundredth and Forty-Eighth year, and an all-scream-glorio[u]s gal she is of her age. She can jump a seven rail fence backwards, dance a hole through a double oak floor, spin more wool than one of your steam mills, and smoke up a ton of Kentucky weed in a week. She can crack walnuts for her great grandchildren with her front teeth, and laugh a horse blind. She can cut down a gum tree ten feet around, and steer it across Salt River with her apron for a sail, and her left leg for a rudder.

1845, p. [5]

# Crockett's Aunt

The Special Collections Library of The University of Tennessee, Knoxville

FIGURE 4. *Crockett's Aunt*

M y Aunt war the sister of Pine Rook, the most rantankerous fighter in the valley of the Massassippy. She war raised in Pine Clearing, and when she war a child, her pap war made of rattle-snake brains and maplesap, well peppered, and biled into a jelly. She growed so fast on that, that she rassled with a nigger in her thirteenth year, and threw him. My uncle war thar when she did it, and he fell in love with her right off, and made her a present of a tame bear, and two eyes that he had gouged out at the last election. She dried the eyes and hung one in each ear, and wore them to church. On the day she war married, she chased a crocodile half a mile.

1848, p. [5]

# Discovery of the Infant Crockett
# by His Uncle and Aunt

The Special Collections Library of The University of Tennessee, Knoxville

FIGURE 5. *Discovery of the infant Crockett by his Uncle and Aunt*

Aunt Ketinah and Uncle Roarious war dreadful tickled when I war born, and thought that thar war never sitch a young one sense acorns growed on trees. Aunt Ketinah held up her hands and sed I war the very pictur of good luck, for I war so fat that it war as good as a meal's vittles to look at me. She sed she knowed that I war cut out to be a great man, and wanted to have the bringing of me up. She said that she would bathe my head every morning with bear[']s gall, as that ar great for bringing forward the intellectures of young sports, and she would have my internal examined every week by the doctor, to see that I war not inclined to the cholera morbus, as that was what her grandmother died on. As for Uncle Roarious he wanted to see me eat, and so they made a smart chance of whiskey pap for me, and broke two rattle-snakes' eggs in it, and give me it in a spoon made of a buffalo's hoof, and an eagle's leg for a handle. When they seed me swallow they declared that I war the flower of the hull family, and would do more execution with my thumb-nail, than any of my posteriors had ever done before me. Arter that, they put me up in a tall tree, and lashed me to the top, so that the wind could swing me about, and that war the cradle in which I war rocked when I war young.

----

1848, p. [8]

# Crockett's Disappointment

When I war a boy I war sent to live with old Grit Plumper, up in Green Swamp. Wunce there war three of us youngsters in a meddo, and all on a suddent we seed a smart chance of gals in a leetle wood only a quarter of a mild off. We sallied out arter em rite off, and when we cum to the plaice war they war, I seed Sal Tuig amongst em. She war a gal that I had a kinder sort o' notion arter, and liked her rite well. Bekase she war knone in them parts, and had got her reppytation up by lickin' a big nigger down on the plantations. She stood six foot and two inches without her shoes; she had a fist like a rock, and the biggest feet in the whole cleering. Besides all this she had lost a eye at a tea-squall, and one ear had been bit off in a fite with two wolves. When we went down to the gals, I seed her amongst em, and she had on her new crocodile skin short gown and looked as pretty as a young buffalo. I begun to wauk up to her, when Sam Snag jumped round the other side and begun to tauk to her. Sez I, "what purtensions have you to this gal?" "He is my bo," sez Sal, "and has a rite to me." That was the fust disappointment in love, I ever had. At fust I konkluded to p[u]t an end to myself; but finally I wauked down to the Massissippi and drunk out of the stream. I spose I swallowed a gallon or two. I then took a swett under seven bear skins, and ett a crocodile's tale roasted. Arter that I keered nothin' about Sal.

---

1843, p. [8]

106

# Crockett's First Love

The Special Collections Library of The University of Tennessee, Knoxville

FIGURE 6. *Crockett's first love*

I must confess that I've had a smart chance of sweethearts in my days. The first one that I ever had war the pride of old Kaintuck, and lived up in Gum Hollow, on Goose Creek. Every winter she fatted up on bear's meat, so that when she turned out in spring, she war bigger round than a whiskey barrel; and when I put my arms 'round the cretur, it war like hugging a bale of cotton. Her two legs war like a cupple of hemlock trees, and when she sneezed it shook the leaves from the trees, and skeered setting hens off thar eggs. She war a very varchus gal, too; for when a Yankee pedlar undertook to come the soft soap over her, she kotched him by the heels and poked him up the chimbly till his head come out the top. Thar never war a gal that liked me as she did, till I had a few words with her brother; and arter I had put one of his eyes in my pocket, she thought I didn't act like a friend to the family. Her name war Florinda Fury, and she belonged to the church, and used to set off for meeting that war held up in Deer Meetin' House, every Sunday morning, and carried her vittles with her. She always took a rifle, to argufy with the varmints when she met 'em on the road; and sometimes she carried a rooster in her pocket, as they used to have a cock-fight in the meetin' house arter sarvice war over. Finally she married Ralph Leaf, a fifteenth cozzen of mine, and the same gentleman what 'lectioneered for me when I war up for Congress, as he sed that it would be an honor to him to have a relation in Congress.

---

1848, p. [7]

# Gum Swamp Breeding

The Special Collections Library of The University of Tennessee, Knoxville

FIGURE 7. *Gum Swamp breeding*

The most unpolite trick that ever was done up in Gum Swamp, tho that is the most unpolite place inside of the Massissippy, was done when I was playing possum for a gal in my young days, before i had ever heered of Congress. This gal was named Jerusha Stubbs, and had only one eye, but that was pritty enough for two, and besides it had a grate advantage in our parts, where folks must rise arly, as she could wake up in haff the time that others could, as she had only one eye to open, while other folks had to open two.

One of her legs was a little shorter than the other, but I telled her I shouldn't make no fuss about that as the road to my house laid all along on the side of a hill, so that the short leg seemed as if 'twas made a purpose for walking to my cabin. She had two cancers cut out of her breast, so that she was as flat as a board up and down there, which I couldn't have got over no how, only she had a beautiful grate hump on her back, and that made up for having nothing of the kind in front. Enenmost all her teeth had rotted out, but then she had a pesky grate swallow, so that she could take down her vittles without chawing. I forgot to say how she had a hare lip, but then she had a long nose, which almost covered the place from sight. There was a grate bunch on her left arm, but then she had a monstracious wen on the right side of her neck, that balanced that difficulty and made it all even agin. She was wonderful neat at pulling up parsenips, and could shake a dog by the ears, and they did tell how she chased one till his tale drew out and war left behind. She could lick two foxes, and make a wolf feel pesky unsartin. She once busted a pare of bellusses by blowing in at the nose of 'em, and smothered a chimney that war o' fire by setting on the top of it. You may suppose such a gal as that would be scarce in courting, for she could put a hole through any man's hart at seventy pases distunce. Onluckily i warnt on very good tarms with her father, tho he war with me. So i got akquainted with the gal a leetle at a time. I knowed her pritty well from her shoulders and upwards, but she kept her mind to herself, and that made me feel as oneasy as a steemboat with one wheel. But i felt hugeously mad, when a feller from doun east cum into Gum Swamp, and put up at her father's house with all his plunder. He was a skool-master, and tho i say it myself he was kind of good looking, and as slick as an eel standing up on his tale. I sot and lookt on whilst he was talking to the gal, and didn't know what to do about it for a good while; but when i begun to git over not knowing what to do about it, i felt an almighty notion to shove my thum nail into his left eye. Jerusha seed i was getting to be very odoriferous about it, tho a word from her would have laid my bristles in a minnit. At last she sot down to table one day, with her good eye next to the stranger, and her blind eye next to me. I took that for the most onrespectful thing that was ever done to me, and looked rite at the stranger, as if i war thinking whether it war best to swallow him or the dinner. You might as well try to play a game of cards on the back of a running deer, as to keep the run of how he looked. I cant ritely say how many colors he turned, but i know i seed three or four colors in his face that i never seed onnywhere else. I've heered tell of fellers that felt blue, but he felt all colors, besides a spot on the eend of his nose. So he axed me what i was grinning at, and i threw out one log and scraped the heel of the other foot as i says, says i, "Stranger, I dont want to onsult you be 4 the gal, but if i had you in the forest i'd hang you on the limb of a tree by your onquestionable ugly nose.'['] He then axed his gal if it would be imperlite if he jist took the tip of my nose between his thum and finger and giv it a small pull. He telled her he would do nothing more, and would make no noize about it, and that he could do it all in haff a minnit. She telled him he might do that if he chooze, but she wouldn't allow onnything else to be done about it, only that; and so she leaned back in her cheer, to let him put his arm out before her, and do what he sed. That wos the fust time i wos so mad i couldn't stir, to think the kussed varmint shood tork of pulling my nose as if it was only snuffing a kandel that couldn't strike back agin. I wos thinking whether i shood eat him with salt, or take him in his boots jist as he wos, when i seed him lay down his nife and fork and reech out his hand. I sot as still as a clam till he got his hand close to my mouth, and then I opened shell and took his flipper between my teeth. He yelled like a nest of young wild cats struck with litening, and insinnivated it hurt him beautiful. The gal begun to bawl out and take the feller's part, and that astonished me so much that i forgot to let go the feller's hand till my teeth almost met through it. There was a smart chance of hot soup on the table, and that was kicked over rite off, for he floundered about like a speared sammun, without stopping this time, to ax the gal whether it would be imperlite or not. She ketched hold of his coat tail to haul him away from me, but that only hurt him wuss, and so to git cleer of her he kicked backwards, and put his heels into her bowels like he was going to walk over her. Pritty soon the hot soup begun to run down into his boots, and then he danced wuss than ever and upset the table, and all the dishes went to smash. At last he got on his nieze and axed my pardun, and then i let him go. Now i went home and thot it was all over, but what does the gal's father do but send me a bill of the crokkery, that the feller broke when he upsot the table. I thot this was the most unpolite thing that ever i heered on, and so i sent the munny bekase i thot 'twould be a disgrace to me for sich a mean feller to think i owed him any thing.

1839 Nashville, pp. 21, 28

# The Flower of Gum Swamp

FIGURE 8. *The flower of Gum Swamp*

Courtesy, American Antiquarian Society

The flower of Gum Swamp, war a gal by the name of Lotty Ritchers. She stood six foot in her shoes; but as she hadn't 'em on very often, she war not quite so high. She used to brag that she war a streak of litenin set up edgeways, and buttered with quicksilver. She chased a crockodile one evening till his hide cum off, and one day I met her in the forrest jist as she had killed a monstracious big bare[;] I seed it war too much for her great strength, so we laid holt together, she took the tail, and I the head part, and for this she treeted me to a slice of genuine steak. She still wears the shift that she made out of the varmint's skin. It is told on her that she carried twenty eyes in her work bag, at one time, that she had picked out of the heads of certain gals of her acquaintance. She always made them into a string of beads, when she went to church, and wore 'em round her neck. She never pared her nales, and had holes cut in her shoes, so that her toe nales could have room to grow. She war a real beauty; but the young fellers war shy of her, bekase she never cood kort long befour she wanted to box with her bo, and her thumb nale war grate for pullin out eyes. Finely she cort her death by standing two days up to her chin in the Massissippy to hale the steem botes as they past by.

---

1841, p. [21]

# [The Puke's* Wife]

Thar war a Puke that cum into our parts who used to exhibit his wife as she could scold agin a harrycane. She could outscreech a Painter and yell louder than a wild cat. She war the true grit for a hunter's wife and he wouldn't take no money for her whatsomever.

---

*A "puke" is a person from Missouri.

1850, p. [24]

# [The Corruption of Frontier Ways]

The gals about our plaice ar gettin' wonderful perlite and perticklar. They used to have combs with iron teeth, and do up thar hare with wooden skewers; but now they must have pewter combs, and do up thar hare with spike nales. If they puts on a crocodile-skin shift, they must have the ruff side outwards, and thar bear-skin pettykotes must be combed as offen as wunst a month. I have heered in kongress that Rome was ruined by luxuriousness and all that ar, and I'm afeered that old Kaintuck will be ruined by them ar gals that can't keep up the old ways of thar four-fathers.

---

1843, p. [21]

# Ben Hardin's* Description
# of His Sweetheart

She is a square-rigged craft, about as thick threw as she is tall. One leg is a little shorter than the 'tother, and that maiks her look more interesting. She lives up near Duck Creek, and may be heard to scream down to Mile Village when the wind is fare. She can bite a spike-nale in two and grin chess-nuts out of the bur. When she sneezes it lifts the roof of the house about one foot, and brakes the crockery. She dresses most butiful, and wares an apron made of willow twigs wove together. She sez she loves me from the top of my head downwards, and I loves her lengthways and across, and cood eat her alive, close and awl.

---

1843, p. [5]

*Ben is Davy Crockett's faithful companion and seagoing counterpart in the Almanacs. This swaggering fictional sailor serves as the supposed editor and publisher of the second series of "Nashville" Crockett Almanacs (1839–41) and is featured in a group of out-landish adventures throughout these and other Crockett Almanacs second only to Davy himself. (See Michael A. Lofaro, ed., *The Tall Tales of Davy Crockett: The Second Nashville Series of Crockett Almanacs, 1839–1841* (Knoxville: University of Tennessee Press, 1987). First introduced in the first series of Nashville Almanacs as "Ben Harding [sic], Member of Congress from Kentucky" (1836, pp. 14–19), the portrayal was more clearly linked to the actual colorful Whig politician from Bardstown, Ben Hardin. In all the other stories, Ben Harding/Hardin is a sailor and bears no resemblance to his more refined middle-class namesake, who, interestingly, was nicknamed "Old Kitchen Knife" because of his cutting, rough-honed speaking style. In a masterpiece of understatement, Hardin's biographer, Lucius P. Little, noted that "the comic almanac maker of his day made Mr. Hardin the unwilling vehicle for communicating jokes rather broader than he ever indulged in the most unreserved moments" (pp. 63, 288). For further information, see Lucius P. Little, *Ben Hardin: His Times and Contemporaries, with Selections from His Speeches* (Louisville, KY: Louisville Courier-Journal Job Printing Co., 1887) and John Seelye, "A Well-Wrought Crockett; Or, How the Fakelorists Passed Through the Credi-bility Gap and Discovered Kentucky," in Michael A. Lofaro, ed., *Davy Crockett: The Man, The Legend, The Legacy, 1786–1986* (Knoxville: University of Tennessee Press, 1985), pp. 26–28, passim.

# Battles
# with
# Animals

# Perilous Situation of Mrs. Crockett: Discovery of an Eagle's Nest

FIGURE 9. *Perilous situation of Mrs. Crockett.*
*Discovery of an eagles' nest*

St. Louis Mercantile Library Special Collections Department

My wife, Mrs. Davy Crockett—whose maiden name war Sally Ann Thunder Ann Whirlwind—always had a nat'ral taste for Eagle's eggs: kase she war edicated to the idee that they give the blood the true sap o' freedom an' independence—made them that fed on 'em able to look the sun or lightenin' in the eye without winkin' or squintin'—an' likewise encouraged the growth o' that all daren disposition to stand no nonsense from man, woman, beast or Beelzebub, while they also hatched in the heart the spirit of fly-high-ativeness and go-ahead-ativeness.

W-a-l-l, the first Easter mornin' arter the annexation of our State [Texas] that we licked out o' Mexico, Sal war determined to du honor to the occasion by havin' a drink o' *Eagle egg nog* from the top o' one o' the tallest trees in the country, whar thar happened to be a nest of a kind of a republic of eagles. So she took a bottle o' my blue lightnin', flogged a she Buffalo and milked her, and then walked up to the Eagles' nest to get the eggs to make her *nog*. But it happined that the hull Senate and House o' Representatives o' the eagle nation war then in session, and they met her with a deputation o' *bills* and claws, that quite turned her hair out o' comb; but the gal went into 'em bite, smite an' claw, an' made the feathers fly like a snow storm or a geese picken; but arter she had flogged the wings off of about a dozen on 'em, her foot slipped, and havin' to use her hand to keep from fallin', two fresh cock eagles flew right at her eyes, an' would a made a week's provision of her if I had'nt a walked, and shot 'em both through with the same bullet. Arter that I walked up the tree, and we both drank to our victory in *Eagle egg nog!*

1854, p. [7]

# Terrible Fight with Three Panthers*

The Special Collections Library of The University of Tennessee, Knoxville

FIGURE 10. *Terrible fight with three panthers*

Having gotten my wife, I thought I was completely made up, and needed nothing more in the whole world. But I soon found this was all a mistake—for now having a wife I wanted every thing else; and worse than all, I had nothing to give for it. My Irish mother-in-law gave me two fine cows and calves. I hired a small cabin and some land, and went to work hard. My wife had a wheel, and knowed exactly how to use it. And in this way we went on several years. I now got plaguey restless, and determined to cut out for the Duck and Elk river country, which was just beginning to settle, I took my family and plunder and removed safely to Lincoln County, on the head of the Mulberry fork of Elk river. I found game here plenty. But the wild varments were very savagerous and troublesome. The wild cats kept us awake with the noise they made in sharpening their claws against the logs on the side of our house, and with their infernal yelling. I now had a touch of the fever and ague, during which time my wife tended the large steel traps which were set for foxes and raccoons. One morning she returned in great terror, and said there were two great spotted varments surrounding a trap in which a still greater one was taken by the leg. My eyes! here was a pretty predicky-ment! I knowed they were panthers, and that they would be easier to master if it wasn't for their divilish sharp claws and teeth. Besides, letting alone my fever, the ague made me shake so I couldn't take aim. But there is no back out to my breed, so we loaded up both rifles; I took one, and my wife the other, and an axe, and we started for the traps. When I had got within forty yards, they saw me and set up such a yell that it rung in my ears for a month. I rested my rifle over my wife's back, and fired at one of the loose panthers; it hit him, he jumped up ten feet and fell down dead. I instantly took the other gun to fire, when the other one made towards us. I fired, and hit his fore leg; he now closed in with us, and a rough time we had of it. With one spring he seized me by the arm, and bit it terribly; I have the marks of his tarnal teeth there to this day. My wife now gave him a cut over the back with the axe, which broke his back-bone; this disabled him so that we made out to despatch him. The other my wife shot in the trap. We dragged one home at a time, and skinned them; the largest weighed over four hundred pounds.

---

1835 Nashville, p. 8

*This story is an excerpt from a longer tale called "Davy Crockett's Early Days, Severe Courtship and Marriage," pp. 3–8. The other part of the tale is reproduced with that title on pages 184–87 of this volume.

# The Panther and the Squaw

The Special Collections Library of The University of Tennessee, Knoxville

FIGURE 11. *The panther and the squaw*

Once, when I war in the forest, down by the Great Bog Swamp, I war going along slowly with kill devil in my hand, and thinkin of my next speech in Congress when I seed an Indian woman and her child lying asleep in the shade of a big rock. I stood a minit looking at 'em: for the woman war one that had brought Mrs. Crockett some good venison soup, when she was sick with the fever and ager [ague]. But she had a jug of whiskey by her side, and so I concluded that she was sleepin pretty sound. While I stood thar I heard something stir up over my head, and when I looked up I seed a pesky g[r]ate painter crouching down o[n] the top of the rock, and watching the woman. I knowed that the painter war expectin to have a good meal off the woman's ribs, and take the child for a desert. So I jist raised kill-devil and d[r]ew a lead on the varmint. It wounded him in the side, and he turned over and made a spring at me. I hit him over the nose with kill-devil, but he minded that no more than a fl[e]a bite, and in a minnit he war combing my hair with his nales. I fell down and he atop o' me. The squaw woke up, and she knowed what it meant in a minnit. She came up with a tommyhawk, and jest as the infarnal varmint war setting his teeth into my windpipe, she split open his head with the hatchet. Then she was very thankful to me for saving the life of herself and child, and if Mrs. Crockett had seed how she hugged me and kissed my hands, I guess that she would have felt her dander rise rather higher than it ever did before in all her life.

---

1851, p. [28]

# Crockett a Prisoner

FIGURE 12. *Crockett a prisoner*

I never got treed but wonce, and that war by a stareiferous big painter, near
the fork of Great Red River. I went up into the tree to get a nest, and left
my rifle at the bottom of the tree. When I got up thar, I seed the tree war
hollow, and I then heared the bra[n]ches close by begin to snap and crack,
and when I lookt up, my eyes! thar war a grate wild-cat steping toward me as
dainty and polite as a dancing master. I lookt out of won corner of my eye,
and woodent take any notice of her; but I war keerful to put my feet down

the hollow of the tree, and let my corpse settle down endwise as fast as its own wait would take it. I had but just got down when the hole at the top war darkened by the cretur's nose. Then she put her paw down and just tutched the top of my hare, for I couldint git down enny furder. I felt very rediculous, and when one of the painter's nails jist scratched the top of my skalp, I thort of Mike Fikkers whose wife used to comb his head for him. I kept still so long that I didn't know as I shood be able to revive agin. The painter liked the smell of my meet, and she owd me a grudge as I had walked into [killed] all her arthly relations;—she being the last of her race bred on the fork of Great Red River, so she stuck close; but I should have spiled before [s]he could have got me. It begun to be dark, and I knew the painter would have company soon, and so [s]he did, for I heered a gun go off and the cretur fell from the tree. I looked out, and seed my wife who had cum to look for me, and shot the varmint, for she smelt a rat when she seed my rifle on the ground.

This war the last time I went a nest hunting; and my wife often holds out that she saved my wife [life], and this makes my blood bile reeling hot; 'cause I always afore this considered myself equal to any she painter that ever yelled, on the universal arth.

———

1842, p. [5]

# Mrs. Cuttle and the Catamount [Mountain Lion]

The Special Collections Library of The University of Tennessee, Knoxville

FIGURE 13. *Mrs. Cuttle and the Catamount*

One day I fell in with Jo Cuttle. Jo war an honest ruft-and-tumble sort of a chap, and arter we had jogged on a little way, sez he. "Karnel, thar war a pesky queer scrape onct happened to me in these diggins. It war arter this sort: It war late one arternoon when my wife war cuming home from a tea-squall [tea party]. She war passing rite thro' the forrest, and had forgot to bring her rifle with her. But she never war afeard of any thing less than a bull mammoth, and so she jogged along as merry and contented as a she bear. She cum to a deep hollow whar war a large pond of water, and she saw a big log lying near, and she rolled it in. As soon as the log war afloat, she got on one eend of it with her face towards the opposite shore, and begun to paddle across. When she got about haff way over, she happened to hear a low growl, and when she looked behind she saw that a great catamount sot on the other eend of the log. He had took passage with her when she fust started, but she did not see him then. As my wife war sitting straddle, it took sum time for her to turn round, and face the catamount. He showed his teeth and grouled because she had left off paddling; so she concluded that he meant to behave civil, if she wood only carry him safe across; but she had an idee that arter they war fairly landed, he would try to make a breakfast of her. So she would not paddle another stroke. He kept growling, as much as to say, "Row away you infarnal jade!" That made her mad, for she cood understand his language jist as well as if she had been born to it; so she dashed water on him with her paddle. This made him wink a little, and he showed his teeth. When she seed he war going to spring rite at her, she jist canted the log and he tumbled into the drink, but he put his paws up to get hold of the log agin, and kept trying to gain a foothold on it, which kept it turning round and round like a grindstone, till my wife's legs war chafed most ridiculous. At last she found she must get upon her feet, and then she war forced to keep hopping up and down all the time—she danced while the catamount fiddled upon the log— She then stomped on his paws, but he minded no more about that than a flea bite. So she watched a chance and gave a jump rite on the feller's back, and caught hold of both of his ears. When ever he tried to bite her, she wood bowse [dowse] his head under and haff drown him. Then he set out to swim for the shore, and she kept upon his back, and guided him by pulling his right or left ear, jist as she wanted he shood go. Well, he got safe ashore with her, and she didn't dare let go of his ears, or to get off, for fear he wood be into her like a buck-shot.

Now I happened to be out hunting, with one Kit Weatherblow at this time, and Kit cum running to me, and told me he saw the strangest cretur going through the woods that he ever seed in his life before. He said it war a wild varmint in petticoats. I told Kit to go with me to hunt it up, for I had seen every cretur in the forrest, and this must be a stranger. We soon cum in sight of it, but I new my wife's petticoat as soon as I got a glimpse at it, and then I seed her head a little while arterward. So sez I to Kit, sing dumb, and let me get a blizzard [volley of shots] at the obstropolous varmint, for he's runing off with my wife. I lifted my rifle and put a hole rite through his gizzard; but I shot away one of my wife's cap-strings at the same time, which war made of buffalo sinew. The varmint tumbled amongst the leaves pretty quick, and my wife picked herself off the ground in less than no time. When I seed she want [wasn't] hurt, I felt a little mad, and told her never agin to clasp around the neck of any living thing but her own lawful husband.

1841 Nashville, p. 32

# Whipping a Catamount

The Special Collections Library of The University of Tennessee, Knoxville

FIGURE 14. *Judy Finx whipping a Catamount*

There war a gal named Judy Finx, that lived down to Mud creek. Every body has hearn on her, and every body has seen her, too, except them what her brother carries their eyes in his pocket. It's concluded that she takes the rag off quite, all along up and down the creek and something of a piece beyond. Judy went out one arternoon to a tea squall. As it war at a near neighbor's who lived only about five miles off, she did not take her rifle with her; she only put her butcher knife in her bosom; but she wore that as much for ornament as anything else. On the way home it war quite dark, and her neighbor where she had been let Judy have a tame bear to see her home, as there war no other beau present. They were going through a piece of woods together, when they heard a squalling like a woman's voice, and Judy knew it was a catamount right off. So she jumped on the bear's back, being intarmined that the varmint should have a chase before he got her. The bear knew what she wanted, and he set out at full speed. They had not gone fur before a great snake seized the bear by the hind leg and stopped his progress. The bear turned around and caught the snake by the neck with his teeth, and held on upon it.

The snake thrashed about, and jest as the catamount came up, Judy caught the cretur by his long tail, and begun to chastise the catamount with it as if it had been a cowskin. The catamount squalled and grinned and snapped at the snake's tail whenever it came down upon his head and shoulders, and at last he caught it in his teeth. The bear then let go of the sarpent and he wheeled upon the catamount. The way them two made the leaves fly war a caution, and Judy did not stop to see which would gain the victory. She drove forward [on] the bear and soon got home, safe and sound.

1839 Nashville, p. 10

# A Thief of an Alligator

About as outrageous a thing as ever happened to me or mine in all the western country, was done by a tarnal alligator on a Sunday morning. My wife was getting ready to go to a meeting, that was to be held about fifteen miles from our clearing by old Lorenzo Dowe.* So says she, "I'll just go and wash out my best bear skin petticoat, and I'll be ready to cut out for to hear the sarmont." Well my wife had just got the garment washed out, and had hung it on some bushes to dry, when a monstratious great he-alligator having scented it, came on a ranting gallop out of the water, seized it, and made off with it. As several of my dogs were near, my wife set them on him, and catching up a big club, cut out after him. The dogs by biting hold of his hind legs soon brought him to bay. I had just started on a coon hunt, but hearing the music of the dogs and wife, I started down the hill to where they were, and saw the tussle. I got a blizzard [shot] at the deuced varmint, but the ball flew of[f] his cursed hide as if I had shot at a rock. So I run down and jumped on to the varmints back near his head, so as to be beyond the reach of his tail, and stuck my knife into his eye, he thrashed about his agony most ridiculous. At length we mastered the critter, and I was enabled to cut his throat. He had swallowed the petticoat, and such is the roughness of these critters palates, that when I got it out of him the hair was all off of it.

---

1836 Nashville, p. 44

*Lorenzo Dow (1777–1834), one of the great eccentric, itinerant preachers of his day, was a Methodist minister said to be the inventor of the camp meeting. He preached in most states from Connecticut and New York to Georgia, as well as in Ireland and England. He delivered the first Protestant sermon in Alabama and visited with Indian tribes in about 1803. In the last thirty years of his life, he issued a stream of pamphlets, revised his journals, concocted medicines for biliousness, and raged against Catholics, Whigs, anti-Masons, and finally, Methodists, because he felt they were tainted with popery. For more information, see Charles Coleman Sellers, *Lorenzo Dow: The Bearer of the Word* (New York: Milton, Balch, & Company, 1928).

# A Tongariferous Fight with an Alligator

The Special Collections Library of The University of Tennessee, Knoxville

FIGURE 15. *A Tongariferous Fight with an Alligator*

When I first went to live on Bean Creek at the Mulberry fork of Elk River, in the spring of 1813, during the great freshets of that season when all the bayous were overflowed that lead from the Mississippi, but a short distance from our log house, there was a large fathomless pool, called the "Alligator's Sink," situated on the "barrens," where the quantity of these monsters was so great that when they ascended in the spring from its unknown recesses, the whole circle was as full as a tub of eels. In the first of the evening a sound like a long drawn sigh announces the presence of the Alligator; but his proper time for singing is about dawn, when you may hear him and his brethren roaring like a distant herd of bulls. We had some of the most rageriferous fights with Alligators. For the infarnal critturs would get atop of our house, where the old bulls would have such fights, for the females, that we could get no sleep at all. They not only knocked off the chimney level with the roof, but in their rampoosings they broke the ridge pole of the house, and scratched off all the bark and shingles. This happened in a bad time, for I was confined to my bed with the spindle fever—my legs were swelled up as big as broom sticks. My sons were all absent; but my wife and

131

two darters [daughters] at home. We had a fine litter of sucking pigs, and the only way we saved them from the varments, was to put them in a big holler log and plug a big stick and spike it in every night. But the critturs kept rolling the log about the front yard all night, scratching it and endeavoring to get at the pigs, so that they squeeled most beautiful. As the varments got upon the roof they would first put a fore foot and then a hind one on the window frame outside. I told my wife to bring me the great cart rope, and I made a strong slip noose in tother eend on't, and desired her to lay it out on the window seat just as a big one was coming to mount. As soon as he got his fore feet on the eaves, he stepped his hind foot on the window seat, when my wife gave a pull, and secured his leg in the noose. As this varmint is not very quick of apprehension, and considerable slack was given to the rope, he did not at first mind it, but quickly began to dispute with another for the favors of a female, and got into a divil of a rage and fight, and the uproar they made on the roof was a caution. We made the rope fast to a beam, and when the strain came upon it, it bent double. The crittur finding something to pay, bit as though he had teeth in his head. At length the rope got tangled with another varmint, when they rolled off the roof together tother side of the house, and left him hanging by the hind leg with the fore part of him on the ground. In this way we kept him till morn, but he knocked off all the clapboards on the side of the house. The women then slacked the rope a little and made it fast round a hickory stump, when my oldest darter took the tongs and jumped on his back, when she beat up the "devil's tattoo" on it, and gave his hide a real "rub a dub." He found it was sharp work for the eyes, as the devil said, as a broad-wheeled waggon went over his nose.* My wife threw a bucket of scalding suds down his throat, which made him thrash round as though he was sent for. She then cut his throat with my big butcher knife. He measured *thirty seven feet* in length.

---

1837 Nashville, pp. 8,10

*This saying is called a Wellerism, named for Sam Weller, a character in Charles Dickens's *Pickwick Papers* (1837), who frequently uses these ancient and sometimes obscure proverbs that often involve the devil, a monkey, a blind man, or an old woman, as in "'Neat but not gaudy,' said the Devil, as he painted his tail blue." For a comment on "Figure 15," please see the note on page 250.

# Sappina Wing and the Crocodile

The Special Collections Library of The University of Tennessee, Knoxville

FIGURE 16. *Sappina Wing and the crocodile*

The biggest thing that ever happent in our cleering war the time that Oak Wing's darter Sappina war mopping up the floor won day, and she war all alone in the house as her mother had gone to a tea-squall and had took a tame wolf with her: for it war one that she had cotch an tamed, an she loved it as she did her own child. Her mother had agreed to scream as soon as she got down to Gander Creek, which is about three mile from the house; an Sappina heered a scream an she couldn't rightly tell whether it war her mother or a cat[a]mount as the voices of the two war a like. At last she heered something rubbing an scratching along the side of the house, an she turned towards the door an seed a big crocodile crawling right in at the door. She backed up in one corner till he got in, an opened his mouth as if he would ax her to walk into a ball room. Then her dander riz, an she lifted the mop an pointed rite at his infarnal tongue, an rammed it down his throat. He struggled about five minuits most butiful, an broke all the crockery with his tale, but his breathing hole was stopt up, an the cretur died.

1847, p. [23]

# A Dangerous Situation

Courtesy, American Antiquarian Society

FIGURE 17. *A dangerous situation*

W on day when I war gone off from home, and my wife sot a nitting by the fire, she heered a sort of a growl behind her; and when she looked around she seed a big bear that had walked in at the dore, and sot down close by her cheer. She looked rite into his face, and he lookt very surprised. She war afeered to git up, lest he should put his teeth into her, so she sot and stared at him. In a minnit he put his paw on her sholder, and she felt the nales begin to sink into her flesh. Nothing on arth is quicker thorted than a woman, and she seed thar war no time to lose. So she drawed out her two nitting needles, and while the bear war looking up at her she stuck 'em both into his eyes. He jumpt about three feet off the floor, and roared out like a stuck pig. He then tride to spri[n]g at her, but he couldn't see, and jumpt rite into the fire. Before he got fairly out of the fire, he had kicked the brands and coals all out upon the floor, and when he cum out, he sprawled round and kicked till he had put everything up in heeps, and broke the crockery; but my wife soon brought the rifle to bear upon his pesky carcase, and straitened him out like a corpse in December. The way she had pork stakes, for a month arterwards, its not worth while to explicitrize about.

1841, p. [17]

# Perilous Adventure with a Black Bear

FIGURE 18. *A Desperate Contest with a Great Black Bear*

The first year I cut out for the Obion [River] near the lower branch of Gizzard creek; it was late in the spring. I turned in, and cleared a field and planted our corn, but it was so late in the season we had no time to make rails, and therefore put no fence round the field. There was no stock, however, nor nothing else to disturb our corn, except the wild varments; and the old sarpent himself, with a fence to help him, could not keep them out. I made corn enough to do me, and during the spring killed many bears and abundance of deer. One day as I went into a small grove on the prairie to cut some birch saplings, for pea-sticks, I had nothing with me but my large hunting-knife. As I was busily engaged on the top of a small knoll, I heard a sudden and sharp growl under me. I jumped up a rod; but recovering myself, I walked down to the side of the knoll. The varmint was in the bottom of a big fissure in the ground. As soon as I got sight of the crittur, I took a large stone, and stepped down one foot to see his eyes; as the place was dark, and as they glared at me, I threw it at his head; it hardly reached him before he sprang upon me. I retreated as fast as possible, but all the way he was snapping his teeth so near me, that I felt his breath warm on my face. He might have seized me at any moment, but did not, as he appeared somewhat mystified for a few moments from the blow on his head by the stone; he quickly recovered and took after me—I ran for home, hollering with all my might. Luckily a neighbur was at the house, who, hearing my music, ran out with my big dog Rough, and wife. I had become almost exhausted. But old Rough seized him by the hind-quarter, so that his pace was slackened; the man now reached the spot, and gave him a blow over the head with his axe. My wife, although she could but just use her left hand as it was hardly healed, as she had lost her thumb and fore finger. They were bit off by a cat fish as she attempted to skin one alive. But she caught up a hickory rail, and as the bear rushed at her with his mouth wide open she ran it down his throat. He corfed as if he had swallowed something the wrong eend first. His attention was now taken from me, and although completely broken winded, I turned and jumped on to the varmint's back, when I reached his vitals with my big butcher; and after a most desperate contest, in which we were all more or less bitten and my wife had her gown torn nearly off of her, we succeeded in killing him. He was a real fat one and weighed six hundred lbs.

---

1837 Nashville, p. 19

# [Mrs. Crockett's 800 Petticoats]

Mrs. Crockett has made as high as eight hundred barr skin petticoats in two years time; from this you can see that we've had a smart sprinkle of barrs in our neighborhood. I have had great experience in, that line of business all my born days.

1850, p. [20]

# [Selling Mrs. Crockett's Petticoats]

Mrs. Crockett and I always sallied out in the fall to sell her barr shin [skin] petticoats which war warranted not to fade in washing and doin up. That war all the shopping she done in the whole year.

1850, p. [19]

# [Oak Wing's Aunt Jerusha]

The most beautiful woman that ever lived in old Kentuck, war Oak Wing's aunt Jerusha. She had a wooden leg, and when she war attacked by a pesky wolf, she gave him a crack over the back with her wooden leg and broke the varmint's back short off. She had a shift made of the critter's hide that lasted her ten years.

1847, p. [28]

# One of Crockett's Infant Children, Grinning Lightning at a Bear

FIGURE 19. *One of Crockett's infant children grinning lightning at a bear*

St. Louis Mercantile Library Special Collections Department

I always had the praise o' raisin the tallest and fattest, and sassyest gals in all America. They can out run, out jump, out fight, and out scream any crittur in creation; an for scratchin, thar's not a hungry painter, or a patent horse-rake can hold a claw to 'em. The oldest o[n]e growed so etarnally tall that her head had got nearly out o'sight, when she got into an all storm fight with a thunder storm, that stunted her growth, an now I am afraid that she'll never reach her natural size; but still, it takes a hull winter's weavin to make her walkin and bed clothes; and when she goes to bed, she's so tarnal long, and sleeps so sound, that we can only waken her by degress [degrees], and that's by choppen fire wood on her shins; but the youngest one o'them takes arter me, and is of the regular airthquake nater. Her body's flint rock, her soul's lightnin, and her fist is a thunderbolt, an her teeth can out cut any steam mill saw in creation. She is a perfect infant prodigy, being only six years old; she has the biggest foot and widest mouth in all the west, and when she grins, she is splendifferous; she shows most beautiful intarnals, an can scare a flock o' wolves to total terrifications. Well, one day, this sweet little infant was walking in the woods, and amusin herself by picking up walnuts, and cracking them with her front grindstones, when suddenaciously she stumbled over a thunderin great hungry he barr. The critter seein her fine red shoulders bare, showin an inviting feast, sprung at her as if determined to feast upon Crockett meat, he gin her a savaggerous hug, and was jist about bitin a regular buss ont [out] on her cheek, when the child resentin her insulted wartue, gin him a kick with her south fist, in his digestion, that made him buss the arth instanterly, and jist as he war a comin to her a second time, the little gal grinned sich a double streak o' blue lightnin into his month [mouth], that it cooked the critter to death as quick as think, an she brought him home for dinner. She'll be a thunderin fine gal when she gets her nateral growth, if her stock o' Crockett lightnin don't burst her biler, and blow her up.

---

1845, p. [33]

# The Tame Bear

The Special Collections Library of The University of Tennessee, Knoxville

FIGURE 20. *The tame bear*

The creturs of the forest is of different kinds, like humans. Some is stupid and some is easy to larn. The most knowing cretur that ever I seed war a barr that my darter Pinetta picked up in the woods. It used to follow her to church, and at last it got so tame, it would cum into the house, and set down in one corner of the fire-place to warm itself. I larned it to smoke a pipe and while it set in one corner smoking, I sot in the other with my pipe. We couldn't talk to one another; but we would look, and I knowed by the shine of his eye what he wanted to say, though he didn't speak a word. The cretur would set up o'nights when I war out late, and open the door for me. But it war the greatest in churning butter. It did all that business for the family. At last it got so civilized that it caught the hooping cough and died. My wife went to the minister and tried to get him to give the barr a christian burial: but the skunk war so bigotted that he wouldn't do it, and I told him the barr war a better christian than he ever war.

1850, p. [24]

# A Desperate Fight between Two Women, One Man, and Two Bears

The Special Collections Library of The University of Tennessee, Knoxville

FIGURE 21. *A Fight between two Women, a Man, and two Bears*

Having arrived, one afternoon, at a solitary log cabin in Lenawee County, M. T. [Michigan Territory],* in the autumn of 1834, the owner was absent, but his wife and sister were at home. They were at supper, when I entered, upon their invitation. I sat down with them, and helped myself with an iron spoon from a dish of suppawn, and fishing up a cup from a huge pan of milk, I poured the snowy liquid over the boiled meal that rivalled it in whiteness. I now took off my leggings, and stretched them on the andirons to dry. After a sociable evening was passed with the females, I had taken off my coat to ascend into the loft of the cabin, when the hogs, which ran at large around the house, set up a terrible squealing, and ran for the house. One of the women sprang up and opened the door, when she sprang back and screamed out that two bears were coming. In rushed two pigs, and before I could reach the door, the bears bolted in, knocking the door off its hinges, and upsetting the churns and stools. Luckily there was a large fire at the time, as the women were boiling maple sugar; one of the women had just dipped out a bucket of the hot liquor; snatching it up, she let the foremost bear have it full in his face and eyes, whilst the other female seized up an axe and buried it in his skull. A terrible struggle now ensued; the wounded bear, blinded by the hot liquor, clawed hold of one of the women, and scratched her terribly—but the other one wielded her axe to so good a purpose, that the brute was quickly dispatched. The other one was so intent after the pigs, which ran up between some logs in the corner of the room, that I seized up a great shovel of burning coals and threw on to him; this made him instantly abandon the pursuit of the pigs, and make for the door, roaring with pain. I instantly applied a large burning log to his posterious, as he galloped out, and seizing a rifle which was hanging on hooks on the side of the room, I ran out and fired at him. The ball took effect, but although he appeared to be badly wounded, he escaped over the fence into the forest. We now barricadoed the door, and passed the night without farther interruption. In the morning, upon the arrival of the owner of the house, we tracked the bear for about half a mile, and found him, very much disabled; we soon dispatched and butchered him. Both of the bears were fat, and fine eating.

---

1838 Nashville, p. 40

*"M. T." could be either the Michigan or Missouri Territory, and the Almanacs deal with both wolverines and pukes, the respective names for their citizens. It was likely Michigan, because there is currently a Lenawee County in that state. Michigan was admitted to the Union as a state in 1837.

# Sal Fink's Victory over an Old Bear and Cubs

Courtesy, American Antiquarian Society

FIGURE 22. *Sal Fink's victory over an old bear and cubs*

Sal Fink went out one morning to gather acorns for her pet pigs, and upon approaching a huge hollow oak tree, and taking a characteristic peep into the opening, she was instantly startled by a loud growl, which was followed by the sudden egress, from the aperture, of a huge she bear, followed by her cubs, who instantly arrayed themselves for an attack upon her. The old bear made a grab at her fair and inviting shoulders, while the young ones sprang and snapped at her exposed extremities, with the fury of wild cats, while Sal greeted their repeated approaches with a furious kick, worthy of a two-year

145

old colt, which sent them rolling over each other, and causing them to bite the ground. But how was the girl managing the mother bear all this time? Springing upright before her, the old one most zealously endeavored to lock her in one of those close embraces or *hugs* for which Bruin is so famous. With her naked fists, (for she scorned the use of her side arms on the occasion) did the intrepid Sal Fink send the creature such a succession of ponderous thumps in the chest, and under the wind, that the old bear became too weak to rise erect before her, although, in the last effort, she so far succeeded as to get her forepaws and teeth entangled in Sal's hair, which she held on to with terrible tenacity—and the brave girl struck and kicked to effect her release, like an enraged wild cat—and, darting back to the full length of her hair, she seized on a piece of loose rock, with which she dealt Bruin a death-blow—and dragged her home to her father, Mike Fink.*

---

1853, p. [19]

*For more information on Mike Fink, see Walter Blair and Franklin J. Meine, eds., *Half Horse Half Alligator: The Growth of the Mike Fink Legend* (Chicago: University of Chicago Press, 1956).

# Skinning a Bear

The Special Collections Library of The University of Tennessee, Knoxville

FIGURE 23. *Skinning a bear*

One day when Oak Wing's sister war going to a baptizing, and had her feed in a bag under her arm, she seed a big bear that had come out from a holler tree, and he looked first at her, then at the feed, as if he didn't know which to eat fust. He kinder poked out his nose, and smelt of the dinner which war sassengers [sausages] maid of bear's meat and crocodile's liver. She stood a minute an looked at him, in hopes he would feel ashamed of himself an go off; but he then cum up and smelt of her, an then she thort twar time to be stirring. So she threw the dinner down before him, an when he put his nose to it, to take a bite, she threw herself on him, an caught the sc[r]uff of his neck in her teeth; an the bear shot ahead, for it felt beautiful, as her teeth war as long an as sharp as nales. He tried to run, an she held on with her teeth, an it stript the skin clear off of him, an left him as naked as he was bors [born], she held on with her teeth till it cum clear off the tale. The bear was seen a week arterwards up in Muskrat Hollow, running without his skin. She made herself a good warm petticoat out of the pesky varmint's hide.

1847, p. [8]

147

# Nance Bowers Carried over
# Mud River by a Bear

The Special Collections Library of The University of Tennessee, Knoxville

FIGURE 24. *Nance Bowers carried over Mud River by a bear*

Nance Bowers, the youngest daughter of my sister Aggy, war about as fair a sample of full grown female flesh, as ever flourished outside of the garden of Eden; she war seven feet tall out of her stockins, and hair comb. She could outscream a thunderbolt, outscream a dozen wild-cats, wipe her feet with her hair, swing on the top of a fifty foot hickory tree, and eat more wild cat steaks raw, than any other livin critter in creation. She had one of the most universally useful mouths in her face that ever fell to the head of humanity; she could eat victuals with one corner, whistle with the other, an scream with the middle; she could grin with her upper lip, and frown all sorts of temptation with the under one; she could scratch the skin off of an alligator with her toe nail, an snap a ten foot sarpint's head off by a single galvanic jerk of his tail. I'll never forget the trick of her usin up, an civilizin the great king bear, of mud forest. You see the great critter took it into his head, one

148

day, to walk into her smoke house, an fodder himself upon a smoked ham or two, an naturally growin more impudent, he walked one day into her kitchen, an grabbed her around the bosom, thinking to squeeze the gizzard out of her afore she could say who or boo; but I tell you what, the bear-faced varmint war taken by surprise, for she had jist taken hot dumplings out of the pot, for dinner, an she turned her head suddenaciously round, smacked a big red hot smoking one into the critter's throat, an the way it made his eyes wink boilin water, war a caution to a high pressure steam boat boiler, arter that, she took an grabbed him by the tail, and licked him till he shed enough of bear's grease through his hide to supply twenty-seven perfume shops, an the critter become so docile an domestic, that he sarves, to this day, both for dog an horse; he tends to all her cows an niggers, supplies her with bear's oil for her family, lends her his paws for tongs, ovens, rakes, grid-iron an hoes, and when she wants to cross big muddy river [the Mississippi River], he takes her in his paws, as a nurse takes a baby, an carries her across as upright as a Yankee soldier, an brings her on shore, as dry as a smokin fire poker.

1851, p. [19]

# An Evening Visiter

The Special Collections Library of The University of Tennessee, Knoxville

FIGURE 25. *An evening visiter*

I bleeve i never told the reeder about a little affair that cum about shortly arter i got married and went to settle on the north side of the big Muddy [the Mississippi River]. Thar war a kuzzin of my wife's that took his plunder and went with me. He had ben to Cincinnati and had got a grate eddication for them days. He could grammarize and geografize and fillossofize, and would wear out a slate a siferin in one weak. Then he had his square roots and his round roots, and I bleeve he had the root of all evil, for he war jist sich a pesky feller as it wood take five hundred like him to make an honest man. But i dont want to explicitrize him too hard seeing that he is dead, and when one is in his grave he cant harm nobody, for he is a quiet citizen then, if he never war befour. I sed when i fust begun this story that he war a kuzzin to my wife, but that war a lie, for he only maid me bleeve he war, but i found him out arterward. He wanted to go and settle with me in the cleering, and we packed up and went. When we got to the big Muddy, i begun to make a hole in the forest, and i built a log house as fast as i could, tho i wos obleeged to hav killdevil [Davy's rifle] at my side all the time, as the painters had a grate deel of curosity to see how a white man's flesh tasted. Them varmints had got tired of Indian meet, for their red skins war so tuff it sot their teeth on edge, and so they war very dainty arter a peece of my bacon. But i couldn't obleege them in that way no how, tho i war willing to do ennything in my line that war reesonable seeing i war a stranger in them parts and didn't want to be on bad tarms with the inhabitants. They put me to grate expence for amminition, and i sent some of them to the divil without benefit of clargy, and sum of them i shot in the starn and they went off shaking their tales as if they felt ridiculous. All this time the feller that war with me kept poring over his books, for he sed he intended to open a skool as soon as our clearing had got peepled, and be [he] looked to me and my wife to supply him with a smart chance of skollars.

Arter i had got my log house rigged up in pritty good style, we all moved into it. It war rite enuff all but one winder that war not finished. One dark evening I sot in one corner and the skoolmaster sot in tother, befour a roaring fire. My wife had gone to bed and war fast asleep in a crib i had bilt up on one side of the room. Well, while we sot there talking about nothing at all, i heerd a sort of scratching noise outside of the house, and I looked up to where killdevil hung; but before i could git up to take it down, a monstropolus grate wild cat bounced in at the winder, and in a minnit she war in the middle of the floor, and crouched down and wagged her tale, and kept her eyes rolling in her head fust at me and then at the skoolmaster. He looked obflisticated, and i seed he could not sifer himself out of the scrape. The varmint was the most saverageous beast that i ever sot my 2 eyes on, and her teeth looked as white as if she had cleaned 'em every mornin. But her eyes grew bigger and wilder every minnit. We sot as still as two rotten stumps in a fog. I did not dare to move my head to look at killdevil, for i couldn't hav time to take it down befour the varmint would have her teeth in my carkass.

So we didn't stir, and the wild cretur kept squinting fust at me and then at my frend, not knowing which to choose, and she lookt mighty proud to think she could have the pick between us. I felt so mad i kood have bit through a five inch plank. The skoolmaster nor i didn't nary one of us want to be ete up, for i had dun a hard day's wurk, and war too tired to go through with sich a job befour i had a good night's rest. The skoolmaster war hugaceously oneasy, and i seed he thort it war a very ridiculous peece of bizziness; so he speeks to me, and sed, "What do you think we had best to do, Crockett?" I told him that depended mostly on the varmint who seemed to have the casting vote on this okkasion, but it war most likely one of us wood be chawed up befour we war a minnit older, and as he had good larning, i spose he knowed how to make his peece with God in real book fashion; but as to me i had no purtensions to larning, but bleeved i war never guilty of desarting a frend or turning my back to a hungry feller-critter, and must trust to God's mercy to make it up to me where i war lacking. Then he begun to blubber rite out, and sed if we could only direct the varmint's eyes to the place where my wife laid, he might ete her up, and so our lives would be saved! When i heered that, i forgot all about the danger and jumped rite up on eend like a rumping* alligator. I war going to ketch the mean-spirited infarnal coward, that wanted to turn off the danger on a woman, rite by the throat, but i seed the wild cat war making his spring at me. So i jumpt towards killdevil and war reeching out my hand to take it down, when i seed it war gone. I felt as streaked as a bushel basket for haff a second, but jist as the varmint touched me with her teeth, i heered killdevil speak and the wildcat tumbled doun dead at my feet! I war amazed at fust, but in the next minnit my wife had her arms around my neck. Killdevil had hung close to her crib, and when i jumped up it woke her, and she had kotched the rifle like a flash and fired it in time to save my life. Then i seed she war worthy to be the wife of Davy Crockett.

---

1840 Nashville, pp. 8, 10

*The meaning of "rumping alligator" is unclear. "Rumping" may be "romping." However, "to rump" is to flog on the buttocks, which would certainly cause anyone to jump up. There is also the possibility of a slang sexual allusion.

# The Heroine of Kaintuck

The Special Collections Library of The University of Tennessee, Knoxville

FIGURE 26. *The Heroine of Kaintuck*

Of all the ripsnorters I ever tutched upon, thar never war one that could pull her boat alongside of Grace Peabody, the herowine of Kaintuck. When she got her temper fairly up, she war more like seven thunder bolts, withed together with chain lite[n]ing, than a human cretur. Her father war a squatter; but she ganed a residence as she war born in the plaice. I reckon that all the varmints in the state stood in fear of her, and would sooner stick their tales in a steal trap, than feel the gripe of her thum and 4 finger around their throttles. She had a most abstemious eye, and when she gave one look at a painter or a bear, he thought the sun had riz within rifle shot of his nose. She minded no sort of weather. She would go through a snow-bank without looking for the path, and would shed rain like a duck. It took seven women to hold her when she sneezed, and they said that when she was insulted by a Tennessee bully in the month of March, she jumped clean out of her close [clothes], she war so furce [fierce] to cum at him. She cum pritty neer gitting discharged one onlucky morning in September. She war going to carry home some work, for she got her living by making Prarie pillows, which war bear-skins stuffed with buffalo horn scrapings, and they war made for two conveniences, to sleep on for one, and for tother, when your head itched in the nite, you could skratch it by rubbing it agin the piller. So she did her arrant, and then sot out to cum home through the woods, as it war gitting late in the arternoon.

She hadn't got fur before she perseeved she was follored by something of the four-legged kind. She war not skared at all, and it would be a dangerous predicament for the bridge of a man's knows [nose], who should tell her she war ever skared at enny thing. But she kepp one korner of her eye open, and wawked on. In a little while she kinder thort she saw about fifty wolves coming around her and jumping at her throat. As she coodent kill 'em all at once, she run up a tree that grew slanting, and when she got to the top of it she begun to break off pieces of the limbs and throw at 'em; and she killed two or three of the pesky creturs in this way; and made one of 'em gape for fourteen sekonds, as she hit him between the two ize with a twig as big round as her leg. But jist as she was killing them off by degrees, a bear cum up out of the tree, which war holler inside, and he bolted out so quick that he took her with him, and they cum down together on the ground; but Grace hung on upon the bear and cum down astraddle of his back. The wolves got out of the way when they cum down, like when you throw a stone in the water; but they closed up as the bear begun to run. Grace had a bit of stick in her hand, about as long as my rifle, and as thick at one eend as a cat's body. The bear didn't like to have a rider, and the wolves tride to help him git her off; and as he cut through the dry leaves, with the wolves all around him, jumping at Grace, the leaves and twigs flew about, so that you couldn't see nothing but Grace's cudgel as she swung it over her head, to bring it down upon the profile of some infarnul wolf, that was left rolling in the forrest behind them, and spouting the bloody foam from his lips. But the wolves cum thicker and thicker, and Grace begun to git tired in the arms. She held on upon the bear's wool as well as she could; but he run and jumped and roared, bekase he knew it was all Grace's fault that the wolves rained around him like a snowstorm. Grace's cudgel begun to splinter, and the pesky varmints took advantage of that sarcumstance, for ther is no onor about 'em, and they care no more for fare play than an injun kares for the sarmont on the mountin. Grace begun to think her time had cum, for one wolf had tore off the soul of her shew, and another one had got the skirt of her gownd in his teeth. She was jist about letting go of the bear and dropping down among the wolves, when help cum. I had been out that arternoon with Grizzle a hunting. Grizzle told me as plane as he cood speak, that thar war something to pay in the bushes, and I run down that way; and sure enuff, I seed the twigs and leeves a-flying like thar war a small arthquake running along the ground. In a minnit the bear cum bolting out from a thicket, with wolves all around him, and I seed the cudgel agoing, but couldn't see Grace till I got close to her. I pulled trigger upon the varmints, and shot two. Then Grizzle and I went in among 'em like the wonderful workings of Providence in a thunder storm, and the wolves scattered jist as Grace cum to the ground. The bear got off cleer, for I sposed he had done good sarviss, and tis not the fashun with Davy Crockett to do an ongrateful axeshun. Grace told me I had saved her life, and a fortnite from that day, she sent me a pair of new stockings that she had gnit out of wolf-sinues.

---

1840 Nashville, p. 20

# Katy Goodgrit

FIGURE 27. *Katy Goodgrit's Fight with Wolves*

Katy Goodgrit war a favorite of mine, bekase when her spunk war up, she could grin a wild cat out of countenance, and make a streak of lightening back out. She didn't care for anything that went on four legs, nor anything that went on two legs. One day she war going out into the woods, and seed two wolves shying along like a snake in the grass, not a grate ways off; and she intarmined to put a stop to 'em, for they looked very obnoxious, and seemed to want to be tasting sumthing of the human kind. So she took up a club, and walked in between 'em. They begun to feel amazing skitish when they seed her coming with the club, but at last they come towards her.—She gave one of 'em a monstracious tap on the head with her club, and he squawked rite out. Before she had time to hit the other, she heered a pattering amongst the leaves, and when she lookt around, thar war about fifty wolves cuming towards her on the full trot. Sum gals wood hav ben skeered out of thar seven wits, but Katy always knowed it war the fust duty of a gal of Kaintuck to stand up to her lick log, salt or no salt.* So she just squatted low for the present, and got up into a holler stump whar the wolves couldn't quite reach her, and they cum roaring around her, like the water boiling around Crocodile Rock, at Tumble Down Falls. They jumpt up evenmost to her face, and she spit at one so wiolent that it nocked his eye out. She cotch anuther by the scurf of his neck, and whipt his hed off agin the tree. So she kept stopping their wind, till the fust she knew thar war a pile of dead wolves around the tree, high enuff for the others to climb up on. Then she war obleeged to squat down, or they wood hav tore her hed off. She staid thar all nite; but early the nixt morning, she stuck up her head, and crowed, till she crowed and screamed all the wolves deff, and then they begun to cleer out, but she went arter 'em with a pole and killed haff of 'em before thev [they] got away.

1842, p. [20]

*To "stand up to her lick log, salt or no salt" means that she is determined to stand her ground no matter what the consequences.

# The Methodist Parson and His Eels

The Special Collections Library of The University of Tennessee, Knoxville

FIGURE 28. *The Methodist parson and his eels*

A Methodist parson was once travelling in our parts, and he put up at a
log house in the woods, where there was a woman of his way of thinking. So them two fell to religionizing for two or three hours; when, at last, he
fetched a sigh, and said how he wished he was on the sea board where he
could have a fresh mess of eels for his supper. So she says right away, 'you can
have eels ready in less time than skinning a badger, if you want,' and out she
run to get him some for supper. While she was out the minister heard strange
noises that he did'nt know what to make on. He thought somebody was playing dice, for he heard a tremendous rattling as if a dozen men were shaking

dice boxes at once. At last he got up and went out to see what it meant, intending to preach them a sarmont against gambling, when what should he see but his landlady with a big knotted club in her hand batterfanging a dozen rattle snakes that were squirming and twisting around her in all manner of shapes and fashins. One big fellow fetched a leap at her when she dodged him, and wrung off another one's neck that was about to spring on her. The minister thought she was in great danger, and got hold of a stick to help her. 'Don't worry yourself, holy sir,' said she, 'you go into the house and write out your sarmont, and leave me to get your supper.'

'Supper!' cried he, 'I don't understand you!'

'Did'nt you order eels?' said she, 'and aint I a preparing a nest of the varmints, as fast as I can?'

The minister flung down his club, and run right off, and never stopped till he got home again. He told all the brethren it was no use to go into Kentucky to preach, the very women sarved up rattle snakes for supper.

1836 Nashville, pp. 12–13

# Battles
## with
# Humans

# Mike Fink Trying to Scare
# Mrs. Crockett by Appearing
# to Her in an Alligator's Skin

The Special Collections Library of The University of Tennessee, Knoxville

FIGURE 29. *"Alligator, bulligator, woman hater, or woman eater,
you've got to feel this Crockett steel in your ugly nater, darn you."*

You've all on you, heered of Mike Fink, the celebrated, an self-created, an
never to be mated, Mississippi roarer, snag-lifter, an flat-boat skuller.
Well, I knowed the critter all round, an upside down; he war purty fair
amongst squaws, cat-fish, an big niggers, but when it come to walkin into wild
cats, bars, or alligators, he couldn't hold a taller candle to my young son,
Hardstone Crockett. I'll never forget the time he tried to scare my wife Mrs.
Davy Crockett. You see, the critter had tried all sorts of ways to scare her, but
he had no more effect on her than droppen feathers on a barn floor; so he at
last bet me a dozen wild cats that he would appear to her, an scare her teeth
loose, an her toe nails out of joint; so the varmint one night arter a big freshet
[rain] took an crept into an old alligator's skin, an met Mrs. Crockett jist as

she was taken an evening's walk. He spread open the mouth of the critter, an made sich a holler howl that he nearly scared himself out of the skin, but Mrs. Crockett didn't care any more for that, nor the alligator skin than she would for a snuff of lightnin, but when Mike got a leetle too close, and put out his paws with the idea of an embrace, then I tell you what, her indignation rose a little bit higher than a Mississippi flood, an she throwed a flash of eye-lightnen upon him that made it clear daylight for half an hour, but Mike thinkin of the bet an his fame for courage, still wagged his tail an walked out, when Mrs. Crockett out with a little teeth pick [hunting knife] and with a single swing of it sent the hull head and neck flyin fifty feet off, the blade jist shavin the top of Mike's head, and then seeing what it war, she throwed down her teeth pick, rolled up her sleeves, an battered poor Fink so that he fainted away in his alligator skin, an he war so all scaren mad, when he come too, that he swore he had been chawed up, an swallered by an alligator.

1851, p. [16]

# The Indian and Crockett's Grandmother

Courtesy, American Antiquarian Society

FIGURE 30. *The Indian and Crockett's grandmother*

Arter all their boastifferous spoutin, preachin, lecterin an song makin, about the splendifferosity o' the injun character, its all a full blown up bladder o' humbug, for as nigger will be nigger, so injun will be injun, the tarnal head cutter, blood drinken, rum drinkin, humanity cookin varmints. Why, the tarnal cunnin cowards are always pugnaciously valorous whar thar is least danger, an they'll scalp any defenceless crittur, a minute high and about as old, to any old granny so old that she can't feel what time o' year it is. You see my Grandmother was an all-standin tough gal, in her 129th year; but she'd a damned stubborn cough, and so echoaciously loud, that it used to set the cider barrels rolling about the cellar, an her only relief was to go into the woods once a day, and chaw hickory limbs; well, one mornin while she was settin on a stump, and usin up the last limb o' hickory, a tarnal sneak of a tator nosed injun walked most audaciously up to her and collered her by the cap, and prepared his execution iron for true injun valor in carvin off old Granny's top knot. Now Granny being a regular fotched up Kentuck gal, did-n't mind her scalp no more than a cherrystone; but her family cap bein of the true Martha Washington's pattern, she'd sooner parted with life, cough and all; so she hung out her eyes at him, obstinaaiously [obstinaciously] wicked, while he squinted at her, scalpaciously cruel, she gave him a kick on the shins that made him loose his grip, and cut away the briars, thinkin it war them; he then grabbed her by the cap, hair and all, Granny bit her hickory an spit it at him, he flourished his execution iron sarcledicularly,* and giving a most valorous and romantic war-hoop, whar just goin the hull scalp Granny's cap and all, when she give one o' her all shakin coughs that sent the red nig-ger rollin in the leaves, as if struck by the bare foot of an earthquake; he leaned agin a tree, an shivered an panted like a steam bellows, an then tried to cough back at Granny, but it warn't no more use, he couldn't cough back her cough, kase it war a coffin to all that she coughed at; he now cut his arm, an drunk a little warm blood as a renovator, an agin moved for Granny gain-nin all colours, of antymosity at her; the old gal set still, extendin her left eye at him, and chawin hickory considerably, which the injun took for a cough producer, an so he cut off a hickory limb and begun chawin it like a bark machine; arter that he thought he'd try its power, so he give Granny three or four jumpin coughs, but Granny grinned an gummed at him, an didn't mind 'em a sneeze, an bit away at her hickory, now an then spittin a cheek ful at him, as he walked forrid at her; at last he flourished his execution iron and made a painteracious [panther-like] grab at her mouth, thinkin to stop it while he walked into her top knot, but Granny's patriotism an valor for her Martha Washington's cap, jist drawed open the cressent part o' her counte-nance, an give another double breasted cough that sent him about twenty feet into the air, an he come down about as blue as a bruize, if he didn't singe me. He coughed, an then whooped like an alligator with the whooping cough, rolled over among the leaves, an tried to take his leave, but Granny had coughed him fast, so he laid still an tarned up the two knot holes of his face, (meanin his eyes,) and whimpered like a palsy-struck painter, scraped his knife with his lips with a savagerous greedification, that showed how all-fired greedy he war for a drink of the old gal's blood, to renovate his spirits; being detarmined to have a drink of her vital revolutionary sap, he agin crawled towards her, an got as fur as a holler log that he held fast to it to breathe by, when Granny's revolution begun to rise in her at the rate of old 76, an she settled upon coughin him to his coffin instanterly; so she jist walked up near to the log, give ahem! or two by way of introduction to the operation, an' drawin' up her hickory life basket, gave another cough that would h[a]ve silenced a forty-eight pound cannon, an if that same red nigger didn't roll rite into the holler of a log about as slick as a corps into a coffin, then petrify me for grave stones. Granny walked safely home with her hickory, and he died of the full-gallop consumption, if he didn't then tan my hide for injun moccasins.

You romantic an full head o' steam authors, what write with such a perfect looseness on the bravery of the Injuns, think of the scalpin of my granny's night cap, an paint the red niggers in thar true colours, jist call on me, her Grand-son, Davy Crockett, an if I don't give you the true circumstantial caracter of these upright squadrupeds, then torpify me with alligators in frozen mud. Why thar boasted humanity is a little bit thinner than city milk, and they like a drink of white baby's blood nearly as well as whiskey, an the only reason why they don't eat up each other is bekase they're of the buzzard disposition, and couldn't begin to stomach their own carron acrousness. I never seed but one decent injun in all my life, but he war part white, just about half breed, an was a purty well behaved sort of a critter, till one day he got in with a party of rale red sarpents, and was goin to do some Injun trick, when the white blood in him got ashamed of [the] tarnal injun company in him, an it burst a vein and run rite out, if it didn't cut me into meat blocks.

---

1844, p. [4]

*The word "sarcledicularly" is coined from "circle" and "perpendicularly."

# Crockett's Daughter Guarded
# by a Lot of Panthers

FIGURE 31. *Crockett's daughter guarded by a lot of panthers*

I shall never forget how all horrificaciously flumexed a hull party of Indians war, the time they surprised an seized my darter, Thebeann, when she war out gatherin birch bark, to make a canoe[.] The varmints knew, as soon as they got hold of her, that she war one of my breed, by her thunderbolt kicken, an they determined to cook half of her an eat the other half alive, out of revenge for the many lickens I gin 'em. At last they concluded to tie her to a tree, and kindle a fire around her; but they couldn't come it, for while they war gone for wood, a lot of painters that war looking on at the cowardly work an war so gal-vanised an pleased, with the gal's true grit, that they formed a guard around her, and wouldn't allow the red niggers to come within smellin distance, an actually gnawed her loose, an 'scorted her half way home.

1851, p. [25]

167

# The Celebrated Heroine

The "Great Western" thus tells of an adventure with some Indians:—One day as I wandered outside of our lines in search of excitement, who should I meet but two strapping Indians. One of them pointed with great interest to my head, and the other, drawing his fingers over the edge of his knife, said, 'come here, white squaw, I want your hair.' I could not stand that at all, as my hair was always my particular pride, and deemed it like Sampson of old, the very root of all my courage; so I walked right over to them, with a knife in one hand and a pistol in the other. 'Now,' said I, 'if you are for a scalp, here is my head with all the hair on it; take it or touch it, you that dare.' They commenced moving all round me as a hawk hovers round a chicken; at last one of them made a grab at my topknot in the rear, and another in front, the others on my right and left.* I fired, thrust, kicked, and sent the one part of them reeling, but the other got hold of my topknot, as if to fight for the prize. At last off it came, they yelled with joy. 'Good,' said I, 'you have scalped a black mare's tail.' It was a *wig* made of this article, to save my precious black mane.

---

1855, p. [8]

*The tale begins with "two strapping Indians," but at least four seem to be involved in the fight.

# A Single Combat

FIGURE 32. *A single combat*

The Special Collections Library of The University of Tennessee, Knoxville

Sal Fungus war one of the most pounderiferous gals in the old Alligator clearing, which lies between Roaring River and Dead Man's Holler. Once I war a going out to take a little walk in the morning, and breathe the fresh air, about ten or fifteen miles into the forest—when I heared a pesky rustling and thrashing amongst the dry leaves and bushes. I cut down to the place

169

whar the voice come from, and I seed Sal Fungus thar, and a big injun, who war jest a goin' to take off her scalp, for they had had a few words together. Sal had kicked his fundaments [buttocks], and he had slapt her face, then she had wrung his nose till the blood spurted, and that whar what made him so mad.

I war so mad when I seed his pesky hatchet lifted over her head, that I cotch holt with both arms round a tree for fear I should bust all to pieces. I screamed and crowed at the same time. The injun give one yell and flung his tomahawk at me—it stuck in the tree. The idee of being fired at by a red-skin varmint made me madder yet, and I telled Sal to kotch hold of him and hold him fast, while I skinned the uncarcumsized [uncircumcised] cretur alive. He jumpt at me with his tomahawk and I slipt down; he sprung on to me with his hatchet in his hand, and I grabbed his face, and took a twist in his hair—then my thumb slid into his eye most beautiful, and at the same time he put his hand into my mouth to haul out my tung; but I held on his hand with my teeth, and took his wrist about half off. I gave his eye to Sal arter it come out. He dragged me about ten rod with his hand in my mouth, and hollowed so that two pukes [Missourians] heard him four miles off, and they cum down and helped me tie the scandiferous varmint and carry him off.

Well, after that, my attachment for Sal grew taller and wider every day, and we courted, hunted and walked together night and day. Bime by, she could scalp an Injun, skin a bear, grin down hickory nuts, laugh the bark off a pine tree, swim start up a cataract, gouge out alligator's eyes, dance a rock to pieces, sink a steamboat, blow out the moonlight, tar and feather a puke, ride a painter bare-back, sing a wolf to sleep and scratch his hide off. But her heart growed too big; and when I left her to go to Texas, it burst like an airthquake, and poor Sal died. She died with a bursted heart—it war too big with love for me, and it's case war not big enough to hold it. She war buried with the honors o' war. I used to go every nite for a week arterwards and fire a salute o' 100 guns over her grave to show my respect for so much true grit. A week arter that I went to Texas.

1848, pp. [10, 25]

# Sal Fink, the Mississippi Screamer, How She Cooked Injuns

St. Louis Mercantile Library Special Collections Department

FIGURE 33. *Sal Fink, the Mississippi screamer, how she cooked Injuns*

I dar say you've all on you, if not more, frequently heerd this great she human crittur boasted of, an' pointed out as *"one o' the gals"*—but I tell you what, stranger, you have never really set your eyes on *"one of the gals,"* till you have seen Sal Fink, the Mississippi screamer, whose miniature pictur I here give, about as nat'ral as life, but not half as handsome—an' if thar ever was a gal that desarved to be christened *"one o' the gals,"* then this gal was that gal—and no mistake.

She fought a duel once with a thunderbolt, an' came off without a singe, while at the fust fire she split the thunderbolt all to flinders, an' gave the pieces to Uncle Sam's artillerymen, to touch off their cannon with. When a gal about six years old, she used to play see-saw on the Mississippi snags, and arter she war done she would snap 'em off, an' so cleared a large district of the

171

river. She used to ride down the river on an alligator's back, standen upright, an' dancing *Yankee Doodle*, and could leave all the steamers behind. But the greatest feat she ever did, positively outdid anything that ever was did.

One day when she war out in the forest, making a collection o' wild cat skins for her family's winter beddin, she war captered in the most all-sneaken manner by about fifty Injuns, an' carried by 'em to Roast flesh Hollow, whar the blood drinkin wild varmints detarmined to skin her alive, sprinkle a lee-tle salt over her, an' devour her before her own eyes; so they took an' tied her to a tree, to keep till mornin' should bring the rest o' thar ring-nosed sarpints to enjoy the fun. Arter that, they lit a large fire in the Holler, turned the bottom o' thar feet towards the blaze, Injun fashion, and went to sleep to dream o' thar mornin's feast; well, after the critturs got into a somniferous snore, Sal got into an all-lightnin' of a temper, and burst all the ropes about her like an apron string! She then found a pile o' ropes, took and tied all the Injun's heels together all round the fire,—then fixin a cord to the shins of every two couple, she, with a suddenachous jerk, that made the intire woods tremble, pulled the intire lot o' sleepin' red-skins into that ar great fire, fast together, an' then sloped like a panther out of her pen, in the midst o' the tallest yellin, howlin, scramblin and singin', that war ever seen or heerd on, since the great burnin' o' Buffalo prairie!

1854, p. [21]

# The Bravery of Mike Fink's Wife

One day a Snake Indian walked into Mike Fink's cabin, when he was out hunting, picked up a venison ham, and ran off with it. Mike's wife hearing a noise, looked out, and saw the robber making off with his booty. She picked up a gun and a hunting-knife, and started in pursuit. Finding that he could outstrip her in running, she fired a ball into his right thigh, which disabled him. She then came up to him, secured the ham, tied the villain's hands together, dragged him back to the cabin, and kept him prisoner until her husband returned; who, thinking that the poor devil had already suffered enough, let him go. He went limping off, saying he would never steal anything more from Mrs. Fink.

1852, p. [24]

# [Oak Wing's Daughter and the Yankee Pedlar]

Oak Wing's youngest darter war true grit, and hated a Yankee pedlar like any other varmint that is found in the forest. Once, when one of 'em was sassy to her, she took the axe, made a split in a log, and shoved his nose down into it, and drew the axe out, and kept him thar until he begin to squawk.

1850, p. [19]

# A Rail Herowine

The Special Collections Library of The University of Tennessee, Knoxville

FIGURE 34. *A rail herowine*

Speeking of human natur, thar's more of it to be seen aboard of a broad horn than enny whar else except in Kongress; tho I think thar's much resemblance between 'em, only the won that steers the broad horn is called a skipper, and him as steers the Kongress is called a speeker. Ruel Gwynn took a broad horn for won seezon, and I used to like to go down the Mississippi with him, tho I didn't let the peeple aboard noe that I war Kurnell Crockett, or I should a had no piece nor elbow room, as thar is alwise a squirminiverous jam to get site of me when I'm vissuble.

I war standing on the shore won day, and I seed Ruel's broad horn poking down the river, and I hollered out for him to stop. So he laid as stil as he could while I swum off to him. As soon as I got in the bote, thar war a passle of fellers cum round me; for they had heered how my name was Crockett, and they stared at me as if I war a mammouth from forty leag [leagues] beyond the head of Salt River. Won feller cum up rite be 4 me, and leened on his rifle, and gaped at me with his mouth wide open, as if he war going to swaller me up like an arthquake taking down a meetin house. "Mister," sez I, "I take it people are scarse in your diggins."

"How so?" sez he, and then he shuved his nose up to me as sassy as a hungry wolf.

"Why," sez I, "you is so free with your squintifications that I ar thankful your eyes aint a gimblet [gimlet*], or I should ha' been bored threw be 4 long."

"I take it you ar a public man," sez he; "and the peeple has a rite to xamine thar representatives."

Howsever I telled him he needn't xamine me as a Yankee jokky xamines a hoss, for thar war won way to inspeck hosses and niggers, and another way to inspeck white humans. That war like putting a butt behind his ear, and he lookt as mad as a cat up to her neck in a snow-bank. Fust he turned red, then he turned white, and then he looked blue, and arter that, he pushed his hand into his hare. I lookt rite at him, and felt hungry. Thar war a nawing at my stumark like when I feel sharkish arter a day's hunt.

"Stranger," sez I, "do ye meen enny insinnivations?"

Sez he, "I'll see you agin at the 'lection whar I can hav fare play, and I'll chaw you—I'll dubble you down, and screw you into the shape of a cork screw—I'll persuade you I'm pluck and grit united in won individdle."

"Don't tantavrillize me," sez I. "If you arn't reddy to fite now, jest obsquat-ulate—stand cleer, I tell ye, for I'm rising inwardly. Thar's a hot place in my gizzard, and my gall is reddy to bust, and besides all this my feelins is hurt."

He nodded his head, and stepped back, and sed, "I tell you Kernill Crockett, I'll see you agin about this." So he strutted off like a tree standing perperendicular with the branches lopped off. I sorter kynder got an idee that the feller warnt true grit, but I never judges a stranger, only I ment to give him a chance to meet me agin, for I took it that it war a fare challenge. They called his name Willikins, and I got Ruel to rite it down on the seat of my trowsers with a peace of chork so that I needn't forgit it.

The bote had gone on a smart distance further when we turned Great Puddle Point, and thar won of the fellers seed a painter squeezing in among the bushes. So we stopt the bote and a passle of us what had rifles went ashore. This Willikins went ashore with the rest of us, bekase he had a rifle. We went up a smart peace, but didn't see nothin of the painter, and wile we war going back to the bote, that pesky Willikins thort he seed a white burd jest over the bushes, and he drew a lead upon it; but it war an old woman's cap that he fired at, and if he had fired strait, he would hav put haff an ownse of lead under her hare, but he mist her hed, and hit a bran new shift that she had on the line. She riz rite up, for she had been leaning down over her close basket, and when she seed the feller cuming to look for his burd, she picked up a club, and went at him. Now it's no lye that I'm tellin on, deer reeder, but it's a sartin truth, that he showed this old woman the tale of his cote, and run as if a hole tribe of wild injuns war on his tale, and he bawled for help, but our fellers stood and laft at him: and as for me, I war so mad to think I had been challenged by sich a fauk [fake] that I grit my teeth till they struck fire.

---

1841 Nashville, pp. 31–32

*A gimlet is a small, T-handled tool for boring holes.

# Crockett's Description of the Joint Occupacy of Oregon

FIGURE 35. *Crockett's description of the joint occupancy of Oregon*

I expose the reader has heered o' them diggins out West, that are called Oregon, and how the British wants to hav a joint occupacy of that ere clearing. It's a sort of sinivation that we can't take keer of it alone, and it puts me in mind o' the joint occupacy of me and a painter when we both found ourselves together on the branch of a tree. The place war big enough for us both, but we couldn't both agree to stay there together. Thar war wonce a pesky Yankee pedlar that put up at my house, and had as much bears meat and whiskey in his long guts as he could carry, but he wasn't satisfied with that, for he wanted to have the joint occupacy of my wife too. So, when I got out of bed early in the morning, he crept along to the disputed territory, and begun to turn down the coverlid. My wife heered him, and made blieve she war asleep, but kept won eye open. Jest as he put one leg into bed, she took a close line that hung close by, and tied it round his ankle, and made him fast by one leg to the bed post. Then she got up and opened a hive of bees on him. He danced and roared most beautiful; and I think John Bull will do the same, when he gits among the Yankee bees of Oregon.

1847, p. [31]

# A Love Fight—by Ben Harding

FIGURE 36. *A Love Fight.—By Ben Harding*

Praps, Kurnill, sed Ben Harding won day, as he filled his pipe, you never heered about the gals in other parts. Howsomever I can spin you a yarn about 'em whilst your doxy\* is gittin supper. When I was in Kuby [Cuba], there was a capital gal that had a sorter notion after me, tho' I say it—a fine gal, and as pretty as a figger head.\*\* She stood six foot without her shoes, and her waist was as big round as a windlass. So I couldn't help loving her, you know. But there was another craft about four feet long, from stem to stern. She was good what there was of her, but I take it that two hundred pounds of wife is better that [than] forty pound, and so I went with the majority as our bosun used ts [to] say. But I used to drop down to the cabin where the short one messed jist to keep her sperits up, and she got an idea that I was entered for life on her log book. Arter a while she began to get her peepers open, and she got a notion that I exposed of my evenings sumwhere else. So, one night she dropt into my wake, and kept close to my starn, when I was going into dock with the long gal. I had got sot down when my long gal begun to back and fill before the winder, as if she seed sumbody she didn't like. In a minnit my short doxy dove into the door like a fly-fish through a

Courtesy, American Antiquarian Society

skupper-hole, and the long one turned round to meet her. The two gals fixed their eyes on one another, and their backs both riz at wunst. With that they sot sky-sails, and run down together. The long one aimed her nippers rite for the short one's peepers, and stuck her thumb in her eye. With that she jumped up to the short one's face, and caught her nipple between her teeth, and held on. I thort there was some loud squalling about that time, and I was going to dive into the muss and see fair play, when I was cotched by a big nigger named Tony that belonged to the house, who held me fast. So the gals was left to fite it out. Pretty soon the long gal had the short one's nose between her teeth, and then there was a yell. In the next minnit their hair was flying, and their rigging was tore ennermost off their backs. Then [t]he nigger parted 'em, and they hauled off to repair damages. The long one had lost her cloze and one nipple, and the short one lost an i and haff her nose. So I married the short one for the present, bekase she had suffered so much in my cause.

---

1842, p. [32]

*Doxy is a disparaging term for a woman.

**A figurehead, the carving of a woman on a ship's bow. Since Ben Harding is a sailor, a slew of other nautical terms follows in his story.

# Ben Hardin in a Dancing Match

FIGURE 37. *Ben Hardin in a dancing match*

The Special Collections Library of The University of Tennessee, Knoxville

Ben Hardin war always considered a hull hurricane on a breakdown [dance], an it was bragged on him by the old sailors, that he could dance all gals in sea-ports from Cadiz to Cape Cod, out of thar stockings; but it took me to gin him enough of dancin, that set his teeth on edge, and drawed his feet into fly-blisters. You see, Ben come out to the West once, on a visit to me, and used to dance so much that he wore all the stone steps away from the front of my house, and Mrs. Crockett used to swar that his tarnal toes

180

and heels war pieces of thunderbolts, for he struck lightnin at every step. So thinks I, old Salt-rope, I'll gin you a breakdown enough to last you for a seven years cruise. So I got a fat squaw, half Injun an half Mexican nigger that I brought from Texas, and she war a cantankerous tornado at all sorts of breakdowns, from a Fandango to an Airthquake reel, or a square-toed double trouble shiver shuffle, or a storm-spike. So I took 'em both out to Asphaltum Flats, that war so etarnal hard that the thunderbolts used to glance off. I had a hemlock fiddle made to play by steam, and some new tunes that went so fast that a humming birds wing couldn't keep time with it, an then I set 'em at it, an away they went, like hungry hogs into tater swill, an the way the fire flew out of the ground, an the hot perspire rolled down an smoked, war a caution to a mount Vesuvius, or a prarie on fire; arter the first three times through, Ben begin to grunt like a saw goin into a pine knot; the next, he staggered, an tried to grease his heels with terbacker juice, and the way the hot tar smoked on his trowsers war equal to a pine forest on fire. The Squaw sed nothin, but kept up grinnin and leadin out every new tune, while her eyes winked all sorts of never-give-up-ishness. Ben, arter the 115th tune begin to roll like a ship in a sea storm, and finally fell over an fainted in his pig-tail.

1851, p. [5]

# Courting Stories and Amorous Adventures

# Davy Crockett's Early Days, Severe Courtship, and Marriage

I was born in August 1786; at the mouth of Lime stone, on the Nola-chucky river in the State of Tennessee. My father was an Irishman and by profession a farmer. The name of my mother was Rebecca Hawkins, an American woman of the State of Maryland. I was pretty *well born* from my size which is over six-feet. The first thing I recollect was an event which so badly scared me that it seems to me I could not have forgotten it if it had happened the day after I was born. At all events it was before I had any knowledge of the use of breeches, for I had never worn any.

The circumstance was this; My four elder brothers, and a well-grown boy of about fifteen years old, by the name of Campbell, and myself were all playing on the river's side, when all the rest of them got into my father's canoe and put out to amuse themselves on the water, leaving me on the shore alone. Just a little distance below them, there was a fall in the river, which went slap-right straight down slantindicular with a descent of *sixty feet*. My brothers, though they were little fellows, had been used to paddling the canoe, and could have carried it safely anywhere about there; but this fellow Campbell would n't let them have the paddles, but fool like, undertook to manage it himself. I reckon he had never seen a water craft before; and it went just any way but the way he wanted it. There he paddled, and paddled, and paddled—all the while going wrong,—until, in a short time, here they were all going, straight forward plump [plumb] to the falls, and would have gone over slick as a whistle. I was so infernal mad that they had left me on the shore, that I almost wish'd they would go over the falls a bit. But their danger was seen by a man of the name of Kendall, who was working in a field on the bank; who ran to their assistance like a cane-brake on fire, throwing off his clothes as he ran. When he came to the water he plunged in, and where it was too deep to wade he would swim, and where it was shallow enough he went bolting on; and by such exertions as I never saw at any other time in my life, he reached the canoe, when it was within twenty feet of the fall, and so great was the suck and so swift the current that he had a hard time to get the canoe to the shore which he at last did with the most desperate efforts.

While [I was] yet a small boy my father removed to Jefferson county, Tenn., and kept a tavern on a small scale, as he was poor and his accommodations were only for the waggoners who travelled the road. When I was twelve years old, an old Dutchman, named Jacob Siler, in passing made a stop at my father's house. He had a large stock of cattle, and wished some assistance in driving them. I was hired to go four hundred miles on foot. After staying with him some time; I took French leave of him [deserted him] and joined a party of teamsters, and arrived safe at my father's. Having gotten home, I remained with my father until the next fall, at which time he took it into his head to send me to a country school. I went four days; and had just learned my letters a little. I had an unfortunate falling out with a boy; which I way-laid and gave a whipping, so instead of going to school after this, I started with my brothers and laid out in the woods all day, not going to school, this way I did for a week. At length the school-master wrote a billet [note] to my father inquiring why I had not been to school. When he read this note, he grew as savage as a meat-axe, for he had been taking a few horns [drinking], and was in a good condition to make the *fur* fly. Said he if you don't instantly go to school I'll whip you an eternal sight worse than the master. I tried to beg off; but nothing would do but to go to the school. Finding me rather too slow about starting, he gathered about a two year "old Hickory," and broke after me. I put out with all my might, and soon we were both up to the top of our speed. We had a tolerable tough race for about a mile; but mind me not on the school-house road, for I was trying to get as far as possible tother way. And I yet believe, if my father and the school-master could both have levied on me about that time, I should never have been sent to Congress, for they would have used me up. But fortunately for me about this time, I saw just before me a hill over which I made headway like a young steam-boat. As soon as I had passed over it, I turned to one side, and hid myself in the bushes. Here I waited until the old gentleman passed by, puffing and blowing as though his steam was high enough to burst his boiler. I lay hid until he gave up the hunt, and passed back again: I then cut out and went to the house of an acquaintance a few miles off, he was just a starting off with a drove of cattle, and I accompanied him. After working in different places and driving cattle and teaming for three years, I went home and nobody knew me, I had grown so.

I now went to work for an honest old Quaker named John Kennedy, who lived about fifteen miles from my father's, and worked for him two or three years. And in that time a young woman from North Carolina, who was the Quaker's neice, came on a visit to the house. And now I'm just getting on a part of my history that I know I can never forget. For though I have heard people talk about hard loving, yet I reckon no poor devil in this world was cursed with such hard love as mine has always been, when it came on me. I soon found myself head over heels in love with this girl; and I thought that if all the hills about there were pure chink [money], and all belonged to me, I would give them if I could just talk to her as I wanted to; but I was afraid to begin, for when I would think of saying anything to her, my heart would begin to flutter like a duck in a puddle; and if I tried to outdo it and speak, it would get right smack up in my throat, and choak me like a cold potatoe. It bore on my mind in this way, till at last I concluded I must die if I didn't broach the subject; and so I determined to begin and hang on a trying to speak, till my heart would get out of my throat one way or tother. And so one day at it I went, and after several trials, I could say a little. I told her how well I loved her, that she was the darling object of my soul and body; and I must have her, or else I should pine down to nothing and just die away with the consumption. I found my talk was not disagreeable to her; but she was an honest girl, and didn't want to deceive nobody. She told me she was engaged to her cousin, a son of the old Quaker. This news was worse to me than war, pestilence, or famine; but still I knowed I could not help myself. I saw quick enough my cake was all dough, and I tried to cool off as fast as possible.

My next flame was a pretty little girl that I had known when quite young. I made an offer to her and she took it well. I soon got to loving her as bad as the Quaker girl, and I would have agreed to fight a whole regiment of wild-cats if she would have said she would have me. I gave her mighty little peace, till she told me at last she would have me. I thought this was glorification enough for one while. We fixed the time to be married; and I thought if that day come, I should be the happiest man in the created world. I started on Tuesday to ask for my wife, Thursday being the wedding-day. I had put off asking her parents as long as possible, dreading the asking so badly. When I arrived at the house, I went in and saw her sister; and asked her how [to ask her parents?] as [they] were at home. She burst into tears, and told me her sister was going to deceive me; and that she was to be married to a man the next day. This was as sudden to me as a clap of thunder of a bright sun-shiny day. It struck me perfectly speechless for some time, and made me feel so weak that I thought I should sink down. I however recovered from my shock after a little, and rose and started without any ceremony, or bidding anybody good-bye. My appetite failed me, and I grew daily worse and worse. They all thought I was sick, and so I was. And it was the worst kind of sickness,—a sickness of the heart and all the tender parts, produced by disappointed love.

I continued in this down-spirited situation for a good long time, until one day I took my rifle and started a hunting. While out, I made a call at the house of a Dutch widow, who had a daughter that was well enough for smartness, but she was as ugly as a stone fence. She began to banter me about my disappointment, and seemed disposed to comfort me; and told me to be of good heart as "there was as good fish in the sea as ever was caught." I thought this was a hint to court her!!! the last thing in creation I could stomach, for she was so homely it almost gave me pain in the eyes to look at her. She said if I would come to their reaping, she would show me one of the prettiest little girls there I had ever seen, and that the one that had deceived me was nothing to be compared to her. I didn't believe a word of this, for I had thought that such a piece of flesh and blood had never been manufactured, and never would be again. I went to the reaping, and was introduced to the little girl, who was very pretty. As soon as the dancing commenced, I asked her to join me in a reel, she readily agreed to. I found her very interesting; while I was sitting by her, making as good use of my time as I could, her mother came to us and jockularly called me her son-in-law.

I went to see her in a few days. She was at a tea-squall at one of the neighbors. When she came home there was a young man accompanied her, who I soon found was disposed to sit up a claim to her, as he was so attentive to her that I could hardly get to slip in a word edgeways[.] I began to think I was barking up the wrong tree again, but I was determined to stand up to my rack, fodder or no fodder. And so to know her mind a little on the subject I began to talk about starting, as I knowed she would then show some sign from which I could understand which way the wind blowed. It was then near night, and my distance was fifteen miles home. At this my little girl soon began to indicate to the other gentleman that his room would be the better part of his company. At length she left him and came to me, and insisted mighty hard that I should not go that evening; and from all her actions and the attempts she made to get rid of him, I saw she preferred me all holler.

I commenced a close courtship, having cornered her from her old beau; while he set off looking like a poor man at a country frolic, and all the time almost gritting his teeth with pure disappointment. But he didn't dare to attempt anything more, for now I had gotten a start, and I looked at him every once in a while as fierce as a wild-cat. And in an extacy of joy I slapped my arms, and crowed like a cock. My opponent could stand this no longer, but taking from his mouth a great chaw of tobacco he hollered out, 'I say stranger, I don't value you that,' at the same time throwing it full drive at my face; it missed it by an inch, and hit my girl slap on the cheek. At this I jumped up a rod, he did the same, and when we lit he was uppermost. I now found I had a pretty severe colt to deal with, we took it "rough and tumble." He got a turn in my hair, and his thumb in my eye, and gave the ball such a start from the socket, that it has squinted ever since. By a desperate jump I regained my feet, and with one kick sent him clear into a gourd-patch, where he laid kicking like a tortoise turned belly up. The coast being clear, I staid a courting till Monday morning, and then cut out for home.*

---

1835 Nashville, pp. 3–6, 8

*The bulk of this tale is extracted from Crockett's autobiography, A Narrative of the Life of David Crockett of the State of Tennessee (1834; Knoxville: University of Tennessee Press, 1973), pp. 14–62. Since it was published in early 1834 (its preface is dated February 1, 1834, and the advertisements for other books for sale by the publisher are dated March 1834), it would have been available to the authors of the 1835 Nashville Almanac. Although unnamed in this story, Polly Finley does become Mrs. Crockett. The present tale condenses the materials in the Narrative and adds in more "local color" in such episodes as the fight at its conclusion. Its concluding adventure, a separate tale in itself, is reproduced on pages 120–21 of this volume.

# A Love Adventure and Uproarious Fight with a Stage Driver

In the spring of '34 when I was going home from Congress I came the nearest being chawed up, that ever I did. After staying all night at Memphis, where I slept so *sound*, (i.e. made such a noise a snoring that the neighbors could'nt sleep for some distance from the hotel.) From fatigue I was so drowsy they were obliged to open my eyes with a pickaxe. Well arter breakfast I started in the stage alone with the driver. At the distance of two or three miles from the house, at a point where the road was covered with stumps of trees, he drew up, and tying the reins up at the front window, he said to me, 'look to the reins till I come back.' He was obliged to go a little way to give out some sowing he said. Before I could say a word he was out of sight behind the trees. He kept me holding on to the reins for nearly half an hour, when I began to smell a rat, and was just on the point of getting out to go arter him, when he made his appearance from behind the trees. After he got on his box, I began to blow him up for staying so long. Says he 'the fact is I have a girl a little ways off; I always stop when I pass and make some of the passengers hold the horses. I have built a house and got a negro wench to wait on her.' Thinks I what would the Post Master General say if he knowed that the great Southern Mail was stopped half an hour every day or two to let a stage driver see his doxy. But says I to myself, Crockett keep dark and squat low. So on our arrival at the next hotel, instead of going on with him, I pretended I should stop till arternoon and take the stage to Natches and go down the Mississippi. But no sooner had the driver started than I cut out for the gal's house in the woods. I quickly got into her good graces, as she was 'nothing loth,' as the poets say. I kept her company for two days, when as we were up in the loft of the house which had a ladder and trap door to get to it, all at once, whose voice should I hear but the stage driver's below, inquiring for his doxy. Zounds! here was a pretty predikyment. I must either play possum by jumping out of the window and running off, or jump down and fight. I found I must do the latter, as the window was so small I culd'nt get out of it. As quick as the critter saw me, he flew into such a rage that he crooked up his neck and neighed like a stud horse, and dared me down. Says I, stranger! I'm the boy that can double up a dozen of you. I'm a whole team just from the roaring river.—I've rode through a crab apple orchard on a streak of lightning. I've squatted lower than a toad; and jumped higher than a maple tree; I'm all brimstone but my head, and that's aquafortis. At this he fell a cursing and stamping, and vowed he'd make a gridiron of my ribs to roast my heart on. I kicked the trap door aside, and got sight at the varmint; he was madder than a buffalo, and swore he'd set the house on fire. Says I take care how I lite on you; upon that I jumped right down upon the driver, and he tore my trowsers right off of me. I got hold of his whiskers and gave them such a twitch that his eyes stuck out like a lobster's. He fetched me a kick in the bowels that knocked all compassion out of them. I was driv almost distracted, and should have been used up, but luckily there was a poker in the fire which I thrust down his throat, and by that means mastered him. Says he, stranger you are the yellow flower of the forest. If ever you are up for Congress again, I'll come all the way to Duck river to vote for you. Upon this I bade them good morning, and proceeded on my journey. This adventure I never told to Mrs. Crockett.

---

1836 Nashville, pp. 43–44

# A Blackberry Frolic

It happened that on one o' these blackberryin frolics that a sartin long haired feller, with a leetle bunch rite over his mouth—lookin at a distance jest as though he'd been among the pots an kittles, and got a great gob of crock on his upper lip—was a visitin down our way, an appeared tu have taken an amazin fancy tu Sally Ann; the Sally Ann that I'd been payin 'tentions tu; kep a chattin to her the hull live long time, an I snum,* if I could scarcely believe my own natural senses, when he begun to pick berries an put 'em intu her basket, and she not sayin a word agin it. Wal, I guess as how I was a leetle riled, tu see myself cut an set adrift in that fashion, an I had a gret mind tu go off and shine round some other gal jest for spite, but somehow or other, I wanted to keep an eye on that dandy. So tu Sally, says I, "there's a smart sprinkle o' berries over here, I guess a *leetle* thicker than they grow around your way.["] "Oh, they're thick as puddin here," says she. "I kalkilate that you *are* pooty consumedly thick," says I. "*You-aur remarks aw demd superfluous,*" says the long haired cretur. Suz alive! but wa'nt my dander up, to hear myself called a "demd suporflus,"—down I slat the basket, an upsot all the berries—marches rite up to him jest as brassy as a hull malicious trainin, an I says, "ony you call me a porpus or a superflus again, an see how I'll go tu work an spile your hansum countenance for ye." With that, Sally, she bust out a cryin, an I v[ow?], if I could help a hoo-hooin a leetle myself, I felt so conflusticated.

---

1843, p. [24]

*"I snum" may be a dialect rendering of "I was numb."

# A Bundling Match

The Special Collections Library of The University of Tennessee, Knoxville

FIGURE 38. *A Pretty Predicament*

When I was a big boy that had jist begun to go a galling* [courting], I got astray in the woods one arternoon; and being wandering about a good deel and got pretty considerable soaked by a grist of rain, I sot down on to a stump and begun to wring out my leggins, and shake the drops off of my raccoon cap. Whilst I was on the stump I got kind of sleepy, and so laid my

192

head back in the crotch of a young tree that growed behind me, and shot [shut] up my eyes. I had laid out of doors for many a night before with a sky blanket over me—so I got to sleep pretty soon and fell to snoring most beautiful. So somehow or somehow else I did not wake till near sundown, and I don't know when I should have waked had not it been for somebody tugging at my hair. As soon as I felt this, though I wan't more than half awake, I begun to feel to see if my thum nail was on, as that was all the ammunition I had about me. I lay still to see what the feller would be at. The first idee I had was that a cussed Ingun was fixing to take off my scalp, so I thought I'd wait till I begun to feel the pint of his knife scraping against the skin, and then I should have full proof agin him, and could jerk out his copper-colored liver with the law all on my side. At last I felt such a hard twitch that I roared right out, but when I found my head was squeezed so tight in the crotch that I could not get it out, I felt like a gone sucker. I felt raal ridiculous, I can assure you; so I begun to talk to the varmint and told him to help me get my head out, like a man, and I would give him five dollars before I killed him. At last my hair begun to come out by the roots, and then I was mad to be took advantage of in that way. I swore at the varmint till the tree shed all its leaves and the sky turned yaller. So in a few minutes I heerd a voice, and then a gall cum running up and axed what was the matter. She soon saw what was to pay, and told me that the eagles were tearing out my hair to build nests with. I told her I had endured more than a dead possum could stand already, and that if she would drive off the eagles I would make her a present of an iron comb. That I will, says she, for I am a she steamboat and have doubled up a crocodile in my day. So she pulled up a small sapling by the roots, and went to work as if she hadn't another minnit to live. She knocked down two of the varmints, and screamed the rest out of sight. Then I told her the predicament I was in, and she said she would loosen the hold that the crotch had on my head. Up she went into the tree, and spanned her legs over my head like a rainbow. She put one foot agin one side of the crotch and the other foot agin tother, and pushed as hard as she could. I was always as modest as an unweaned calf, but I could not help looking up as my head was held in one position. But I soon felt the limbs begin to loosen, and then I jerked out my head.

As soon as I was clear, I could not tell which way to look for the sun, and I was afeared I should fall into the sky, for I did not know which way was up, and which way was down. Then I looked at the gal that had got me loose. She was a strapper. She was as tall as a sapling, and had an arm like a keel boat's tiller. So I looked at her like all wrath, and as she cum down from the tree, I says to her, 'I wish I may be utterly onswoggled if I don't know how to hate an ingun or love a gal as well as any he this side of roaring river. I fell in love with three gals at once at a log rolling, and as for tea squalls my heart never shut pan [closed to love] for a minnit at a time; so if you will bundle with me to-night, I will forgive the tree and the eagles for your sake.' Then she turned as white as an egg-shell, and I seed that her heart was busting, and I run up to her, like a squirrel to his hole, and gave her a buss that sounded louder than a musket. So her spunk was all gone and she took my arm as tame as a pigeon, and we cut out for her father's house. We hadn't gone fur before one of her garters cum off, but she soon made up for that by taking a rattling snake from his nest, and having knocked out his brains agin a stone, she wound him around her leg as brisk as a Yankee pedlar would tie up his budget [sack]. She told me that her Sunday bonnet was a hornet's nest garnished with wolves' tails and eagles' feathers, and that she wore a bran new goun made of a whole bear's hide, the tail serving for a train. She said she could drink of the branch without a cup, could shoot a wild goose flying, and wade the Mississippi without wetting her shift. She said she could not play on the piano nor sing like a nightingale, but she could outscream a catamount and jump over her own shadow; she had good strong horse sense and knew a woodchuck from a skunk. So I was pleased with her, and offered her all my plunder if she would let me split the difference and call her Mrs. Crockett.

She said she would try bundling fust, and that she must insult [consult] her father before she could go so fur as to marry. So I shut pan and sung dumb till we got to the house. We went into a room where there was a bed, and, by this time, it was quite dark. She consented to haul all off but her under petticoat and so I thought I had a fine bargain. But I soon found my mistake. Her under petticoat was made of briar bushes woven together, and I could not come near her without getting stung most ridiculous. I would as soon have embraced a hedgehog. So I made an excuse to go out, and then I cut out for home, leaving my coat and raccoon cap behind. I never went that way since.

1839 Nashville, p. 14.

*The phrase "a galling" is best understood as "a gal-ling," to go out looking for "gals."

This is one of the few tales in the Almanacs that exists in a substantial variant. There is no variation in the title page information to denote the different versions. With the title "A Pretty Predicament," the same as that given to the illustration, the second version differs only in a few words except in two critical situations. Instead of "spanning her legs over my head like a rainbow" to help Davy get his head free from the crotch of the tree, and giving him an unintended view that evidently does not lessen his passion, she adopts a more modest approach:

> So she took and reached out her arm into a rattlesnake's hole, and pulled out three or four of 'em. She tied 'em awl together and made a strong rope out of 'em. She tied one eend of the snakes to the top of one branch and pulled as if she was trying to haul the multiplication table apart. The tightness about my head begun to be different altogether, and I hauled out my cocoanut, though I left a piece of one of my ears behind.

In a similar desexualizing of the tale, only the first sentence of the concluding paragraph is retained. The bedroom scene, complete with briar-bush petticoat, is replaced with the following:

> So she took me into another room to introduce me to another beau that she had. He was setting on the edge of a grindstone at the back part of the room with his heels on the mantle-piece! He had the skull bone of a catamount for a snuff-box, and he was dressed like he had been used to seeing hard times. I got a side squint into one of his pockets, and saw it was full of eyes that had been gouged from people of my acquaintance. I knew my jig was up, for such a feller could outcourt me, and I thort the gal brot me in on proppus to have a fight. So I turned off, and threatened to call again; and I cut through the bushes like a pint of whiskey among forty men.

No priority can be established between the versions, but it seems likely that the more sensual one printed in its entirety in this volume was issued first and then revised. For the complete version of the snake-rope and rival suitor text, see Michael A. Lofaro, ed., *The Tall Tales of Davy Crockett: The Second Nashville Series of Crockett Almanacs, 1839–1841* (Knoxville: University of Tennessee Press, 1987), 1839, p. 14.

# Larned Courting

FIGURE 39. *Larned courting*

Courtesy, American Antiquarian Society

If the reeder ar had any expereunce, he aut to kno as thar ar more kinds o' courting than won. Won kind ar where you shin up to a gal and give her a buss rite off, and take her by storm, as it wur; and then thar ar won kind whar you have a sneaking regard, and side up to her as if you war thinkin about sumthing else all the time, till you git a fare chance to nab her, and then you cum out in good arnest. Thar ar one kind whar you ax the gal's pareints, and

jine the church, and ar as steddy as a steembote, till arter marriage, when you
may do as you like, seeing as how the game is run down, and you have nothing more to do; but the gratest kind o' courting that ever I seed war the
Larned Courting. It ar a most beautiful thing for them as knows how, and I
never had a try at it but wonst, and never want to agin; bekase it war so difficult to keep up my eend of the log. Thar war a gal cum into our parts when I
war a young man, and lived on the little eend of little Salt Creek. She war
very short in stattue; but she war monstracious high in her notions, for she
war always torking about the moon and the stars, and all them kind o' things
what you cant tutch with a ten foot pole. When she lit down in our parts,
thar war a grate stir among the young-fellers, for she war fairer in the cheeks
than our gals, and bekase she had sich little feet, it woodent take much
leather to keep her in shuze. Now I had an old dame living up in Carim
Holler, and I thort it wood be a sort of ridiculous to go to see this gal. Her
name war Kitty Cookins, and she lived within a rifle shot of my kabbin; and
my gal's name war Rueliana Drinkwater. Howsomever, I squatted low, and
kept one corner of my eye open. Thar war some almity ripsnorters that lived
up near the south fork of Salt River, who war as broad between the two eyes
as a New Orleans cat fish; and when they smelt out Kitty, they rubbed up
their coonskin breeches, and went down to see her. This put a kink into my
idees at wunst, for I lookt at it as a sort of a stump, seeing as I lived closer to
her than they did, and had the best right to set my trap for her. So I took
killdevil on my shoulder, one day, and sallied down to the Great Notch
where she burrowed. When I got there I war all twisted up at sight of her,
and didn't know which leg to put forward fust, for she war settin on a green
bank under a hemlock tree, dressed in a purty yaller frock, and had a book in
her hand. She lookt up, and seed that I war in trouble, and she spoke rite
out, and sed good morning; and when she showed her teeth, it war like two
rows of mother pearl. I felt streaked all over, and wood sooner have faced
seven hungry painters in the forrest; but twas too late to hang fire, and so I
walked rite up to her. Sez I, "How fare ye; I've heered that you war cum into
our cleering, and thort it wood be no more nor naburly to cut out for your
lodge, so here I be. Mebby you never heered of Davy Crockett; but come, its
dry torking, and here is a bottle of whiskey." I hope I may be shot if she didn't
turn up her purty nose, and pout out her red lip at my whiskey, which you
must know I took as a great insult, seeing it war the best whiskey in them
parts. So I took twice as big a horn of it myself, as common, jist to be
revenged, and then I [s]ot down by the side of her. Then she begun to tork;
but I don't know as I can give her exact lingo, for it war never heered in the

forrest befour. She axed me if I war fond of reeding, and I telled her that I had red the catekise when I war a child; but thort it only fit for children, that I could draw a lead on a squirrel at three hundred paces, and swim the Mas-sissippy blindfold, and dubble up any he, this side of Roaring River. She lookt down and begun to trot her little foot, and sed thar war no defined peeple in the cleering, and how she inferred litter-a-toor and novelties, and loved to look at the moon, and the clouds, and how she liked cun-gineral sperits, and Sally Tude and vartoe, and war going to cultivate bottiny and larn the use of yarbs; and then she red a little out of her book, and axed me if I war fond of poetness and duplicity. I telled her I didn't know about them kinds of varmints; but I liked a bear stake, or a horn of mountain doo, and had drunk two sich fellers as her sweetharts drunk in won evening. Then she opened her big blew eyes and lookt at me so arnest, that I begun to think I had gin her a sort of a notion that she wood like to stay with me, and so I war jist a going to put my arm round her neck, when I heered a noise in the bushes, and I ketched up old killdevil, as I expected it war a painter. Purty soon I heered a squall, it sounded some like a painter; but it sounded more like my gal, Rueliana. I should know her squall from a hundred others, by moon light, or in pitch dark midnight. So I jumpt up from the place war I war setting, as I seed thar would be a breeze directly. Rueliana broke grownd through an elder bush, and cum at me with her mouth wide open, and it scared the little gal Kitty so terrifficasciously that she run into the house and fastened the door; and it war well she did, or Ruey would have chawed her up like a wad, and wiped her teeth with the yaller frock. Then she flew at me like a mad alligator, and so I seed she loved me most horrid, and nobody ever dared to say Davy Crockett war ungrateful. So I never went to see the larned gal agin; but stuck to Ruey like a chesnut burr.

1841, pp. [12, 13]

# Crockett Paying Off Two Frenchmen for Insulting His Sweetheart; Taming a Lioness, &c.

FIGURE 40. *Crockett paying off two Frenchmen for insulting his sweetheart*

The mounseers are particularly purlite but when they come out in Kentuck, they leave all thar purliteness behind 'em, an go the whole hog in insultin our gals. Two of these frog eaters come our way once, showing a parcel o' beasts that had I think, a little more manners than thar masters. Now these two chaps one mornin followed my sweetheart, Sal Sugartree out to the chestnut woods, war they begun thar purliteness by offering kisses, but Sal suffered nothing to come that close to her unless it smelt o' Crockett, an

Courtesy, American Antiquarian Society

FIGURE 41. *Crockett taming a lioness, &c*

she did hate the smell o' garlic amazin, an the way she kicked an spit fire at 'em was equal to painter; but jist as one was trying to hold her while t'other did the bussen, I walked up, knocked the head o' one agin t'other, till they run off with the lockjaw, an so all-scratchin savage that they let out thar she lion an her two young ones at us; but I took Mrs. Lion by the two jaws and chopped her tarnal tongue off with her own teeth, then stov 'em in, pared off her claws, and shook her young ones out o' wind, an give 'em to Sal for pet kittens.

1845, p. [24]

# Driving Ahead; or, How
# Davy Crocket[t] Got His Wife

FIGURE 42. *Driving ahead; or how
Davy Crocket[t] got his wife*

I have always found out in the affairs of this world, that when things wont go they must be driv; an' no mistake. Now the way I got my wife, now Mrs. Davy Crockett, M.C. [Member of Congress], was by the true drivin' go-ahead principle. You see the gal liked me just about as much as a cat likes cream, but then her daddy hated me just about as much, if not more, an' said I

Courtesy, American Antiquarian Society

shouldn't have her no how; but one day the old chap, arter he had driv his team to a market in Kentuck, he suddenly found that his hull unanimous team o' horse-flesh bolted, an' wouldn't be driv home; so he hired seats for himself an' darter in a stage, an' just as he was going to start off, he happened to see me, an' knowen that I was death on a drive, he said that if I could only drive that *team home*, I might have everything in the wagon for my trouble. Well, seein' that he had forgot to take his darter an' my sweetheart out o' the wagon, "Why agreed," says I, "Major;" "Done," says he, "Davy;" so I jumped in, put the gal beside me, an' if I didn't reach his house about two hours ahead o' the coach, why saw me. As soon as he come, "Well done, Davy," said he; "take all that's in the wagon." "Thank'ee, Major," said I, an' led out his *darter*. He stared a few; swore a few more; then whistled, and said, "You've driv ahead o' me, Davie, so take the gal, team an' all!"

———
1856, p. [5]

# Crockett Popping the Question

The Special Collections Library of The University of Tennessee, Knoxville

FIGURE 43. *Crockett popping the question*

Every human in our clearing always thought it war thar duty to take a var-tuous gal, and replenish the airth, especially in our parts o' the world whar folks war pesky scarce, and the painters and bears war ennermost all the population, speckled with crocodiles and rattle-snakes. Thar war a gal that lived a smart piece from my cabin that I had seed flog two bears, for eatin up her under petticoat; and every blow she hit 'em, war a Cupid's arrow goin into my gizzard; so I put on my best raccoon skin cap and sallied out to sce [see] her. When I got within three miles of her house I began to scream, till you could see my voice a goin through the air like flashes of lightning on a thunder-bolt—it sounded most beautiful to her, for it went through the woods like a harrycane, and I warn't far behind it; when she heered it pretty nigh, she come out, and climbed up the biggest tree thar; and when she reached the top, she took off her barr skin petticoat, the one she died red with tiger's blood, the day her mother kicked the bucket; and then she tied it fast to a big limb, and waved it most splendiferous, and then I soon come up to her, and she made one jump down to meet me. I cotch'd her in my arms, and gin her such a hug that her tung stuck out half a foot, and then we kissed about half an hour, and arter that I popped the question. She 'greed to have me if I'd promise to have no babies; but she let me off from that agreement pesky quick arter we war tied together.

1848, pp. [29, 32]

# A Snake Story

The Special Collections Library of The University of Tennessee, Knoxville

FIGURE 44. *A snake story*

When I war courting Ann Hunky, up in Dog's Paradise, it war a hot summer's evening, an we sot in doors without anything around one another's necks, an I war feeding Ann with the eend of a sassenger [sausage] and a pig's tale. She held open her mouth while I poked it in. All of a sudden we looked around, an the room behind us war full of snakes as it could hold; I took up Ann and sot her on the shelf out of the way, but I war in sich a hurry that I sot her behind into a plaitern o' hot soap, an she jumpt down pesky fast, an squirmed most beautiful, for it burnt her sum, I think. Then the snakes cum at me an twisted around my legs, an arms an body, like a Yankee pedlar when he wants to cheat you out of a dollar. Thar war a smart chance o' snakes that chased the gal too: but she jumpt out of the window, and got off. Then I seed I couldn't do nothing with my arms, for they war fastened by the snakes like ropes. All at once I begun to scream. I screamed till the chimbly fell down on the roof; it upsot the bed, an turned over the tea-kettle, and the snakes begun to unloose themselves, an they trotted off most beautiful. Every one o' these snakes war hard o' hearing arter that. I forgot to count 'em, but I think thar war over two thousand; every time that I war out huntin arter game, I could see these snakes runnin in all directions to git out o' my road.

1847, p. [20]

# A Corn Cracker's Account of His Encounter with an Eelskin

FIGURE 45. *Encounter between a Corncracker and an Eelskin*

Of all the cursed Adam varments in creation, keep me clear of a yankee pedler. They swarm the whole valley of the Mississippi, with their pewter watches and horn gun flints, peppermint drops and essences. Although the greatest chaps in creation for brag and sarce [sauce], they always play possum when there is danger; and skulk out the back door over the fence in no time. With their ribbons and dashy trash they are enabled to make love to the gals with every advantage over the real natives. I was once courting a fine little gal on Swamp Creek, in Old Kaintuck. I went once a fortnight as she lived twenty miles off. One day I took my rifle and cut out for bears. Having taken the direction of her house, I got so near it that I determined to make a call on my doxy. On arriving at the house and opening the door what should I see but my little gal sitting in the lap of a tarnal pedlar. The little jade as soon as she saw me jumped out of his lap, blushing like a red cabbage. I looked firce and the feller looked as slunk in the face as a baked apple. Said I, stranger, do you make purtensions to this gal; what are you? "I'm first rate and a half and a lettle past common. I can blow through a pumpkin vine and play on a cornstalk fiddle with any man, and whittle the leetle eend of a stick

207

to nothing. But mister you hav'nt seen nothing of no horse with crop ears and a switch tail in the woods aint ye? I lost a sleek two year old mare in the woods yesterday." Said I, stranger you are a dam red eel: and if you aint off in no time, I'll take off my neckcloth and swallow you whole. He had a basket of essence vials on the floor. I gave it sich a kick that the vials flew about most beautiful. The fellow now found it was time to be off, and if my gal hadn't interfeared, I was so wrothy I should have scun him alive. Arter the critter was off, I looked glum enuff but the little varment come and sat down in my lap and put her arms round my neck and gave me a sweet buss, so I got over the huff directly. In his hurry he left some ribbons, and as he didn't dare to come back for them, my doxy rigged herself out with them.

---

1837 Nashville, p. 17

# The Yankee Pedlar

FIGURE 46. *The Yankee pedlar*

The Special Collections Library of The University of Tennessee, Knoxville

Thar war a Yankee pedlar that use to come in our cleerin, and he war arter all the gals in our parts. He would make them presents of ear-rings and sich nonsense, and get them to bleeve that he war something better than us, that war brought up in the forest. That made us as mad as a hornet with his tail chopped off, and we vowed to take vengeance on the critter. My darter Chloe war a match for any Yankee Pedlar that ever war born, and she and Zippoworth Cloud's darter intarmined to fix him out. So one nite when he war up in Crow cleering, they got an ungrateful big owl, and the owl had a darter that war haff as big as herself. So they tied the big owls to a tree whar the Pedlar war going past that nite, for they had sent for him to come to Zip-poworth's cabin, as they wanted to see his things[.] But the vain critter thought that the gals cared more about seeing him than his clothes and trin-kets, and he dressed himself out in the best clothes he had, and brushed up his hat and sot out in the evening to go to the cabin. Jist as he got to the tree whar the owls whar, they both begin to holler "Hoot! hoot! hoot!" and flap their wings. The pedlar war astonished. He looked round and seeing thar big fiery eyes lookin at him, he flung down his trunks and run, and the owls kept on hooting, for he heered 'em til he got to the door of the cabin. The gals run out, and pertended to be astonished, and axed him what war the matter? He telled 'em that he war attacked by a whole army of savages, and then they pertended to be frightened, and told him that some injuns war expected that way that same night, and that he must stay and protect them. But he cleered like a fox with his eyes sticken out a feet, and war never heered of arterwards. The gals went back to the tree an got the owls, and brought away the pedlar's boxes. They stowed 'em away to save 'em till he comes back, but I hardly think he will come back.

1851, p. [9]

# Severe Courtship

The Special Collections Library of The University of Tennessee, Knoxville

FIGURE 47. *Severe Courtship*

I wonst had an old flame that I took sumthin of a shine to, bekase I had nothing else to do, and bekase other game war skarse at that seeson of the year. And she lived rite alongside of the path where I used to go to look for bears. When I coodent find nothing else that war worth sending to, I got upon the trail of Zipporina. She war a most partikeler skreemer, and I named her the wild cat of the forrest. She noed how to taik good keer of number one, and never cook a peece of meet that she hadn't kilt with her own hand. She cood jump up and strike her heels together twice, while a rifle war taking time to flash, and cood grin a nigger white. She cood ride a krokodile till he swet, and her hare war alive. She was a most butiful peece of woman flesh, and when I lookt at her I used to feel as if sumbuddy war running off with my rifle, and I didn't ker nothin about it. But sumhow it so fell out or fell in, that I found out a new hunting ground whar the bears war as thick as mull-asses, and so sum how I didn't go that weigh, where the gal lived. May be I got the bag, but if enny pesky he that wauks on two legs war to tell me so, I would put his rite i in my poket. Shawtly arter I shifted my tracks, thar war a feller cum down into them parts to chawlk down figgers and keep akkounts at the Wisskonsin mines. The way he didn't no nothing was most butiful, and he poked snuff into his knows, like he war a going to charge it and fire it off. He got a squint at Zipporina, and lookt at her thru his green spektakles, and so I spose he took her to be *green*, jist bekase she lookt so, when he seed her threw the green glass. But Zipporina squatted low, and pricked up her eers like a squirrel when he sees a rifle lookin at him endways. One nite he went to her father's door and rapt, and the dore opened of itself, as all the dores in old Kaintuck is tort to do when a stranger kalls. Zippy sort of had a notion what he war cum arter, and she put up her hair with a iron comb which I had guv her, and put on her bearskin shawl to look as grashus as she cood, but he lookt at her as if he war going to the gallus [gallows], and her ize war like two koles of fire, and when she lookt at him, she grinned like a red hot gridiron. But he pulled off his hat, and made his obedience to her, like a long sapling when the wind blows it over like a rainbow. Then he sot down and begun to tork to her about the sun and the moon and about her eyes that he sed were like the seven stars. She noed that war a lye, bekase her eyes were like her mother's. Then he went off; but he kept kolling all the time, and stuck to her like a buzz to a sheep's wool. At last he grew as furce as a bear with his tale chopt off, and swore he wood put his arm round her neck if she would taik off that ruff bare-skin that she wore. This was a leetle too much for Zipporina, and she intarmined not to bare it.

One day he axed her to take a walk with him. She shouldered her rifle and slung her powder horn, and went out with him. He was pesky polite, and he offered to carry her rifle for her which she thought was a great affront, and so she war intarmined to pay him for it. She seed he was a green one and didn't know nothing, but her eddication, as I said before, had been most beautiful. She took him to a place where there was a bear's nest, and by this time it had got to be darkish. She pretended she wanted to go a little ways off, and told him to wait till she come back. So she went down to the bear's nest and begun to stir up the bears with a branch. They made a terrible noise, and the young spark run for his life. He wandered about in the woods all night, and the next day, he fouud [found] the house. He told Zipporina that he heard a noise as of wild beasts, shortly after she left him, and that he thought she was in danger, and hunted after her, but that he got lost in the dark. She knew how much of this to believe, but squatted low, and did not say a word. He went on courting, and she pretended to be mighty tickled with his fine speeches. At last he got rail saucy, and was as obstropolous as a Yankee pedlar. He proposed to Zippy to meet him in the dark one evening and make him happy. She was as mad as a buffalo, but she hung fire and sung dumb. She agreed to meet him; and as soon as it was dark he sneaked out of the house and went to the place to be made happy. He waited about half an hour, and then he heard a rustling among the leaves. Zippy had told him she should wear her bear skin cloak, and he thought he seed her coming. It was alfired dark, and so he couldn't tell a great black bear that Zippy had driven along before her from Zippy herself. So he went up to the bear, and the feller put his arms around the varmint's neck, and it stood right up on its hind legs, and give him a most beautiful hug. So he begun to talk to it, and thought all the time, it was Zippy. She heard him say, "Dont hug me quite so hard, dear Zipporina! Oh! Oh! Zippy—Zip—Zip, you will choke me with your love!" At last the bear begun to scratch, and he bawled right out like a calf that has lost its mother. Then Zippy went up behind the bear, and stuck her knife into his side, and the varmint tumbled down, but the young spark didn't see her, and he run off with a bloody shirt, and his coat torn off him. He went back to the mines, and never came near our place agin; but he told his acquaintances all along the Massissippy never to go up into our parts a courting, for the gals up that way loved so hard they would have squeezed his bowels out if he hadn't got away from them.

---

1840 Nashville, p. 14

# Account of a Goose Pulling.
## As Related by Col. Crockett to a Yankee, Who Did Not Know What the Thing Was

The Special Collections Library of The University of Tennessee, Knoxville

FIGURE 48. *A Goose Pulling*

My eyes, stranger, how illiterate some people is! Whar in the universal world war you broughten up, not to know what a goosepulling ar? No wonder you Yankees is despised all over the world. Howsever, you seem to be a clever sort of a feller, quite a conception to the general rule, and I dont care if I waste a few words in instructing you. You see thar war a little dust of a jollification at Luke Logroller's improvement in Rumsquattle Bottom, for Luke had got married to one of them cornfed Connecticut Hooshur gals, that you'll see sot a-straddle on every fence in Ohio. Luke's wife war a complement to her broughten up, for she war a lady every inch of her, six feet high in her stocking feet, that is she would have been, ony she'd got no stockings. Her hair war the color of raw flax, and hung round her neck and sholeders like Spanish baird [beard, or moss] on a magnoly. The parson war not come wen I lit down, and Luke and his wife war divartin themselves and the company with a ressle on the grass afore the door, and I wish I may be flung myself if she didn't fling him three times hand running. When will you find one of your Yankee gals that would do that, Stranger? I cant say tho I think it

214

war altogether rite, for the husband ort always to be uppermost in the family—that ar a fact, and Mrs. Logroller tore her best gingham, and the seat of Luke's onmentionables in the tussell. When the parson cum and put the yoke on Luke and his lady, thar war scrub races and dancing that beat cock-fiting. And then thar war rassling and shooting at a mark, and I suppose it's enough to say Davy Crockett war on hand—and you needn't ax whose ball cut the cross* the most oftenest. Thar war not a gentleman thar that war a sarcumstance to Davy Crockett at rassling, and I'm the man what sez it. Howsever, when the whiskey begun to fly round, the boys begun to look at each other like so many wild cats, and if Luke hadn't have thort of something to keep 'em quiet, his lady would have had a bushell of eyes to sweep up off the floor, thar'd have been such gougeing. So he axes the gentlemen if they wouldn't like a goosepulling, and they all hurrahed for the goose as I've since heered 'em hurrah for Jackson.

But it war not a goose pulling after all, for it war a gander pulling. Mrs. Logroller picked out a gander that didn't lay eggs before Adam war a little boy; but he mought have done it if he'd been a goose. It was as much as she could do to hold him between her knees while she pulled the feathers clean off his neck and smeered it with soft sope as beautifull as Jinerall Jackson did the people. The way he squawked war a caution—you'd raly have thort that something war the matter with him; but what can you expect from a goose. I've seen a feller lay still and have his sculp taken off and make less noise. But Luke tied him by the legs to the eend of a long branch of a scrub oke, and those gentlemen what had horses got on to 'em. 'Look out! for I'm a cummin!' sez Hugh Horsefoot, and dashed at the gander as if the devil had kicked him on eend. But goosey wasn't to be had that time, for he dodged as if an Injun had been taking a squint at him, and the way he run his nose agin a bough war ridiculous. He fell off and bled like a stuck pig. And thar war a good many more what tried it; but goosey dodged, and the limb surged backward and forward, and up and down, and his neck war well soped and so tough it mought have sarved to cordell [tow] a keel boat of two hundred ton. So thar war few that got hold on it, and them that did couldn't hold on. At last a feller, not knee high to a chaw of tobacco got hold and wouldn't let go, but hung on to goosey like death to a dead nigger, and his horse went from under him, and left him hanging like Absalom in the midst of the oke. But the bough wouldn't bear him and the goose too, and down he come and barked his shins, and the goose played away about his head with his wings, so that he almost rumsquattled him. By this time he was as wolfy and savagerous as a rattlesnake in a circle of ash leaves and fire, and he got goosey between his feet and pulled away at his head with both hands. But he sot his teeth to no righteous purpose—the head wouldn't cum off. Then he tried to ring it off, but he mite as well have tried to twist off a cotton wood a hundred year old, and some of the boys offered to bet that goosey would whip him after all. That made him as rothy [wrathful] as a meat axe, and he swore that he could whip every goose that ever was hatched, and he got a hatchet and tried to chop off the poor cretur's mazzard, but it war dull, and the ground war soft, and all he could do war to drive the beast's neck into the mud. But I begun to take pity on goosey, for his sufferings was intolerable, and so I lent the feller a nife, and he sawed his head off with it, and put the animal out of his pain. And now, stranger, I expect you'll be able to tell what a goose pulling is when enny body axes you.

When the gander war dead some of the boys begun to cavail again, and crow for a fite; but the dancing put a stop to that. The whiskey war turned out of an arthen jug and handed round in a mussel shell, for Luke war poor, and hadn't got all his fixins about him. The gentlemen pulled off their coats to it, for it war in July, and it war warm work. Mrs. Logroller's mother gave out the tune, as she sot knitting her stocking in the chimbly corner, for we hadn't no fiddle, and I can tell you, her darter didn't spare shoe leather. The old woman didn't know me, and she had to call out the figgers as well as sing 'em, for the dancers to navigate by. It war somehow so. 'Dance up to that gal with a hole in the heel of her stocking.' 'Down in the middle with the blue check apron.' 'Now chassez with slim Sal Dowdy.' 'Now dance up to the entire stranger.' We danced till Luke begun to git pritty considerably oneasy, and about midnite, 'Gentlemen and Ladies,' sez he, 'I'm a man that wouldn't cum for to go for to be onperlite on enny account whatsomever, and I always expect to do the thing what's rite; but gentlemen and ladies, suppose my case and Molly's war your own, and you'll not take the stud if I tell you that if you live enny whar its time to go hum.' So we took pity on Luke and bid him good night. I expect stranger, if you knew the sport of a wedding in the back woods, you'd want to go there and be married once a week.

---

1840 Nashville, pp. 11–12

*They are shooting at a piece of paper with a cross drawn on it. The part of the tale that deals with the "pulling" was likely inspired by "The Gander Pulling" in Augustus Baldwin Longstreet's popular *Georgia Scenes* (1835; Atlanta: Cherokee Publishing Company, 1971), pp. 110–19.

# The Early Days, Love and Courtship of Ben Harding, Member of Congress from Kentucky, as Related to Col. Crockett by Himself

The Special Collections Library of The University of Tennessee, Knoxville

FIGURE 49. *An Alligator choked to death*

As the public seems to be very anxious to hear all about my friend Colonel Crockett, I don't see no reason why I should not make some stir in the world too, as we are both members of Congress. I have long had an intention to write my life, and tell about the wild varmints that I have killed, and how I got to be elected member of Congress, and all that. I was born in Kentucky and there's where I was reared. I knowed how to handle a rifle before I was five years old, and gouged out four eyes before I was sixteen. I bit off a fellow's nose on the same day that I come of age, and waded a river when I was twenty-five. When I was about twelve years old, my parents sent me to school. It was none of my seeking, for I could never see any use in larning. A man can kill an alligator without larning; he can tree a bear without larning; and lick his enemy without larning—so that a great deal of time is thrown away by going to school, when a boy might be employing his time to better purpose. Well, the schoolmaster was a young flirt that had got his eddycation in

217

some big city, and then cut out to the backwoods to make his fortin by keeping school. He went all round to the parents of the chidren to ax them for
their custom, and the old folks was mighty glad to get him, but the boys
looked at him like he had been a wild varmint, for they knowed he would
keep 'em in the house when they wanted to be out of doors a hunting. So me
and two other boys set out to go to his school though we did'nt mean to take
any of his lip, for ary one of us could double up two such fellows any minute.
But we packed off to please the old folks. The school house was a little log
house not more than twelve foot square, by the side of a large clearing. We
went in and found about forty boys there, and ten gals. All the boys had
brought their rifles and butcher knives with them, so that if they got a
chance to take a blizzard at any thing on the way, they might improve the
time. We all set down on the benches, and the master began to ax us all
round about our knowledge in larning, and when we telled him we did'nt
know our letters, he looked at us as spiteful as if we had been bear's cub's, and
said we was as ignorant as savages. We looked rather striped at this, for every
one in our parts hated the savages as we did pison. But we did'nt make any
answer, for we wanted to see how fur he would go for to provoke us. He then
began to range us into classes—but in the midst of it all, one of the big boys
got to carrying on most uproriously with a big gal, and the master called him
up, and took a ruler and told him to hold out his hand—so he did'nt know
what the master was a going to do with his hand, and he held it out, and
then the master gave him a whack over the hand with his ruler. With that
the boy tackled to him; "root hog or die," was the word, and the master came
to the floor, all the gals cleared out, and away they went over the hills like a
herd of young buffaloes, and the small boys followed them. I cut for home
like a cane-brake on fire—but presently the master was seen coming, running
like a heavy thaw, after us. He had a stick in one hand, and we did'nt care to
wait for him. So that was the last of his school-keeping in them parts. Well, I
staid about home after this, sometimes setting traps for wild-cats, and sometimes shooting bears and deer. At last the war broke out, and then I marched
under General Jackson against the English at New Orleans. When we was
about starting for New Orleans, I composed the celebrated song, well known
to every backwoodsman, and which was wonderfully admired at the time,
beginning with,

> "Come all you bold Kentuckians, I'd have you all to know
> That for to fight the enemy, we're going for to go."*

I believe it was this song that did more than any thing else, towards getting me to Congress, for when it was seen that I had talents, I grew very poplar all at once. Before I went home from the wars, I met a big fellow on the Levee at New Orleans, who thought to take advantage of my youth, and begun blackguarding me about my countrymen, for he did'nt belong to Kentucky himself[.] Says he, 'You call yourselves half horse and half alligator, but I'll let you know that I'm whole alligator with a cross of the wild-cat.' I jumped up and snapped my fingers in his face, and told him that I did'nt care the fag end of a johnny cake for him, and I spit right in his mouth. With that he came at me with his mouth wide open; he just missed my ear, and I snapped at his nose and seized it between my teeth. He roared and struggled but I held on like a pair of pinchers, until at last off came his nose. 'That's into you,' says I, 'for an alligator—you see I'm crossed with the snapping turtle!'

Well, I went home once more, and found every thing pretty much as I left it, and fell to hunting bears right away. In one season I killed twenty-five bears, besides two wild cats and a possum. I was out one day and got benighted, when I laid down to sleep by the side of a river. I laid my head on a great log, and closed my eyes. I had'nt been long asleep before the log began to move, and I jumped on my feet, when what should the log be but a great crocodile. He raised his head and opened his pesky great mouth to bite me in two. I jumped right down his throat. He whisked about and thrashed up the ground like an earthquake for a few minutes, but presently he give over completely choked to death, and I found hard work to get out again.

Having come to the years of maturity, and being a stout lad of his age, young Harding began to look around for a wife. Having heard of one Betsey Buzzard, a good stout gal, not very high, but making up what she wanted in longness by being pretty thick through, and as round as an apple, he cut out for the house where she lived. Ben considered himself a whole team, and went about trapping this gal, just as he would tree a bear. He felt pretty queer when he had got near the house where she lived, and had a good mind to turn back and not go in, as he was afeared she would have nothing to say to him, but he knowed that 'faint heart never won fair lady['] and, so he stood still awhile to wait till his courage got up; but he found the longer he stood, the more his courage went away, and he began to fear if he stood much longer, he should not dare to go at all. So, he thought he would take only one long step towards the house, as there could'nt be any thing decisive in that. Then he took another step, and so on until he had only one step to take to the house, and now he found that that last step was just as much as if he had'nt taken any steps before, for he was puzzled just as much how to go ahead as he was before he stopped at all. The way his heart bobbed up and down was a caution. He dassent so much as look over his shoulder, and much less look ahead; he was stuck in the mud like a Mississippi sawyer [river log], and thought he would rather face a whole regiment of wild cats than look Betsey in the face, but 'twa'nt because he did'nt love her, only 'twas a dubus [dubious] thing to make the first attempt, and not know nothing about how he would be received. Just then the door opened, and Betsey herself come out all rigged up in her best bib and tucker, and Ben was dumb-foundered right away, and his heart came up into his throat, specially as Betsey was cross-eyed, and he thought she was looking right at him, whereas she was looking towards the hovel where the horses was kept. There she stood right on the door stone, and Ben felt it would be impossible for him to speak to her, but, pretty soon, another fellow come out of the barn, leading along a horse towards Betsey. Then Ben forgot his bashfulness all at once, and his dander riz right up. 'I say, stranger,' said he, 'do you make purtentions to this gal?' The fellow let go the horse and looked right at Ben, as if he would eat him up alive! Ben knew what would come next very well, and sure enough the other fellow made a dive at one of his eyes, but Ben jumped up his whole length and lit right on the other feller's head. Both of them tumbled together against an old gate, leading into a watermillion patch, and the way the vines was snarled about their legs and the watermillions got squshed was a caution. Sometimes he was uppermost and sometimes the tother; until at last, Betsey, who had taken a notion to Ben, jumped astraddle of the other feller's back when he was down, and began pounding him with a stone over the head, until he called for quarter. When he seed that, he give over right away, for it went so to his heart that his gal should turn agin him that he could'nt fight. He got [o]n his feet and shook himself, and he turned all colors when he seed Ben go right up to Betsey and give her a smack on the cheek. Says Ben to himself, 'Mister, I think you are most catawampiously chawed up?['] The feller said not a word but turned his tail and went straight off, and was never heered on arterwards. So, the gal then told Ben that she was just a going to set out with that feller for Camp Meeting, and that if he liked, he might take his place on the horse. So Ben got right up on the horse, and took Betsey up behind him, and they drove off to camp meeting, at the distance of about ten miles. On the road they courted with all their might, till Ben got her to agree to have him, though she little thought, all that time, that he would one day be a member of Congress. When they reached the camp, they found the preach-ers all very earnestly engaged, some a praying, and some a preaching and some a singing sams [psalms]. There was one feller in perticular that hollored so you could hear him as far as a catamount, and he stamped worse than a fulling mill. There was guards placed all round to prevent the gals running after the fellers. There was a great many tents where the ministers penned up the gals to convert them; and some on 'em was lollerin [hollerin] like they were going mad. At last one minister come along and asked Ben and Betsey to be converted—so he got up on the trunk of a tree to preach them a sarment, when just in the middle of it, he slumped in, for it was a holler tree, and he sunk clean down out of sight, but he was so arnest, that he kept on preaching in the tree, till a great bear that was inside with him woke up and begun to move, when he hollered out that the devil was gouging him most ridiculous. Then Betsey laughed right out, for she knowed it was a bear; and she climbed up the tree, so as to lower down a rope to him and help him out. Finally, somehow or somehow else, they got the minister out of the holler tree, and he said he had been swallored up in a whale like Jonah. But presently the bare come breaching from the tree like a steamboat. Then such a scratching and hollerin as there was you never see. They thought the devil had broke loose upon them sure enough. They upset the tents in their hurry to cut out, and there was one minister that was so fat he could'nt run very fast, and the bear gained upon him every step he took. When Betsey walked right up to him and stuck him with a knife. Howsomever there was no more praying or preaching that day, and as Ben and Betsey had a great deal of courting to go through with they cut out for home. Ben had some serious talk with the gal, on the way home, but she told him he would be seriouser still, when they were married, and so he was which happened on the very next week.

---

1836 Nashville, pp. 14–16, 18–19

*These lines do not appear in "The Hunters of Kentucky," the famous ballad of the Battle of New Orleans to which Ben Harding may be referring in jest. In full buckskin and fur cap regalia, Noah Ludlow stepped onstage to introduce Samuel Wordworth's song in New Orleans in 1822, celebrating not only Jackson's victory and the sharpshooting of the Kentucky and Tennessee militias, but also the ascendancy of the mythic West, where "every man was half a horse,/And half an alligator." For the words to the song, see Benjamin A. Botkin, *A Treasury of American Folklore* (New York: Crown Publishers, 1944), pp. 9–12.

# Love in a Chest

FIGURE 50. *Portrait of the Girl Who secreted Ben Harding in a Chest, while the crew were in pursuit of him*

"They tell me, Mr. Harding, that a saylor has a wife in every place whar he goes. Now I don't mean to insinnivate enny thing, but as you noes, Ben, praps you could tell how that is."

"Blow my timbers, Kurnill! but that is a hard word, to say it to a seaman too. But never mind. I don't get mad at trifles. You landsmen who has so many women to expose of—why you don't vally a petticoat: you don't know how to feel for 'em. But a saylor always twigs one of 'em when he can. My mother was a woman, Kurnill."

"So you told me before, Ben—but I would'nt hav beleeved it the fust time I seed you floating down the Mississippi, for you hadn't the apperunce of ennything that war ever bora [born] of woman."

Ben rolled up his eyes and turned over his cud with his tung, and after he had settled it to please his mind, he sez, "Then Kern[i]ll, praps you wont bleeve that I've ever been in love, sense you think so hard of my looks."

"I've nothin to say agin that," sez I—"for every critter has his mate. Every thing cums to sum useful purposs, and your face wich is so ruff mite sarve for a gall to scratch her back aginst when it itched. I've no doubt that if you ever war in love, Ben, you loved very hard, bekase you ar a very hard favored man."

"That I did Kurnill!" sez Ben—"I loved so hard that my hart seemed to be skinned and my throte and bowels war all raw. My eyes! I thort I war going to shake to peaces from stem to starn, bekase my insides kept up such a combobolation. You see the way of it was this, that Goverment wanted a draft of men to go to the lakes when we had the last kick up with John Bull [England, the War of 1812]. I got captured among the rest, and was ordered to march into the inferior, and go on the lakes, and you see I'm no fresh water fish, and I felt as savage as a struck porpuss, when arter sarvin a reg'lar prenticeship on salt water, I was transmografied into a fresh water lubber. So when we formed into a company and war put into marching shape, we lookt like a pack of sogers going thro the country, and I got a conceit into my head that I woodn't go fur. So won day when we was turned into a barn to sleep, I jest squeezed off won of the bordes, and my name war o-p-h off. I warked about five mile that nite, and didn't noe whar I war enny more than a codfish off soundins. Towards morning I lade down to sleep, and I hadn't slept long before I war waked up by the sun shining on my eyes: and then I heered the voice of our lefftennent, and I thort my name war Dennis, for they war close aboard of the place where I had cum to an ankur. But I war down in the long grass, and there war sum rocks there-away, and their peepers warnt sharp enuff to twig dungarven. As soon as all war still, I got up and lookt around me; but jest at the minnit an infernal little reefer, who happened to be astarn of the rest, fixt his eyes on me, and he cum runnin towards me and yelping for help. I knowed it was time to drop my courses and set my skysails, and I put one foot before the other as if I was measuring land by the job. I didn't see which way I went, but they war all arter me, like a whole fleet of frigates in chase of a 74 [man of war with 74 guns]. I run about a mile, and as

I hadn't got my land legs on I was tired a little, and then I seed a small house and a fence. 'Any port in a storm,' sez I, and I bounced rite thro the gate into a kind of a garden, and thar war a fine plump looking gal there all alone. She was jest pickin a pare off a young tree; and she turned her head the minnit she heered me cum thro the gate. I telled her not to be fritened, and she stood still. Then I took off my hat, and made about a dozen low bows to her, and telled that I am chased by sum rascals who wanted to make a soger of me, and I put on the soft soap so thick, that she telled me to cum into the house, and it's well she did, for I seed the bosun's head pop up over the fence jest as she shut the door. She took me up garret and put me into a big chist. There I laid as snug as a ground beet butt, and the offissers was soon afoul of the gal, for they swore they seed me dodge into that gate. She told 'em it war a foolish story of theirn, for she hadn't seen no man till they cum, and she wished they would cleer out all of 'em, as it would be agin her karaktur to have 'em there when her father and brothers war away from home. At last, they hauled off grumbling, and then the gal let me out of the chist. So I thanked her kindly, and she smiled and she tauked, and used such dictionary words that I perseeved she was high larnt. I begun to feel strange when I seed her hansum shape, and her plump catheads [breasts],* and all that sort-o-thing, and at last I got in love. In two hours her fokes got home, and I telled 'em how she had slipt off the sharks, and they said she was true blue. I staid there four or five days, and all that time I was in love, and I thort they all liked for the gal to be a sailor's wife; but all of a sudden, they got to drinkin with me, and got me drunk one day, and when I cum to myself, I was about two hundred miles from the place, and never could get the latitude and longitude of it sense I spose they carred me off so that I needn't marry the gal, and they didn't want to hurt my feelins by refusing; so they transferred me. So seein I couldn't ever find the gal again, I took a good cruse on the strength of it, and had a fortnite's drunk, and that cured my love—but it was tremendous while it lasted.["]

---

1841 Nashville, pp. 14, 16

*A cathead is actually a projecting piece of timber or iron near the bow of a ship to which the anchor is hoisted and secured.

# Ben Harding's Courtship

The Special Collections Library of The University of Tennessee, Knoxville

FIGURE 51. *Ben Harding's Courtship*

When me and Ben war out in the forest one day, he got to torking pretty free, and at last he got upon the fare sect. He told me he had been in luv; and when we cum to a plaice called Cold Spring, we sot our rifles up agin a tree, and mixed whisky in our horn, and maid sociable for an our and a haff. Arter Ben had wrenced out his mouth, he put a big cud in one sighed of his cheek and sot his tung upon the wild trot:—

"D'ye see, Kornill Krockitt, I wos niver very much given to overhaul a she craft till I got on the lee side of twenty one. But about that time ther wos one Bets Undergrove who come athwart my hawse so often that, at last, I begun to fix my blinkers upon her. I wos jist on the point of taking a viage to see [a voyage to sea], or I should have got spliced to her without benefit of klarjee, as they say when a thing is to be done in a hurry. So I give Bets a rousing buss, and told her I must go aboard, for the wind wos fare, and the capsun was going round like grinding coffee. The poor gal bawled rite out and stuck her nales into my close like a cat, and she shed teers out of one eye like spray going out of a lee skupper. Her tother eye, you must no, wos as blind as a skupper nale. I jumped into the jolly bote, and my messmates pulled me off to the ship; but we left poor Bets standing on the cliff till the ship got clean out-o-sight-o-land. There she stood in her white gown like Eddystone light-house. She wos a good gal, and I never seed her drunk more than three times in the whole two year that I wos acquainted with her.

We kreuced awf the coast awhile, and then went up the strates, and wile I wos there a thing happuned that let me into the fare sect very clear; and it wos more than I had ever heern on be 4. We kum to an ankur under an ile-and called Yvica. There wos a big black bilding stood on the hill where gals is kept to larn religion. They call it a nunnery. I was ashore on liberty one day, with haff a duzzen other chaps; and we were pretty well corned be 4 night. So we agreed to go on a lark up to the nunnery. We found we koodent get in when we got there. An old woman cum to the door with a bunch of keeze hanging to her waiste, and she acted as bosun over the establishment. Ther wos no gitting aboard without her consent. But jist as I wos turning off like a sick munky, a poor raggamuffin priest cum up softly, and offered to hire me his dress, for a glass of auguadent. I took up with his offer, and was soon rigged out in the friar's gear. He help rig me out; and the rascal shaved off my whiskers and all the hare from the top of my head. I didn't hardly know myself, when I wos finished, and had a grate notion that I war the ship's chaplin who had cum ashore instead of me by mistake. As soon as I was rigged all-a-tanto,* I went up to the gate of the nunnery, and the old woman let me in mighty quick. It war dark in the hall, and she didn't know me from the friar. So she begun to tell me about one of the novisses; that, I take it, wos a gal who hadn't got broke into the fashions. She wanted I should see this gal, and give her sum good sperituel advise. I begun to groan, and hold up my hands, and then she took me to a little sort of locker, where the poor gal was kept. As soon as I seed her I forgot all about Betz; for she wos as pritty as a dolphin, and had an i that cut rite into a feller's hart, like a jackknife going through a bit of salt junk. As soon as I found myself shot up in this place with the gal, I begun to try to tork to her, but somehow I coodent bring my guns to bear, and git hold of the real Scripter lingo; and when I tried to say something of that sort, she laffed rite out in my face. Be 4 I cood get over that and look her in the countenance agin, I got fast asleep, for I had been poring the aguadent and cheechee into me like the whale swallowed Jonah. I spose I slept about three hours, and when I waked up, the gal was gone, and I arterwards heered that she had made her escape from the house, and gone back to her friends. I felt as streeked as a mackarel, and put my hand in my boozum to feel for black Betty [whiskey]; but jist then I heered a whisperin in the next cell to mine and so I hauled my carkase up and looked through the skylite, and there I seed an old feller that called himself a friar, and there wos a a [sic] pritty gal with him who had come to sell oranges. I seed this old rip giv her two or three smacks on the lips, and put his arm around her waste. Then I lay down on a bench close by the skylite, and cood heer every word they sed. The gal agreed to cum the nixt day at 9 o'clock in the mornin, and she axed him how she shood tell his cell from the rest, so that she could find it without any trubble. The old porpus told her he wood put a long nail in the keyhole of the door, and she cood feal the end of it with her fingers. So I laid still till morning, when I got up, and went out of my cell, and found the nail in the keyhole of the old feller's door. I pulled it out softly, and took it into my den, and stuck it through my keyhole. Pritty soon the gal come feeling along at the dores, and she felt the end of the nail. Then she popped into my cell, and I cotch'd her in my arms. She begun to kiss me rite off, and I thort I wos up to my ize in clover, but all at wunce she took a lurch leeward and jumpt back, and lookt at my face—then she seed I war not the man, and she squalled rite out, and shook like a leef. So the tother monk heered the gal skreem and cum running into my cell, and when he seed me and the gal, his holiness wos so kut up that he begun to rore like a bull—for he thort she had took a fansy to me. The gal jumpt into his arms, and begged him to save her from me, and while she was hanging to his neck, all the monks and nuns, and the old woman cum running up. So the monk tride to shake off the gal, but she hung to him like a turcle [turtle] to a nigger's heel, and called him her own true love. I hauled my karkass out of the skrape, and left 'em to settle the bizziness for the old friar, their own way.["]

1840 Nashville, pp. 10–11

*The term "all-a-tanto" is a manufactured one, and its meaning is unknown, though it may mean "fully." "Tanto" means "so much."

# Tar's [Tars, i.e. Sailors] and Injun Feathers or A Squall among the Squaws

FIGURE 52. *Tars and Injun Feathers*

You see my old friend Ben Hardin getten ashore for the first time arter a three year cruize, him an a few on his messmates war determined to see a leetle bit of a land spree among our kentuck injurns an their red gals, an 'known as how I war a sort of a lion in injurn society he got me to interduce 'em to a small shawnee tribe 'o my acquaintence; well, I'm a live crittur among the skull-splitters, that's a fact, and if thars a bit o' fun or fighten to be got among 'em, I'm the poker what can stir it up; I jist shouldered old thunderbolt an execution iron, an led 'em to an incampment in the woods of as jolly a squad o' the red rango'tangs as ever barked a skull, so long as they keep good natered, but when they git their sap up they are about as tearish as harrow teeth in a stony field; well, I giv the interduction an they begun the premonatary civilities by smoken pipes with the chiefs, eatin their broth an vensun, an kissin an huggun the old an young squaws, and I seed that the more the squaws liked it the more the chiefs did'nt like it, so knowin that Ben had a bottle o' the *injun pleaser* [whiskey] with him I giv him the hint, so he out cork and soon had the chiefs squatten and grinnin and at the foot of a tree like tree-frogs in June; by this time Ben and the rest begun to show their sailor natur a leetle more considerabl[e]: Ben and a purty young squaw war

228

gettin as close as buckwheatcakes, he led his red gal out [to dance], an the way they put it down to the melody o' my two lips was a smasher to all creepin insecs about 'em, fin[a]lly the half drunken injins felt their oats considerably and jined in, I followed, an such a mixelaneous assortment 'o sailor hornpipe, country jig, and injun war dance, companied by huggin, whoopin, whistlin, laffin, grinnin, and swearin was never heard in all Kentuck afore er arter, one old red nigger tumbled over a pot o' broth an both tumbled into the fire, and if that are Injun warn't soup-periorly scalded there arn't no virtue in hot venison juice. Arter that B[e]n come to me an sed, "Colonel, I'm arter capturin that ar she Injun, an you must help to do it or you're not Crockett." "Well" said I, "B[e]n, I don't stop a wink about substractin a suckin b'ar from a flock, but I don't go in for kidnappin or abduction human natur, its too much like dog eaten dog." "Dog, be d——d," said Ben. "The gals already struck an made signals to me, an shiver my foretop, but I'll take her in tow, and you shall help me." "Jist you an your salt water cutters put off ahead a few paces," says I, "an if I d[o]n't fetch the she Injun drectly to you, unscalped, then come back an see what a savagerous supper the red niggers will make out of Davy Crockett.["] Now Ben being a sort o' the real reg'lar Yankee grindstone grit, didn't like to go away, and leave me to do all the partiklars, but he knowed that when I do really settle a notion in my head there's no move is [in] me, no how. So he trotted off with his sea-sarpents, an left me to show the Injuns a slick specimen o' human kidnappin—I looked about the tree stumps; an seein a few loaded shootin sticks, I jist spilt a mouth corner full o' old Kentuck juice into the primin, winked a little lightnen at the gal, an tuck her under my arm, jist as snug as a coon, an then I begun to streek it, they missed the gal, whooped like bloodhounds, got all their shootin sticks an pointed em at me, but the juice fixed em, an they put arter me, yellin an grinnin all kinds o' destruction, jist as they war gettin closer than was likely to be pleasant, I levelled old thunderbolt, grinned my death grin at 'em, an it so skeered em that they turned away an begun to gnaw, an butt the trees an howl in hopeless stumpefication, an off I streaked it with the squaw faster than a greased arrow from a bow, till comin to a steep holler, I kicked up the stump of a tree an down rolled gun, gal an I, right across Ben's legs without hurtin a hair o' either, an the hull [whole] e'en give six laughs an nine cheers for Davy Crockett an the squaw, an if they didn't, then saw me into razor hones. Ben married that ere squaw an a fine tribe o' little Hardins she gin him all through the walor o' Colonel Crockett the screamer.

1844, pp. [20–21]

# Ben Harding and the Mermaid

FIGURE 53. *Ben Harding and the mermaid*

Wonst when Ben and I war fishing up in Pitchpine crick, sez I to Ben, "of all the varmints I ever heard on, the mare-maid is the most curous. I have red about it, but I spose you never s[e]ed won."

Then Ben lookt up as mad as if a cat-fish had run off with his bait. He hauled off his tarpolin hat and flung it on the ground. Sez he, "Kernil Krocket, do you take me for a swab or a green horn jist from the mountanes. I tell ye thar's not a craft that ever floated on Salt river that I ain't parfectly acquainted with. Blow my liver into white ribbons, if I haven't bussed the prittiest maremade that ever blinked her eye at a sailor!"

When Ben sed that, I jumped rite off the sod, and struck my heals together, and sez I, "Set rite down, and tell us all about that, for I won't smoke, sleep, or drink a drop of whiskey till I've heern the hull story."

Then Ben, sez he, "You see Kurnill, that I was once croosing in the ship Erdimmeon down along shore, and we went into a place to git wood and water. Wilst we was there, a lubberly mate crossed my horse with sum of his dungarian [coarse]* lingo, and I struck one upon his fresh water cabbige head. That lick persuaded him to tumble down sprawling on the ground. So I thort it best not to go aboard the ship agin, and she went off and left me ashore. I sot down, and began to overhaul my idees, for there was not much grub on the place, and I felt a little down in the chops. Wilst I was holding a talk with myself, I seed a sort of fluttering in the water, off shore, and I thort it was some infarnal black fish, or porpus got among the sea weed. But soon arterwards, I saw its hare and then one of its arms. That was the first mare-maid ever I seed, and I would have thort it was a human, only I seed her sling up the eend of her tale. I dodged behind a rock, for fear she would be skeered, and arter she had lookt around to see as nobody seed her she begin to flop and flop in by degrees. Then I flung a pebble into the water by her, and she turned round as quick as a flash to see what it was. As soon as her back was turned, I jumped out from behind the rock, and run into the drink. She heered me as I cum splashing, and was goin to dive, but the water was too shallow, and I cotched her right in my arms. Lord! what a spattering of water there was, jist like a boarding school miss when you go to kiss 'em. I giv her a buss that was heard by the fokes in the lite-house, but the way she squirmed to get away was a caution to numerous eels. She blushed clean down from the top of her head to the eend of her tale; but she didn't blush red, she blushed green as grass. As soon as she got the buss, she cleared like a rigger. But, my eyes! Kurnill, what a fine tale you might make for your Allmynack, amongst them air creturs if they wunst got sent of it! Arter having that buss everything that I ett tasted fishy for a week."

---

1842, pp. [16–17]

*"Dungarian" may refer to "dungaree," originally a coarse East Indian cotton fabric used for garments for the lower classes, as well as for tents and sails.

# A Sailor's Yarn

The Special Collections Library of The University of Tennessee, Knoxville

FIGURE 54. *A Sailor's Yarn*

I always put grate dependence in my frend Ben Harding, and he never telled me any tuff yarn that warn't true; for I have seen as big wunders in the forrest, as he ever seed on the water. So put that to that, as the cat said when she stuck her tung into the kreem pot, and it proves 'em both true. Ben's last yarn war sumthing like this:—

I have a shipmate by the name of Bill Bunker. Bill was a queer chap, and was up to as many moves as a minnit watch that strikes every second. He want content to get threw the world with a reg'lar breeze and a moderate sea; but war always for having sum shine or another. He wood sooner clime over a coach than turn out for it; and whenever he fell down, he wood make bleeve he war drunk jist to raze a row with the watchmen.

Bill went won seeling voige [sealing voyage] in a little skooner called the Blackbird. I never telled you, Kurnill, how they knock them fellers over the nose; but that's neither here nor thar—Bill's scrape war on an ileand. Arter they had got pretty neer full of skins and see-mammouth ile—sum calls 'em sea-illifants, but I spose when I tork to a Kongressman I must use high-floun lingo—they then steered away for home. They expected to make the land the nixt morning; but they seed nothing but an ileand. It war an outlandish place enuff, so full of scraggy trees and rocks that it looked as if you cood not find room to set down without scratching your fundements to pieces. The Cappen concluded to lay under the ileand a few days, and so they cum to ankur. While they layed there they tarred down the rigging, painted the black streek on the vessel's side, korked the decks, and mended sales. But they didn't go ashore, as the Cappen had seen sum awful lookin Ingens that war so ondecent as to ware very few close. Bill sed he wood be sworn thar warn't a tailor in the ileand that knowed how to make a pare of christian breeches.

So it war won fine sunny day when they war intending to be off the nixt morning, and they had the sales loosed to dry, when Bill, all at once, axed the Cappen to let him go ashore and have a kruice. This war a poser for the Cappen, as Bill was the only able seeman he had aboard, and he felt sartin that if he went ashore, he wood lose the number of his mess: for he wood hav his frolic out, and wood dance a jig if he war hanging on a gallus. He cood dance on a coffin or play kards on a tomb-stone. Bill woodn't take no for an ansur, and so the Cappen let him hav the boat. He skulled her ashore, and then walked into the intereur of the ileand. He found it looked better, as he went on. Thar war a plenty of green grass, and good water, and the birds war so thick, he wood hav thort he had been in the woods, if their wings had only been branches, instead of feathers. But he coodn't find no grog-shop, and so the water war almost as good as none, for every body knows that water without sumthing strong in it, is like a hansum bird that don't no how to sing.

Howsumever, when he got tired of walking about and seeing noboddy, he worked down towards the shore; and now he determined to leeve his ennishawls on a big rok, befour he went aboard. So he got an old korking iron out of the bote, and begun to kut the fust letters of his name. Whilst he war at work, he seed out of won korner of his i, that thar war a little critter behind a tree—and then he watched slyly till he got a glimpse of its eyes. So he flung down his things and run thar. It war a Ingin gal, and Bill swears she war hansum. She tried to run, but Bill got up to her so quick she coodn't. Then she sunk back agin a tree, with her eyes on the ground, and looked as bashful as a monkey with his back broke. That struck Bill all aback, and he coodn't make up his mind rightly how he shood hail her, but he ranged up alongside, and war going to mince up his mouth to speak her fair, when he sum how stuck the end of his queu [queue]* into her eye. He didn't do it a proppus, but she jumped back, and thort he war going to board her in the smoke. He begun to make his polly-gees, and axed her pardun, and all that, but she woodn't trust him for a good while. She chattered away in her own lingo, and every once in a while she wood ketch hold of his queu and give it a twitch, and I spose she war sneering about it in her own language.

At last she got kinder kooled down, and then she let him take hold of her hand, while she led him to the place whar she lived—though she kept a lookout for the queu all the time, as she war afrade it wood be playing its tricks with her agin. She took him to a hut whar war about twenty savagers, and they all got up and run towards them making as big a noise as if the imps of the infarnul reguns had jist got a half holiday on a Saturday arternoon. Bill soon found out that this war the king's dawter, and while she telled 'em about the queu, they listened with their eyes and mouth wide open. As soon as she had done, they seized on Bill and tied him, hand and foot. Then they bro't out a log of wood, and a ax that war made of flint, and sharp as need be. Bill begun to be skared; and then they took and laid him down with his hed on the log, and won grum looking feller caut up the ax. Bill thort his time war cum. His neck felt queer enuff. So he hurried and sed a short prayer and whistled won or two sam [psalm] tunes for the good of his sole. Then the big savager lifted the ax over his hed, and down it cum—not on Bill's neck but on the queu, which it took off smack smooth close to his hed. The gal caught it up, and as soon as Bill war loosed, he didn't stop to see what she did with it, but cut dirt for the bote and got safe aboard the skooner.

---

1841 Nashville, p. 10

*Ben wears his hair in a queue, a braid at the back of his head.

# The Rival Lovers

The Special Collections Library of The University of Tennessee, Knoxville

FIGURE 55. *The rival lovers*

When Hippopotamus Zephyr was a gal, she was courted by a puke [Missourian]—a short feller as ruff as a hemlock log an true grit; one nite while he war coarting her, they heered a noise in the pens, and her lover took the pitch-not [pine-knot torch] and went out to see what it was. In course, he left Hippopotamus in the dark, and pretty soon she thort he cum back and sot down by the side o' her. She axed him what he had done with the light, and he didn't make no answer, but he put his arms round her and squeezed her most beautiful. She telled him that he war squeezin her too tight; but jist then she seed a light at the door, and thar war her lover coming in. So she look'd to sce [see] who it war that had hold o' her, and it war a pesky great black bear that had her in his arms. Her lover screamed louder than a painter, and the gall yelled like a catamount. He begun to tickle the bear behind the ears with his knife, and the varmint left the gal and hugged the lover, till Hippopotamus cotch up the frying pan, which war full of hot grease and pored it down his back, and the critter jumped through the window and cleared; the puke, he got so all-fired hot at having his gal hugged so hard by such a rival, that he married her right off, and folks do say that their first cub war covered with a nat'ral bar skin, and has finger nails that beat all out west.

1847, p. [9]

# The Disguised Yankee

FIGURE 56. *The disguised Yankee*

The Special Collections Library of The University of Tennessee, Knoxville

Them Yankees from down East is the most pestiferous set of varmin's that ever came into old Kaintuck. Thar was a Yankee pedlar that had been round our cleerin for some time, and war arter a darter of Pine Wing. She would listen to the cretur with a nose as sharp as a fox, and an eye like an oval [owl], and so her father told him that if he didn't make tracks, he'd skin him alive. He went off, and in about a week arterwards, a pesky injin come to the cabin, and pertended to be catawampously tired, and wanted a supper. Pine was always as free as a sap maple, and he rolled out the whiskey barrel to him, and telled him to drink out of the bung; but when the cretur stooped down to drink, a mask fell off, and showed the weazen, sallow chops of the infarnal pedlar. With that, Pine Wing jumped up, and screamed like a painter. Then he lit on the pedlar, who fell on his knees and squawked like a strangling goose. Pine axed him whether he would choose to loose an eye or an ear. He begged to loose nary one, and said he would do anything,—he would lick up the dust, or be a slave all his life, if he could be spared. Then Pine drew off, and give him a kick that sent him through the window, and said he war too cussed mean to be shot, and that he war too light to be hung, as thar wasn't meat enough on his bones to stretch his neck. He cleared out and war never heered of arterwards.

1850, p. [25]

# [Snag Darling's Daughter and the Yankee Pedlar]

The greatest courting that war ever done in our parts war between Snag Darling's elder darter and a pesky Yankee Pedlar that had a plenty of money, and had promised her marriage. He war jist going to run away and deceive the gal, but she cotch sight of him at a muster, whar her arms war full of two baskets of eggs, and she couldn't let go of 'em; so she stooped down and cotch hold the slack of his breeches with her teeth, and held on till her father came.

1848, p. [18]

# Tom Towson's Story

Tom Towson was telling me a story, the other day, about the way he was first introduced to his present wife, Col. Ridgely's daughter. Now, I can't tell it as well as Tom told it to me, but I will tell it as well as I can.— —Tom, you see, was poor, and had but a sorry education; but he was very quick to learn, and some said that Tom had the clearest head in the country. Tom lived on Poverty Plantation, as he called it, with old widow Towson, his mother; and the farm, which was small, was all they had between them. The fact is, Tom was a handsome fellow, in homespun or broadcloth. One cloudy afternoon, Tom went down into Silver Valley, to see old Ridgely, about a division line on Joe Gibson's plat of Poverty Plantation.—A storm came on just as he drew up opposite Colonel Ridgely's lane gate. Ridgely was a proud old chap—rich, too—and report said that his daughter Lucy was "almighty" handsome. Now Lucy had been brought up in the best style, and was a high lady in the neighborhood. Some said that she had refused several capital offers, but that's neither here nor there, as Tom, you know, could not think of her.—Well, the storm raged, and in rides Tom—hooks his horse to an apple-tree—goes up the wide steps, and ends with a loud knock at the door. Jim Squirrel opened the door, an old negro, who had carried water to Tom's father, when he (Tom's father) cradled in Ridgely's green field.—"The colonel in?"—"Yes, sir, come in," was the ready response.—Tom was led into a large, old-fashioned parlor, where he found the colonel reading, his wife sewing, and his daughter writing. The old man nodded without rising, and told Tom to sit down; while the old lady very reservedly drew her chair closer to the wall. Tom felt a little curious. The daughter, too, threw two or three beautiful glances at him, which made him feel still more curious. He made so many blunders in telling his business, that a kind smile began to show itself upon the faces of all in the room, which encouraged Tom, who instantly recovered his self-possession, and added to their mirth by many intentional errors and oddities.

"Colonel," said Tom, "It is quite out of the question for us to settle this now."—"Why so?" inquired the colonel.—"On account of your daughter,sir?" replied Tom.—"My daughter!" returned the colonel, astonished, "pray, what has she to do with it?"—"Why," added Tom, "she has knocked me into a cocked hat with those black eyes of hers." —The old lady drew up, although she could not suppress a smile, while the daughter blushed, in spite of her attempts to laugh contemptuously. As for the old colonel, he was so astonished at Tom's impudence, that, for a while, he lost the use of his tongue. They all looked at Tom in silence, and, in the mean time, they remarked his fine figure, high forehead, and intelligent eye; while the irresistible good humor of his countenance entirely disarmed the colonel, who burst out with a hearty laugh at Lucy. Miss Lucy curled her sweet lip into a sort of good-humored scorn, and hastily withdrew.—The next thing we see, is Tom in his homespun, seated at the supper-table, delighting the colonel with his droll stories, complimenting the daughter, and flattering the old lady. The old lady put a plenty of sugar in Tom's tea, and Miss Lucy was a full half hour in drinking one cup.—Tom took leave shortly after supper.—"Plague take the fellow!" cried the old man, as Tom rode out into the lane, and the tears of joy stood in his eye.—"He is quite handsome," quietly remarked the old lady.— "Not he," rejoined Miss Lucy; and a few months after, she was Tom's wife.

---

1842 Improved, p. 18

# A Scienterifical Courtship

FIGURE 57. *A Scienterifical Courtship*

The Special Collections Library of The University of Tennessee, Knoxville

No doubt the reeder has heern of Wicket Finney; and if he hasn't heern of him, of Meg Wadlow. At any rate, between 'em both, he must hav heern of one or tother of 'em. Wicket considered himself inticingly wonderful whar thar war a gal to be treed, and all the female kynd of our diggins war voracious to git him and his plunder. Whenever Wicket axed a gal to set up with him she war rite off as tender as a oak tree with the bark off, and played possum to every feller, for six months arterward. But Wicket didn't take any of 'em for life, bekase why? It war so easy to git 'em, jist as when I war in a whole herd of buffaloes, I didn't draw trigger bekase I war in no hurry. Now Meg Wadlow hadn't cum to them parts then, for she war gone to live with her ant up in Queen's Creek Village, close to the Bluc Notch, and her ant had sent her to bording skool for to finish her eddication. So the tork war all about our parts that she war coming home, and her fokes war in a dreadful fixin about it. Her mother war skeered 1/2 out of her wits, bekase she new that Meg wood xpect to see every thing in the perliterest fashion. She maid her husband wrence out his cap in cold water, and scour up his rifle as bright as two niggers' eyes; and she died her bare-skin pettycoat yaller, and

242

bort two new woodden boles of a peddler for to put into the best room. At last Meg cum in good arnest, and when she got down upon the ground from the karridge, she held up her gound with won hand, jist as if Kaintucky ground war too mean for her to tred upon. Her father stood in the door, and held his breth, for he war so terrificaciously frightened when he seed her skooleriferous perliteness and all her other vississitudes, that he had rather a' faced a painter on the cleerins without his rifle. Her mother run and got behind a fence till the danger war over and peaked at Meg thro a not-hole. I don't no what past arter she got into the house: but in a few days, her father sent to town for a piane, bekase Meg wood hav won; and he went about the diggins torking about northing but the wonderful accomplifications and corruptions of his darter.

Wick Finny heered of all this and it sot his dander rite up. All the other fellers fout shy, and never dast to speek to Meg arter she got home any more than they wood look into Davy Crockett's rifle when his finger war on the trigger. But Wick war not the man to hang fire whar thar war anything of the she kind. He went up into Wolfhead Clearings and got him a soot-o-close that war bran new, and he made the shop keeper show him how to put 'em on. He went home with 'em, and felt so mity odd in his new close that he couldn't hardly turn his hed and lift up his legs, but he noed he war all in the hiter-fashion, and Meg wood have to own it, when she seed him. He war afeered to take his close off for fear he couldn't git 'em on agin, as he had forgot how it war done, and so he slept in 'em all that night.

On the nixt day jist as the sun had begun to squat, he blacked up his boots with a gob of bare's greece, filed sum of the rust off his teeth, and courled his hare with a peace of a broken rake. Then he sot out for Meg's house. He went rite in, and axed for Meg. Her mother didn't no him in his new close, and she curched [curtsied] so hard that she spraint her ankle. She showed him into the room war Meg was, and true enuff she war playing on her piane. He sot down on a kynd of a bench they coll a sophy, and then Meg lookt rite at him. He felt queer enuff when he seed her perlitenes and all that are kynd of personification. But he sez, sez he, "I spose it is a good while sense you hav ben up in these diggins be 4."

"I beg your pardon, sir," sez she, "I war jist sittin down to my piny forty [piano forte; a piano]."

"You needn't beg my pardon, I'm not a going to lick ye," sez he. "But should kindly thank ye jist to play upon that mashine a little; what do ye call it?"

She told him it war a piny forty, and then she begun to make it tork whilst she sung a song that she called *Scots wee hay*.

He sed it war the prettiest thing he had ever heered since his sister broke the conch shell by blowing so hard that she split it in two. When Wick sed that, she held up both of her little white hands, and declared she didn't no what a conch shell war. When Wick heered that, he pulled won out of his pocket, and put it to his mouth and blew sich a winder that she put both her hands on her ears, and jumped up, and hollered rite out; for Wick had as much wind as a race-hoss, and when he blowed on the shell, it shook the hole house and made the wooden dishes rattle. When she sot down agin on the sophy, Wick sez, "Miss Mag'ret I spose you knows that I've cum to to try to—you know what," and then he winked so affectificaciously that she seed trap in a minnit.

"Oh, sir!" sez she, "my trough is invocably plagued to another" [my troth is irrevocably pledged to another], and then she laied her hand right on her stumark, and sed "Oh sir, my hart is deceptible to your honors in axing for my hand, but thar is another won as I is defianced to."

When Wick heered that, he jumpt right up and crowed 3 times, and he sez, "Tell me who the varmint is, right off, and I'll bring ye his two eyes in my pocket before you can wink agin. I'll let him no that when I'm on trail and their's a gal to be fout for, I'm all brimstone from my toes upwards."

When the gal seed that Wick war in arnest, and war going to fite for her, she looked down and blushed up like a red cabbidge. Then Wick sidled up to her, and giv her a smack that might be heered as far as a painter's squall. Then she noed Wick war true pluck, and she begun to feel worser and worser, and she sez, "Alas! my tender heart must yield, sense you will resist that I be your bride," and so she gin her consent.

"I'm glad to hear that," sez Wick, "I'll cum and see you sum times, but you is quite too fast when you sposes I am for yoking on with you. So good bye to ye;" and he jumped up and sallied off whistling thro the forrest. So when Meg seed he didn't want her arter all the fuss, she went into the high sterricks and the rumytiz, and the fainting fits, and all that sort o'thing, wich she had larnt at the boarding skools.

---

1841 Nashville, pp. 23–24

# Colonel Coon's Wife Judy

The Special Collections Library of The University of Tennessee, Knoxville

FIGURE 58. *Judy Coon stomping a nest of Wild Kittens to death*

It's most likely my readers has all heered of Colonel Coon's wife Judy. She wore a bearskin petticoat, an alligator's hide for an overcoat, an eagle's nest for a hat, with a wild-cat's tail for a feather. When she was fourteen years old, she wrung off a snapping turtle's neck and made a comb of its shell, which she wears to this day. When she was sixteen years old she run down a four year old colt, and chased a bear three mile through the snow, because she wanted his hair to make a tooth brush. She out-screamed a catamount, on a wager, when she was just come of age; and sucked forty rattlesnake's eggs to g[i]ve her a sweet breath, the night she was married. It was not at all likely that Judy would throw herself away on any young feller that was a mind to set up a claim to her, and so many of 'em found they were barking up the wrong tree and getting their fingers pricked with a chesnut burr. At last, one Tennessee roarer, that never backed out for any thing short of a mammouth, heard of Judy's accomplishments, and 'tarmined to try his flint agin her steel. So he got into a jumper [one-horse wagon] on a cold winter night, and drove through the woods towards her father's house. He begun to scream before he got within sight of the log hut where Judy lived, and his voice was heard five mile off. Judy's heart begun to beat when she heard him, for she knew who-ever he was, he was a whole steamboat. When he got to the house, he give one leap from his jumper, dashed down the door, and bounced into the mid-dle of the room. "Tom Coon, by Jingo!" cried every one in the house —for he was no stranger by fame, though they had never seen him before. Judy right away set down in a corner of the room to try his spunk, and said not a word, good or bad. He pulled half a dozen eyes out of his pocket, and flinging 'em down on the floor, swore with a round oath he'd place any man's eyes by the side of them that dared to say a word agin Judy! Judy than jumped up like a frog and said, "Tom Coon, I'm yours for life—I know what you've come for, and I'll be your wedded wife without any more fustification about it." So Tom got Judy and all her plunder. Tom took her into Tennessee with him right away, and begun to make a little clearing in the midst of the wood, when Judy soon gave him a speciment of her talents. For, being out one evening to a tea-squall, about ten mile off, in coming home through the wood, she found a nest of young wild-cats in the stump of a tree. She said nothing about it when she went home, but let her toe-nails grow till they were an inch long, when she started all alone, one morning, and went to the nest, and, jumping in upon the young wild-cats, stamped them to death with her feet. It was quite a tough job, and they bit her legs most ridiculously; but she stood up to the scratch, though they scratched her backsides so tarnaciously they've never itched since.

---

1836 Nashville, pp. 33–34

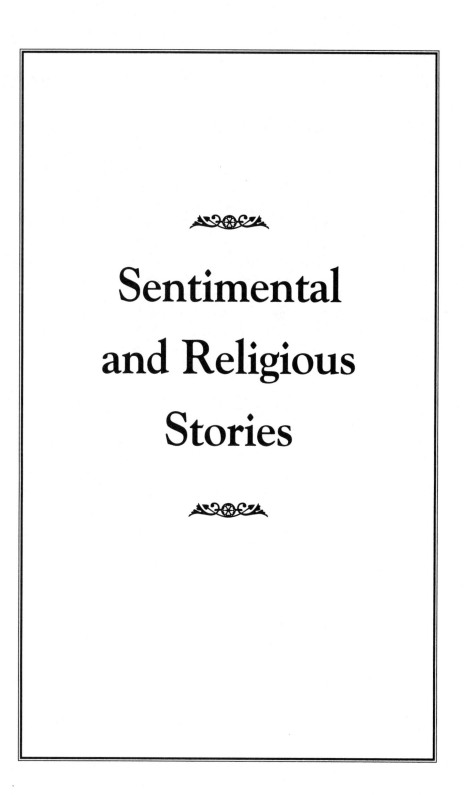

# Sentimental
# and Religious
# Stories

# A Good Wife

Katy Whippoween war the gratest wife that ever lived in our cleering. Her husband war as proud of her as he war of his dog; for she would always put the two ends of every thing together, and help him git along in the world. She brot up a smart chance of children what want no axpense to him, only for thar eddikation. She cut down her husband's trowziz and leggins for the oldest boy, and maid him a jacket of the peases; then she cut 'em down for the nixt bov [boy], and so on. When thar war no cloth in the house, she contrived to keep her boys kivvered. One of 'em had got nothing to ware to shoot but his skin, one cold day in winter. So her husband was as mad as a chimney o' fire, and swore for haff an our. But Katy soon thort of samthing to do. So she opened an old fether bed, and covered the boy with melted glue. Then she rolled him in the fethers, and he cum out kivvered all over with all kinds o' fethers, and looked most beautiful. So she packed him off to skool, and the master vowed he would git himself sich a soot of close, and save the taylor's bills. One winter this woman tride to help her husband along by acting as a wet nuss. Thar war a lady what had took a young bear to bring up and to be treated as one of the family, and Katy offered to taik it to nuss till it got big enuff to feed. In this way she arned enuff to keep her husband in whiskey, and that is saying a good deal, for he was a ripsnorter over the keg. But she got nothing for her panes, for all her children turned out bad. One of 'em s[a]llied off to the east, and sells out cloth and tape and pins, and won of 'em is a minister. They knowed nothin of life in the woods, and is a living disgrace to old Kaintuck.

1842, pp. [8–9]

248

# The "Gold Maiden":
# An Adventure in California

Courtesy, American Antiquarian Society

FIGURE 59. *The "Gold Maiden":*
*An adventure in California*

Upon the placers of Feather River, the early gold seekers in California fell
in with a beautiful brunette maiden, a native of those regions, who sub-
sequently received from them the appellation of *"The Gold Maiden,"* not
merely on account of her bright gold complexion,* but from the fact, that the
young woman, possessed by some instinctive power, the faculty of pointing
out and discovering gold placers or beds, without the slightest turning of the
soil. She was repeatedly seen in the vicinity of the diggins, watching the

249

fruitless labors of the operators, when she would hover round some peculiar spot in the vicinity, point to it, and suddenly disappear—and, upon examination of the designated point, the discovery of gold was the certain result. As soon as this fact, and her wonderful power became known, she was sought out by gold seekers from all quarters—but no one could ever ascertain her place of abode; nor could they trace out to whom she was connected. Frequently, when the disappointed gold seekers, half starved, and worn out with fatigue, would abandon a luckless spot for some other quarter, the dusky California nymph would appear at some distance before them, point to a spot, and vanish like some supernatural being. She was, however, soon observed to hover about in the toiling vicinity of a young miner from the States, who, abandoning his quarters in a fit of romance, followed her. At first, she fled from him, but with a lingering look. Finally, after repeated glances from a distance, she made a downcast pause: they met—and he soon possessed a treasure worth all the gold in California—*a true wife*.

---

1853, p. [32]

*The "Gold Maiden" is here described as a "beautiful brunette" with a "bright gold complexion" and she is later termed "dusky," neither of which provides an exact match for the dark woman with African-American features in the illustration. The illustration also seems more appropriate to a plantation scene than a gold field and may be a case in point of a publisher using an existing woodcut on the same general theme to cut production costs and time. Sometimes publishers will add to or otherwise alter an existing woodcut with apparently the same rationale. See Figure 15 (131), for example, in which the setting seems sub-tropical. Crockett's daughter and the fireplace tongs may be added elements. See also John Seelye, "A Well-Wrought Crockett: Or, How the Fakelorists Passed through the Credibility Gap and Discovered Kentucky," in Michael A. Lofaro, ed., *Davy Crockett: The Man, The Legend, The Legacy, 1786–1986* (Knoxville: University of Tennessee Press, 1985), pp. 38–40.

# A Gold-Ruminating
## upon Ruination

FIGURE 60. *A gold-ruminating upon ruination. A correct picture of the gold diggings—A gold digger, a gold washer, and of everything else except the gold.*

"Curse on the gold and Silver which persuade,
Weak man to follow for fatiguing trade;
The lily peace outshines the golden store,
And life is dearer than the golden ore.["]

Thus sang the great poet of the passions, Mr. James Collins, and thus sings many a disappointed and broken hearted adventurer of thegold [the gold] diggings.— The individual above represented, left a home, family, and

251

a good business, which he disposed of at great sacrifice in order to pay [his] passage and obtain all the necessary out-fit for operating in the mines; put his wife and children with a relation, and shipped in one of the fast steamers for the land of gold. Upon arriving there, he found that getting into California was one thing, and getting up into the mountainous region of the diggings was another. There were deep streams to ford, mountains to be crossed, and there were neither steamboats, teams nor mules at hand. Finally, after a delay of many weeks, in which his funds were almost exhausted, and his patience sorely tried, he at length reached the region of the diggins, when he was ordered in mining phrase to *"dig out,"* or in other words "be off," unless he could pay a certain sum in advance for the right to dig. This he was compelled to comply with, paid the advance and went to work, full of renewed energy and hope; stroke followed stroke—day succeeded day without bringing up the most minute pinch of the golden treasure—months passed on in the same luckless way till his heart and health were almost broken. He stood leaning in despair upon a rock thinking of his little family and praying only for the means to get back to them; the tears mingled with the perspiration on his face—suddenly a female form appeared before him. It was his wife, she had followed, served as a cook in a great hotel in San Francisco, where such persons are well paid. She gave him her earnings, and soon they were once more in their happy home.

1855, p. [33]

# Indian Notions

The Special Collections Library of The University of Tennessee, Knoxville

FIGURE 61. *Indian Notions*

If the reeder never lived in the west, I spose he dont no that the injuns ar all a pesky set of hethens, and has notions that never war set down in the bible. They beleeve that a rakkoon or a painter, or a rok has a sole, and are to be found in tother world, like a kristian what worships God and fites for his cuntry.

One day when I had been for 24 hours on the trale of a bare, and war as hungry as seven wolves tied together by the tale, I lost my way, and cum upon a injun wigwam before I knowed what I had got to. I thort I wood go in and rest myself. So I went and looked in, and seed a very hansum yung injun thar; but it war the only injun that ever lookt hansum to me. He war thinking very serious, and a little she pappoose, about 3 yeer old were setting on the ground klose to his feet and looking up into his face. They lookt more like human creturs with human feelings, than any of the breed that I ever noed before. The injun got up and told me to cum in. So when I had sot down and war eeting a bowl of sowp that the little gal had give me, I notissed that the red skin war very still; and he didn't seem to no as I war pressent; and the gal sot down agin by his feet and lookt up in his face. Then I konkluded to make em tork, and artur a wile I got the injun to speek of his own affares, and he telled me his story so strate that if he had had a white skin instead of a red one I might ha' kinder half beleeved what he sed.

He telled me that his wife and him war married bekase they both had loved one anuther from a child; and that when she died it war like the sun had gone down into the big lake, and ben put out like a wad falling into the Massasippy. He sed he had gone to the place whar she war berried and sot thar all nite, and had prayed the Good Spirit to take him away to the land of ghosts, so that he mite see his wife, for he sed he loved her like the small lake what receeves the streem which cums down from the mountain; and when the streem is dried up, the lake must dry up too, bekase no more water would cum into it. A little while arterward 2 of his children died, and he had none left but the little gal I telled of. He sed how things went on this way for a hole yeer, when one evening that he war goin home to his wigwam, a high wind lifted him off his feet, and carried him over some kuntries what he had never seed before, till he cum to a grate lake, and thar he fell with his own wait, and sunk down for about a mile, when he cum out upon a butiful green plane. The grass war all about two inches high, but lookt more fresh and green than any grass he had ever seed before. He walked along till he cum to a high wall that war made of a sort of rich glass, of a dark blue cullor, and he thort he must stop here; but when he went up to feel of it, he found it war only a apperrition, and that he could walk rite threw it! Then he knowed he war in tother world, and he felt half afeared and half glad. Two painters cum along jist as he got thro' the wall and showed there teeth, but they war only ghosts and coodent bite his solid flesh—but hear he seed beautiful trees and groves, and such blessed perfumes cum up into his nose, that he war made as happy as a lark. Thar war streems of cleer water what run among silver sands, and thar war fruit what war streeked with red and gold colors, and sich birds, and sich music they maid that it war more nor he cood do, to remember his own name. He seed two or three good Indian kings thar who war hunting on beautiful white hosses, and sum of the happy soles war a fishing and leeping, and as happy as a rainbow when the sun shines upon it! He was jist coming out from a whole bed of pretty roses, when he found he war on the side of a cleer and deliteful river. He was looking up and down the river, and seeing the happy soles ketch fish, when all at once, he saw a most glorious woman on tother side of the river who was looking rite at him, and she war droppin teers, and ringing her hands, and holding out her arms to him, as if she wanted to fly rite over the river, but coodent get akross. He lookt at her and seed it was his own wife what he had mourned so long, and had sot on her grave all night, so often. So he jumped into the river, and went rite down to the bottom, as it war only the gost of a river; and he worked over and they run into each others arms, but she war only a spirit, and he coodn't feel her till he war dead too. But they cood tork, and she axed a thousand questions, and so did he, and they put there arms around each other and tried to kiss; and then she led him to a most illigant bower what she had built of boughs and grate roses, and sweet things what he had never smelt till then; and he found his two little dead children in the bower; for their mother had found 'em and took 'em with her. She told him she had built this bower for him, as she new he war honest and always prayed to the good sperrit, and would cum to that happy place when he died, with the other little one.

Davy Krockitt is none of your whimperers, but if I didn't drop tears as big as a bullet, I hope I may be shot. For the injun told it so like the truth that I beleved every word of it—and the little gal too sed she wanted to go thar and see her mother. I bleeve the injun thort it war all true himself. I never seed him agin.

---

1840 Nashville, p. 12

# Indian Virtue

A married woman of the Shawnee Indians made this beautiful reply to a man whom she met in the woods, and who implored her to love and look on him. "Oulman, my husband," said she, "who is forever before my eyes, hinders me from seeing you, or any other person."

1838 Nashville, p. 38

# [Sal Waterman's Pious Tears]

Sal Waterman that lived on the fork of Little Red Creek, war very pious all at once, and shed a grate lot of teers at the preeching; but her mother found out that she had an onion in her pocket and wood put it to her ize when she wanted to cry. So the old lady sed, sez she—"I like that our Sal should be religions [religious]; but I premise that if it takes onions to practiss godliness, it is too expensive. So if she wants to go to heaven that road, she must find onions for herself."

1843, p. [28]

# Crockett's Double-Breasted Gal-lantry, in Rescuing an Emigrant Lady and Child from an Ingin, Near the Rocky Mountain[s]

Courtesy, American Antiquarian Society

FIGURE 62. *Crockett's double-breasted gal-lantry, in rescuing an emigrant lady and child from an Ingin, near the Rocky Mountain[s]*

My mother was a woman, an' so is my sister when she gets to be a mother, an' if she don't be a mother, then she aint no woman. Well, women are Margaret-nificent creeturs—tha're angels without feathers: the werry sugar maple jelly o' creation, an' whenever I see them scandalized, or insulted, then the volcano o' my galantry begins to rumble for overwhelmen eruption.

Now you all know that the black-snake bravery o' the women torturen, baby scalpen, skull peelen, sassagerous bloody skinned Ingins, walk into white babies an' thar mothers like venison. Well one o' these upright wild pusses happened to get an emigrant lady, a splendacious angel, an' her juvenile into his clutches—he had the hot coals ready, and war jist preparing to cut 'em both up for a roast, when I providentaciously happened to drop in that way like a shower to shipwrecked rovers, an' when I seed the knife, the hot coals, and the lady's hot eye-drops, I felt my teeth graten split rock thunder, an' the steam valve o' my disposition begun to snort like an ocean steam biler; he drownded their yells for marcy, with louder yells of savage greediosity, an' sharpened his skull-splitter, lookin' all kinds o' hungry wild-cat animosity at 'em; so I jist gin old thunderbolt a double cloud o' primen, sponged a quart o' salt sap from my eyes with my coat sleeve, and crep along like a wild puss, watchen a possum, an' jist as the red nigger was about dippen the steel taster into the breast o' number one, I dropt down on my two leg hinges, took aim, an' the way I made the back of his skull crack agin his back bone, was double equal to a tree split by sharpened lightnen.

---

1849, p. [20]

# The Celebrated Heroine of the American Camp, "The Great Western"

You have heard of the "Daughter of the Regiment," reader, and also, no doubt, of "Molly Moloony," the great sutler in Napoleon's campaigns; but we doubt whether either of them could compare with the lady at the head of this sketch. She followed the army of General Taylor from Corpus Christi to the Rio Grande, and from thence to Buena Vista and Monterey, and blended with the hardiness of a soldier the tender and careful attentions which only a woman knows how to bestow; while the hair-breadth escapes and intrepid exploits of which she was the heroine, would fill a large volume. While the army was encamped near Salt Lake, fresh water became so scarce, that both officers and men suffered incredibly for the want of it. In this unfortunate state of affairs, the sympathies of the "Great Western" were active, as usual, in devising plans for the relief of the sufferers. Being a female, she knew she could venture to a much greater distance from the lines than the men; so she wandered out in quest of a spring, and at last succeeded in finding one, at the distance of three miles from the outposts of the camp, and, fixing four pails to a large hoop, in which she stood, she made as many as five trips per day, without the camp knowing from whence she obtained the welcome supply of water.

During one of these excursions, she was observed by three Mexican scouts, who, knowing the estimation in which she was held by the General and the whole camp, resolved to capture her at once, thinking that her ransom by the Americans would be an enviable sum. Accordingly, they slipped up behind her, and seizing her by the arms, a furious struggle ensued, in which the Western contrived to free one hand, and draw forth her knife, with which she sent one of them reeling to the earth. The others, enraged at the death of their comrade, immediately released her, and levelled their guns; but, before they could cock their pieces, the Western dashed the contents of a water-pail directly into their gun-locks, and thus rendered them useless; and, drawing a pair of pistols from her belt, she sent the other two limping and howling towards their lines, at the same time calling to them to come back and take care of their dead.

1852, p. [18]

259

# Davy's Sister: Rescuing Adventurers in the Rocky Mountains

FIGURE 63. *Davy's sister. Rescuing adventurers in the Rocky Mountains*

The Special Collections Library of The University of Tennessee, Knoxville

My sister, Comfort, war one of the go to meetin gals' an one of the finest samples of Christianity, an womananity that I ever seed; I says it myself, she swallowed religion hull, an fed on that an do good-a-tiveness all the days of her life, till she war a parfect model of a natural saint; she could preach a few too; her pulpit war the rock, an her sacrament the pure nat'ral element of

Adam; her words would make the coldest individuals heart open like a clam in dog dogs [dog days of summer], an a reprobates hair stand straight up, an bow to her, an when she sung a psalm you'd a thought all the trees in creation war organ pipes, an a harrycane blowin the bellows; she has put her tracks an her tracts all the way from the Alleghany to the Rocky mountains; she is always on hand, with her heart, arms, an pockets open, and she has been the travellers sun, star, an salvation, for the last three years in the rocky mountains, and has worn out seven, out of her nine constitutions, used up four consumptions, an seven fever an agues in saving travelers from freezin, famine, wolves and vultures. The biggest heap of good she ever done was, when she walked the frozen bank of Columby river, for fifteen days, livin on nothin but pure hope to hunt up the fifteen lost men in Col. Fremont's* caravan, that was scattered by a snow storm, an that are gal never rested head nor foot till she explored the hull country, rocks, ravines, an holler logs, an she stuck as true to the chase as an alligator, till she found 'em, an piloted 'em safe to Californy.

---

1851, p. [24]

*Col. John C. Frémont's midwinter expedition of 1848–49, in which he attempted to find a winter route to California through the Sangre de Cristo and San Juan mountain ranges, was a disaster. The intense cold, suffering, and starvation took the lives of eleven of his men. See Allan Nevins, *Fremont: Pathmarker of the West* (New York: Frederick Ungar Publishing Co., 1961), II, 348–68.

# True

# Adventure

# Stories

# Washington's Great Feat of Rescuing the Child of the Indian Queen from the Talons of an Eagle

Amongst the many great feats of strength and address for which George Washington was celebrated in his youthful days, that of throwing heavy stones at an incredible distance, and with unerring aim, was very conspicuous. A feat of this character, illustrative of both his skill and his proverbial nobleness of heart, has been frequently narrated by Indians who lived at that period.

At the time of this well-authenticated incident, young Washington was an assistant to the Surveyor-General, and was pursuing some of his professional operations in the vicinity of the great Natural Bridge, when his attention, and that of his companions, was suddenly arrested by the appearance of the Indian Queen Alaguippa, to whom our hero was known, and who appeared at the giddy summit of the great rock, making the wildest cries and gestures of lamentation to Washington and his friends, who were engaged below. George, who understood enough of the Indian tongue to understand the meaning of her consternation, immediately suspended his labors, and rushed up a portion of the rock near the base of the awful chasm, when instantly an enormous eagle appeared, hovering over the trees, above the bridge, with the young Indian Prince fixed in his talons, while the mother and her attendant squaws pointed upward to the object of their solicitude, in all the grotesque wildness of the Indian character. There was not a single piece of fire arms in the party, and the monster bird was gradually soaring off with his living prey, for some favorite rocky haunt, above which to let it drop from its great height, into some hollow nook below, and then dart down, and feast upon its mangled remains. Fortunately, our hero's ever ready presence of mind was equal to the terrible crisis, and, seizing a pick-axe from one of his assistants, he, with the suddenness of an electric shock, struck a wieldy missile from a part of the rock, and, extending his long and manly arm, he instantly hurled the shattered stone through the whistling air, and with unerring aim and deadly force, that instant it struck the feathered king of the air beneath the shoulder of the wing, and with such effect, that, rendered powerless by the concussion, he dropped gradually downward—his talons relaxed their fixed gripe [sic grip], and the young Indian Prince dropped safely

264

into the extended arms of the man who afterwards rescued Captive Freedom from the IRON TALONS OF TYRANNY AND OPPRESSION!

The spot whereon this incident occurred, was long visited by the various Indian tribes of that region, with awe and reverence: and the spot from which our hero struck this early messenger of liberty, in order to rescue the captive, is still pointed out as *"Washington's Rock!"*

1853, p. [6]

# Terrific Incident in the
# Great Cave of Kentucky.
# A Whole Family Attacked by Wolves

A short time after the discovery of the mouth of the "*Mammoth Cave of Kentucky*," now justly celebrated as one of the wonders of the world, and before its great depth had been explored to any extent, it was found that the part within an hundred yards of the main entrance, yielded large quantities of Salt Petre, and the article being scarce at the time, a small company was formed for obtaining the nitrous mineral, for the purpose of manufacturing gunpowder for our government. One of the principal workmen in this enterprise, with a desire to commence his operations, erected a small house within the cave, for the accommodation of his family, consisting of his wife, mother, and several children. Large wolves had frequently been seen prowling about the vicinity, but no one suspected that they were likely to enter within the hidden jaws of this subterraneous retreat. It happened, however, that one night, the workman, of whom we have spoken, went out to a party with a portion of his fellow operatives of the cave, and did not return, till very late, when, to his horror and consternation, on returning with two of his friends, and passing the dark avenue to his subterranean home, to find the inner passage guarded, as it were, by a number of howling wolves, whose fiery and hideous eyes, glaring in the dim light thrown around by a solitary lamp, gave his abode the appearance of a den of fiends, or a horrid *pandemonium*— but what startled their souls more than the howling of the beasts, was the shrill screams of the poor and defenceless inmates of the dwelling, bringing before their minds all the horrid apprehensions of their having suffered, or were suffering, devouring massacre from the ferocious intruders. Having guns at their sides, they discharged them at random upon the opposing beasts, who, startled by the sudden attack, sent forth a peal of horrifying yells, which, mingled with the loud reverberation of the guns, made the vast cavern roar like an earthquake. The men next out with their knives, and the fight and contest for a passage became too terrific for description, as they tugged together, man and brute, in the darkness—one could hardly distinguish which was which: while the screams and cries of the family were truly appalling. In the midst of the struggle, the only lamp went out, and the general horror was redoubled: presently, the report of one or two guns were heard in the vicinity of the house within, followed by a loud death-groan from some of the perforated beasts: a female was seen rushing from the dwelling with a large torch in her hand, lighting up the scene of conflict and terror, and showing a number of the wolves struggling in their dying spasms—men, bleeding and prostrate, and others still contending. They had now struggled so far into the cave, as to have the animals between two piles of Salt Petre and Sulphur,—when the workmen we have before named, called on all the men to rush, or creep, if possible, inward. They succeeded, fortunately, in doing so, when the workman, seizing the torch which the female held near him, he hurled it suddenly into the piles of nitre—while they all retreated towards the house. The Salt Petre and Sulphur immediately ignited with a sweeping flame, snapping and waving, and sending forth its glare of scorching heat, consuming every wolf who did not escape, into a crisp of flesh and bone. The female who fired, and appeared with the torch, was the wife of the operator, who, by fireing and re-loading a double-barrelled gun, had kept the brutes at bay, and saved the helpless inmates from massacre.

1853, p. [12]

# A Narrow Escape of a Woman
# from a Panther in Texas

The Special Collections Library of The University of Tennessee, Knoxville

FIGURE 64. *A Woman rescued from the Jaws of a Catamount*

In the northern parts of Texas, panthers and wild cats abound in considerable numbers. A woman having been to visit a neighbor several miles from home, set out to return early in the afternoon, and after riding for a few miles over the open prairies, she struck into a burr oak opening; this being the first one she had ever seen, she rode around to admire its novel beauty, as it looked more like a pear orchard than any thing she had seen, the trees being somewhat of the shape and size of full grown pear trees, and standing at regular intervals apart from each other on the firm level soil, as if planted by some gardener. Here too were flocks of deer grazing. She rode for some time amongst the opening, and then entered the dense forest, through which the road lay. She soon heard a cry like that of the human voice some distance off on the right. Listening and hearing it repeated, until she was satisfied that some person was near, she answered it, and the call was repeated two or three times, until she heard a crackling in the bushes, and looking aside she saw a panther up on the trunk of a tree. He had sprung up to reconnoitre. She instantly put her horse to the top of his speed, when the animal sprang down and chased. For some time the horse appeared to gain on the monster, which came howling after them, and made the poor horse snort with terror. Although frightened, she had presence of mind to guide the animal; and being near home, she hoped to reach it before the panther overtook her. But in this she was disappointed, for he now gained rapidly on them—soon came up, and jumped up behind, when he began lacerating and biting her neck and shoulders with his teeth and claws. She was now luckily near home. And her sister and daughter hearing her screams, ran out to meet her, one armed with a rifle and pistol, the other with a rifle. Upon her approach, her sister, a large masculine woman, fired at the monster, and put a ball through his head; but such is the abstract ferocity of these animals that he did not let go his hold, until her daughter had put a rifle ball through him, and her sister shot him in the head with her pistol, when he relinquished his hold and fell to the ground, where he yelled and rolled about till a man finished him with an axe. The poor woman fainted and fell from loss of blood. She was borne into the house, and her wounds were carefully dressed; but it was several months before she was able to attend to her ordinary occupation.

1838 Nashville, p. 4.

# A Terrible Fight with a Snake and Panther, and a Young Lady Rescued

FIGURE 65. *A Woman Rescued from the Jaws of a Catamount and Fangs of a Serpent*

A young lady, after attending a camp meeting in Missouri, was proceeding home without any attendance. She was suddenly startled by a loud hissing behind her, when, turning round, she saw a monstrous snake crawling rapidly towards her. She had the presence of mind to run for a large tree, on which the branches grew down very low. She scrambled up as fast as possible;

when to her horror a large panther was just in the act of coming down one of the large limbs. Her screams appeared to daunt the animal, for he laid on his belly like a cat in the act of springing upon her. The snake had got coiled round the tree, and was in the act of ascending, when her screams being heard by some men who were returning in the path behind her, armed with rifles and tomahawks, they came to her assistance. One man fired instantly at the snake, and wounded him badly; he struck round with his tail, making the dry twigs and rubbish fly in every direction. With some well-directed blows, the man cut through the back bone of the reptile, which so disabled him that he could not ascend the tree, and he darted his head and bit hold of the leg of the man; but with two blows he nearly severed his head from his body, and rendered him completely powerless. In the mean time, one of the other men got a shot at the panther, who, upon feeling itself wounded, sprang upon the girl, and they both fell to the ground. The girl fainted from the scratches and bruises in falling, and the man had his tomahawk struck out of his hands, in endeavoring to hit the animal, which instantly sprang with great agility up another tree, and quickly ascended to some of its upper branches. The attention of the men was now drawn to the suffering girl; as there was a rivulet close at hand, she was quickly recovered, and the blood washed from her face and hands—and although badly scratched, she was not dangerously hurt. The rifles were now reloaded, when both firing at once, brought the monster to the ground. Although mortally wounded, he continued to scratch and leap about; but another ball was sent through his head, when he expired. He was a monstrous large one, and weighed three hundred pounds; the snake was eighteen feet long. The skins of both were stuffed, and sold to the Natchez Museum.

---

1838 Nashville, p. 17

# Lucky Escape of Two Ladies
# from a Catamount

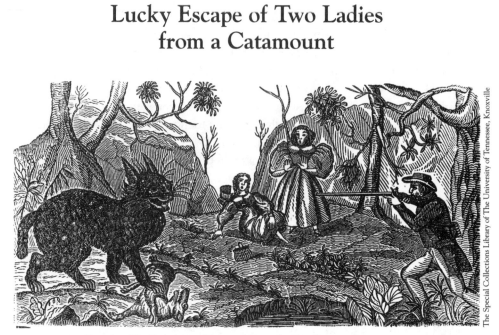

The Special Collections Library of The University of Tennessee, Knoxville

FIGURE 66. *Fortunate Escape of two Ladies from a Catamount*

In the spring of 1829 as two young ladies were rambling among the mountains near Frankfort, Ky. and were proceeding along the margin of a precipice, the oldest suddenly started and exclaimed, "Listen, there are the cries of a child on this mountain! is there a clearing near us, or can some little one have strayed from its parents." "Such things frequently happen," returned the youngest; "let us follow the sounds; it may be a wanderer starving on the hill." Urged by this consideration, the females pursued the low, mournful sounds, that proceeded from the forest, with quick and impatient steps; accompanied by their faithful companion, a large and fierce mastiff. Upon turning by a thick clump of trees, they saw the dog with his eyes keenly set on some distant object, his head bent near the ground, and his hair actually rising on his body, either through fright or anger; it was most probably the latter, for he was growling in a low key, and showing his teeth. "Be quiet Rover," exclaimed one; but at the sound of her voice, the rage of the mastiff instead of being at all diminished was very sensibly increased. He stalked in front of the ladies, and seated himself at the feet of his mistress, growling louder than before, and barking. "What does he see?" exclaimed the oldest, "there must be some animal in sight." Hearing no answer from her companion, she turned her head, and beheld the other standing with her face whitened to the color of death, and her finger pointing upwards, with a sort of flickering convulsed motion. Her quick eye glanced in the direction indicated by her friend, where she saw the fierce front and glaring eyes of a female catamount fixed on them in horrid malignity, and threatening instant destruction. The dog stood firm and undaunted, his short tail erect, and his body drawn back on his haunches. The catamount sprang twenty feet from the branch of a beech on to the back of the mastiff. No words of ours can describe the fury of the conflict that followed; it was a confused struggle on the dried leaves, accompanied by loud and terrible cries, barks and howls. So rapid and vigorous were the bounds of the inhabitant of the forest, that its active frame seemed constantly in the air, while the dog nobly faced his foe, at each successive leap. When the panther lit on the shoulders of the mastiff, which was its constant aim, the noble dog though torn with her talons, and stained with his own blood, that already flowed from a dozen wounds, would shake off his furious foe like a feather, and rearing on his hind legs rush to the fray again, with jaws distended and a dauntless eye. A higher bound than ever, raised the wary and furious beast far beyond the reach of the dog, who was making a desperate but fruitless dash at her, from which she alighted in a favorable position on his back. For a single moment only could the panther remain there, the great strength of the dog returning with a convulsive effort; and he fastened his teeth in the side of his enemy; when they perceived that the collar of brass around his neck, which had been glittering throughout the fray, was of the color of blood, and directly, that his frame was sinking to the earth, where it soon lay prostrate and helpless. Several mighty efforts of the catamount to extricate herself from the jaws of the dog followed, but they were fruitless, until the mastiff turned on his back, his lips collapsed, and his teeth loosened; when the dog appeared dead. Luckily as the panther recovered, and crawled towards the ladies, they screeched so loud as to attract the attention of a hunter, who got up and fired his rifle just in time to save their lives; the bullet whizzed past them and sent the crittur rolling over on the earth biting its own flesh. The hunter kept his position in front of the ladies and loaded his rifle as quick as possible, when he stepped up to the enraged animal, and put a ball through his head and killed him dead.*

1837 Nashville, p. 37

*The panther is female at the beginning of the story; by the end it is male.

# Perils of the Rocky Mountains.
# A Woman Rescued from the Snow-Drift

Courtesy, American Antiquarian Society

FIGURE 67. *Perils of the Rocky Mountains.*
*A woman rescued from the snow-drift*

In the autumn of 1851, a band of California emigrants, upon reaching the great Ridge which separates the Oregon from Upper California, were suddenly overtaken by a most furious storm of snow, in which men, women, children, horses and vehicles became embedded in the piling drift, from which they were finally rescued by their guides and some Indian assistants with the greatest difficulty and peril. One female, however, they were unable to trace out, while her poor, desolate husband was compelled to move forward in despair. It appeared that his heroic wife had, in her laudable effort to recover some money (the whole amount in their possession) became so thoroughly embedded in the snow, that for almost two whole days she was doomed to struggle in her frosty shroud, in order to reach the open air: and upon finally succeeding, she was so overcome and chilled through, that she sank upon the drifted pile exhausted; from this dying position she was fortunately rescued by one of the hospitable missionary monks of that region, who, in company with their faithful dogs, are out amongst the mountains in all storms to look out for distrest travellers. She was found out by the noble animal, with the money secured about her person, and finally conducted to her overjoyed husband.

1854, p. [9]

# Indian Barbarity

The Special Collections Library of The University of Tennessee, Knoxville

FIGURE 68. *Preparations to Burn Miss Fleming*

The craftiness and cruelty of the American Indian is proverbial. Could the victims of their slaughter be numbered, what a countless host they would present! What appalling and horrid scenes could they not recount! The narratives of the first settlers of the Far West present the most thrilling scenes that can move the human soul. Among the most exciting, is the history of a small party that, in 1790, undertook to descend the Great Kenhawa and Ohio Rivers, in a small boat. The party consisted of six persons,—four men and two young women. After being borne down the stream for some days, their attention was arrested by the appearance of two white men on the shore of the river, wringing their hands, and making the most imploring gestures for assistance. The party in the boat were about equally divided in their opinions of the two supplicants, some of which firmly resolved to pay no attention to the entreaties of the distressed men, feeling assured that it was only an Indian stratagem to get them to the land, while the rest as firmly remonstrated against the cruelty and hardheartedness of the act that would leave them to their fate. The pity and entreaties of two women who were of the party at length prevailed, and the boat was headed for the shore. But no sooner had she approached within the reach of a rifle shot, than a volley was poured into and among the hapless crew, by the Indians, who now appeared in great numbers on the bank, and who rent the air with their accursed and furious yells. In a few moments, they had possession of the boat, and all who had escaped death from their murderous rifles, were bound hand and foot. One of the young women was killed at the first fire. The remaining one, and her surviving companions, were carried into hopeless captivity. Two only finally escaped. After enduring the keenest and most frightful hardships, the narrative closes thus: "The small party of Cherokees, to whom the surviving female belonged, suddenly made its appearance in a Miami village, in a condition so tattered and dilapidated, as to satisfy every one that all their booty had been wasted with their usual improvidence. Miss Fleming's appearance, particularly, had been entirely changed. Her dress was tattered, her cheeks sunken, her eyes discolored by weeping, and her whole manner expressive of the most heartfelt wretchedness. Johnston, who had belonged to the same party, but was now ransomed, addressed her with kindness, but she only replied, by wringing her hands, and bursting into tears. Her master quickly summoned her away; and, on the morning after her arrival, she was compelled to leave the village, and accompany them to Lower Sandusky. Within a few days, Johnston, in company with his friend Duchouquet, followed them to that place, partly upon business, partly with the hope of effecting her liberation. He found the town thronged with Indians of various tribes. Upon inquiring for the Cherokees, he learned that they were encamped with their prisoner within a quarter of a mile of the town, holding themselves aloof from the rest, and evincing the most jealous watchfulness over their prisoner. Johnston instantly applied to the traders of Sandusky, for their good offices, and, as usual, the request was promptly complied with. They went out in a body to the Cherokee camp, accompanied by a white man named Whittaker, who had been taken from Virginia when a child, and had become completely naturalized among the Indians. This Whittaker was personally known to Miss Fleming, having often visited Pittsburgh, where her father kept a small tavern, much frequented by Indians and traders. As soon as she beheld him, therefore, she ran to the spot where he stood, and, bursting into tears, implored him to save her from the cruel fate which she had no doubt awaited her. He engaged very zealously in her service, and, finding that all the offers of the traders were rejected with determined obstinacy, he returned to Detroit, and solicited the intercession of an old chief, known among the whites by the name of "Old King Crane," assuring him (a lie which we can scarcely blame) that the woman was his sister. King Crane listened with gravity to the appeal of Whittaker, acknowledged the propriety of interfering in behalf of so near a relative, and very calmly walked out to the Cherokee camp, in order to try the efficacy of his own eloquence in behalf of the white squaw. He found her master, however, perfectly inexorable. The argument gradually waxed warm, until at length the Cherokees became enraged, and told the old man that it was a disgrace to a chief like him, to put himself upon a level with "white people," and that they looked upon him as no better than "dirt." At this insupportable insult, King Crane became exasperated in turn, and each bespattered the other with a profusion of abuse, for several minutes, until the Old King recollected himself sufficiently to draw off for the present, and concert measures for obtaining redress. He returned to the village in a towering passion, and announced his determination to collect his young men, and rescue the white squaw by force; and if the Cherokees dared to resist, he swore that he would take their scalps upon the spot. Whittaker applauded this resolution, but warned him of the necessity of despatch, as the Cherokees, alarmed at the idea of losing their prisoner, might be tempted to put her to death without further delay. This advice was acknowledged to be of weight; and, before daylight on the following morning, King Crane assembled his young men, and advanced cautiously upon the Cherokee encampment. He found all but the miserable prisoner buried in sleep. She had been stripped naked, her body painted, and in this condition had been bound to a stake, around which hickory poles had already been collected, and every other disposition made, for burning her alive at daylight. She was moaning in a low tone, as her deliverers approached, and was so much exhausted, as not to be aware of their approach, until King Crane had actually cut the cords which bound her, with his knife. He then ordered his young men to assist her in putting on her clothes, which they obeyed with the most stoical indifference. As soon as her toilet had been completed, the King awakened her masters, and informed them that the squaw was *his!* that if they submitted quietly, it was well!—if not, his young men and himself were ready for them. The Cherokees, as may readily be imagined, protested loudly against such unrighteous proceedings, but what could words avail against drawn tomahawks and superior numbers? They finally expressed their willingness to resign the squaw—but hoped that King Crane would not be such a "beast" as to refuse them the ransom which he had offered them on the preceding day! The King replied coolly, that he had the squaw now in his own hands—and would serve them only right if he refused to pay a single broach—but that he disdained to receive any thing at their hands, without paying an equivalent! and would give them six hundred silver broaches. He then returned to Lower Sandusky, accompanied by the liberated prisoner. She was instantly painted as a squaw by Whittaker, and sent off, under care of two trusty Indians to Pittsburgh, where she arrived in safety in the course of the following week.

---

1842 Improved, pp. 2, 5

*This story is unrelated to the earlier and perhaps better known captivity narrative, *A Narrative of the Sufferings and Surprizing Deliverance of William and Elizabeth Fleming* (Philadelphia: Printed for the benefit of the unhappy Sufferers, and Sold by them only, [1756]).

# Stratagem and Cruelty
# of a Party of Indians

The Special Collections Library of The University of Tennessee, Knoxville

FIGURE 69. *Massacre of a White Girl by the Indians*

On the night of the 11th of April, 1787, the house of a widow, in Bourbon county, (Ky.) became the scene of an adventure, which we think deserves to be related. She occupied what is generally called a double cabin, in a lonely part of the county, one room of which was tenanted by the old lady herself, together with two grown sons, and a widowed daughter, at that time suckling an infant, while the other was occupied by two unmarried daughters, from sixteen to twenty years of age, together with a little girl not more than half grown. The hour was 11 o'clock at night. One of the unmarried daughters was still busily engaged at the loom, but the other members of the family, with the exception of one of the sons, had retired to rest. Some symptoms of an alarming nature had engaged the attention of the young man for an hour before any thing of a decided character took place. The cry of owls was heard in the adjoining wood, answering each other in rather an unusual manner. The horses, which were enclosed as usual, in a pound near the house, were more than commonly excited, and by repeated snorting and galloping, announced the presence of some object of terror. The young man

280

was often upon the point of awakening his brother, but was as often restrained by the fear of incurring ridicule and the reproach of timidity, at that time an unpardonable blemish in the character of a Kentuckian. At length, hasty steps were heard in the yard, and quickly afterwards, several loud knocks at the door, accompanied by the usual exclamation, "who keeps house?" in very good English. The young man, supposing from the language, that some benighted settlers were at the door, hastily arose, and was advancing to with-draw the bar which secured it, when his mother, who had long lived upon the frontiers, and had probably detected the Indian tone in the demand for admission, instantly sprung out of bed, and ordered her son not to admit them, declaring that they were Indians. She instantly awakened her other son, and the two young men seizing their guns, which were always charged, prepared to repel the enemy. The Indians finding it impossible to enter under their assumed characters, began to thunder at the door with great violence, but a single shot from a loop-hole, compelled them to shift the attack to some less exposed point; and, unfortunately, they discovered the door of the other cabin, which contained the three daughters. The rifles of the brothers could not be brought to bear upon this point, and by means of several rails taken from the yard fence, the door was forced from its hinges, and the three girls were at the mercy of the savages. One was instantly secured, but the eld-est defended herself desperately with a knife which she had been using at the loom, and stabbed one of the Indians to the heart, before she was toma-hawked. In the mean time the little girl, who had been overlooked by the enemy in their eagerness to secure the others, ran out into the yard, and might have effected her escape, had she taken advantage of the darkness and fled, but instead of that, the terrified little creature ran around the house, wringing her hands, and crying out that her sisters were killed. The brothers, unable to hear her cries, without risking every thing for her rescue, rushed to the door, and were preparing to sally out to her assistance, when their mother threw herself before them, and calmly declared that the child must be aban-doned to its fate—that the sally would sacrifice the lives of all the rest, with-out the slightest benefit to the little girl. Just then the child uttered a loud scream, followed by a few faint moans, and all was again silent. Presently the crackling of flames was heard, accompanied by a triumphant yell from the Indians, announcing that they had set fire to that division of the house which had been occupied by the daughters, and of which they held undis-puted possession. The fire was quickly communicated to the rest of the build-ing, and it became necessary to abandon it, or perish in the flames. In the one case, there was a possibility that some might escape; in the other, their fate would be equally certain and terrible. The rapid approach of the flames cut short their momentary suspense. The door was thrown open, and the old lady, supported by her eldest son, attempted to cross the fence at one point, while her daughter, carrying her child in her arms, and attended by the younger of the brothers, ran in a different direction. The blazing roof shed a light over the yard but little inferior to that of day, and the savages were distinctly seen awaiting the approach of their victims. The old lady was permitted to reach the stile unmolested, but in the act of crossing, received several balls in her breast, and fell dead. Her son, providentially, remained unhurt, and by extraordinary agility, effected his escape. The other party succeeded also in reaching the fence unhurt, but in the act of crossing, were vigorously assailed by several Indians, who, throwing down their guns, rushed upon them with their tomahawks. The young man defended his sister gallantly, firing upon the enemy as they approached, and then wielding the butt of his rifle with a fury that drew their whole attention upon himself, and gave his sister an opportunity of effecting her escape. He quickly fell, however, under the tomahawk of his enemies, and was found at daylight, scalped and mangled in a shocking manner. Of the whole family, consisting of eight pesons, when the attack commenced, only three escaped. Four were killed upon the spot, and one (the second daughter) carried off as a prisoner.

The neighborhood was quickly alarmed, and by daylight about thirty men were assembled, under the command of Col. Edwards. A light snow had fallen during the latter part of the night, and the Indian trail could be pursued at a gallop. It led directly into the mountainous country bordering upon Licking, and afforded evidences of great hurry and precipitation on the part of the fugitives. Unfortunately, a hound had been permitted to accompany the whites, and as the trail became fresh and the scent warm, she followed it with eagerness, baying loudly, and giving the alarm to the Indians. The consequences of this imprudence were soon displayed. The enemy finding the pursuit keen, and perceiving that the strength of the prisoner began to fail, instantly sunk their tomahawks in her head and left her, still warm and bleeding, upon the snow. As the whites came up, she retained strength enough to wave her hand in token of recognition, and appeared desirous of giving them some information, with regard to the enemy, but her strength was too far gone. Her brother sprung from his horse and knelt by her side, endeavoring to stop the effusion of blood, but in vain. She gave him her hand, muttered some inarticulate words, and expired within two minutes after the arrival of the party. The pursuit was renewed with additional ardor,

and in twenty minutes the enemy was within view. They had taken possession of a steep narrow ridge, and seemed desirous of magnifying their numbers in the eyes of the whites, as they ran rapidly from tree to tree, and
maintained a steady yell in their most appalling tones. The pursuers, however, were too experienced to be deceived by so common an artifice, and
being satisfied that the number of the enemy must be inferior to their own,
they dismounted, tied their horses, and flanking out in such a manner as to
enclose the enemy, ascended the ridge as rapidly as was consistent with a due
regard to the shelter of their persons. The firing quickly commenced, and
now for the first time they discoveed that only two Indians were opposed to
them. They had voluntarily sacrificed themselves for the safety of the main
body, and had succeeded in delaying pursuit until their friends could reach
the mountains. One of them was instantly shot dead, and the other was
badly wounded, as was evident from the blood upon his blanket, as well as
that which filled his tracks in the snow for a considerable distance. The pursuit was recommenced, and urged keenly until night, when the trail entered
a running stream and was lost. On the following morning the snow had
melted, and every trace of the enemy was obliterated. This affair must be
regarded as highly honorable to the skill, address, and activity of the Indians,
and the self-devotion of the rear guard, is a lively instance of that magnanim-
ity of which they are at times capable, and, which is more remarkable in
them, from the extreme caution, and tender regard for their own lives, which
usually distinguishes their warriors.

---

1842 Improved, pp. 17–18

# A Young Warrior of the Pawnees

The Special Collections Library of The University of Tennessee, Knoxville

FIGURE 70. *A young warrior of the Pawnees*

Petalesharoo, a young warrior of the Pawnees, was one of the handsomest Indians I ever saw. He was about 23 years of age, of the finest form, tall, muscular, exceedingly graceful, and of a most prepossessing countenance. His head-dress of war-eagles' feathers, descended in a double series upon his back, like wings down to his saddle crosp; his shield was highly decorated, and his long lance was ornamented by a plaited casing of red and blue cloth. On inquiring of the interpreter, our admiration was augmented by learning that he was none other than Petalesharoo, with whose name and character we were already familiar. His name is connected with the abolition of a custom formerly prevalent in this nation, at which humanity shudders.

An Indian woman, brought captive into the village, was doomed to the Great Star, by a warrior whose property she had become by the fate of war; she underwent the usual preparations, and on the appointed day was led to the cross, amidst a great concourse of people, as eager perhaps as their civilized fellow-men to witness the horrors of an execution. The victim was bound to the cross with thongs of skin, and the usual ceremonies being performed, her dread of a terrible death was about to be terminated by the tomahawk and arrow. At this critical juncture, Petalesharoo stepped forward into the area, and in a hurried but firm manner declared it was his father's wish to abolish this sacrifice; that he presented himself for the purpose of laying down his life upon the spot or of releasing the victim. He then cut the cords which bound her, carried her swiftly through the crowd to a horse which he presented to her, and having mounted another himself, conveyed her beyond the reach of immediate pursuit.

----

1835 Nashville, p. 20

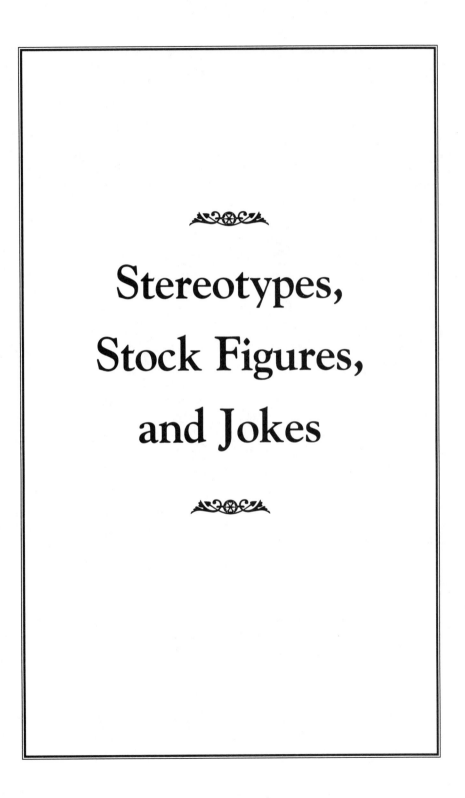

# Stereotypes,
# Stock Figures,
# and Jokes

# Crockett's Account of
# the Concerts in Kansas

One of our extremely sentimental and musical ladies of New York, and who had long run mad after the Italian opera, with its foreign airs and foreign *hairs*, took a notion to emigrate with some of her agricultural relatives to *Kansas*, merely for the romance of the thing, and for some new sort of excitement. Like the fashionable belle who married an Indian, she put up with many privations and annoyances for the sake of the *romance*. She could get along without a street promenade, a fashionable gossip and scandal; "but," said she, "I shall positively expire from want of music and the dear opera. I am dying for the sounds and dulcet swells of a *concert*."

"A consart!" cried Crockett, who happened to hear her; "a consart, Miss! Do you mean for to come for to go for to think that we've not consarts an' operas in Kansas, Ma'am? — Jist you walk along with me to-night, an' you shall hear both, by as *hairy* a set of vocalists as Italian Opera-house can show."

The lady was in raptures, and as soon as the night came on she was in perfect readiness, when Crockett lifted her into his opera-cab, (*a farm-cart,*) and drove out to the neighboring forest, which was alive with all kinds of wild beasts and hideous birds of night. At first, a screech-owl opened the pro-gramme with a direful scream.—"Oh! what's that?" shrieked the trembling listener. "That," said Crockett; "oh, that's only Signorina Screech-Owl-ine." Next came forth the horrid howl of a hungry wolf, who was soon joined by the growls of a grizzly bear. "There, Ma'am," said Crockett, "you hear the two great *Bassos*, Signors Wolfini and Bearini." Next thing, a panther put in his most shrill and horrid scream. "That, Ma'am," said Davy, "is the great *tenore*, Signor Painterini." In a few moments more, the whole and entire natural *menagerie* all broke out together—wolves, bears, wild hogs, wild horses, pan-thers, owls, and Indians, in a mingled roar which made the whole forest tremble with the echo. At the same time, a huge bear walked out upon a fallen tree, with an Indian baby or papoose in his paws. "Thar, Ma'am," shouted Crockett, "thar's the chorus an' fine-alley; ain't it *fine*. An' thar's Signor Bearini come out for a bucket of flowers." The lady screamed, and fell into convulsions, and Crockett drove her home to the *symphony!*

1856, p. [33]

# A Wolfish Affair

The Special Collections Library of The University of Tennessee, Knoxville

FIGURE 71. *The Skeleton of Zebulon Kitchen*

Zebulon Kitchen, a partiklar friend of mine from the Big Black Fork of Little White River in Misouri, came to my house one summer to get a little
insight into the ways of the world and larn civilizashun. So I repeated over to
him some of my speeches in Congress, and told him how they lived in the
big clearings down East. My wife was a little vain and wanted to show off her
breeding to Zebulon, as he was cum from the West, and so she combed out
her new bearskin petticoat, and put on her crocodile-skin short-goun, and
shoes made of buffalo hide, and smoothed down her hair with bear's grease.

289

Then she looked right charming, and Zebulon was so much taken with her that I begun to feel jelus. Howsomever, he got his head so full of notions about what I told him that he intarmined to go down East himself, and tho't he should then get a good deel of noledge about the world and other things and should carry home such a wonder of larning that his naburs would be astonished half out of their census. So he took his gun and his dog and went off alone. I knew Zeb was true pluck and a rail ring-tailed roarer, so I had no doubts he'd make his way whereever he went. So he giv my wife a smack that she has never forgot to this day, and off he went. Well, I thought no more about Zeb till about six weeks arterward, when I was out a hunting, and all of a sudden I cum across the bones of a dog. A little further on I seed the stump of a tree about ten foot high, and on the top eend of it stood a man's skiliton, with his gun in one hand and a piece of paper in the other. It looked rail frightful, and my hair stood straight on eend. I couldn't think how the skilliton could have got up there, and it was no use to ax it for its tongue had been eat out by the birds. Then I seed there was sum writing on the paper, though it was enymost washed out by the rain. I took it out of the skilliton's hand, and read as follows:—

"Deer Krokkit—i am surrounded by wolves. I had to run and got upon this old stump. I have shot away all my amminition and my dog is kilt. So I see no chance of my gitting away at all. If I go down the cussed varmints will ete me up, and if I stay here i shall git nothing to ete myself. So if you find me when ded, see me decently in turd [interred], and i remane Yourn til deth, Zebulon Kitchen.

P.S. I rite this with blood from my finger."

I vow I was completely explunctificated when I red this, for it was as plain as preeching that the wolves had treed poor Zebulon, and he had stain on the stump the whole enduring six weeks. So I took down the bones of poor Zeb, and carried them home with the bones of his dog. I buried them both in one grave, and sent his gun and powder horn home to his family. My wife begged hard for one of the skilliton's hands which she said would make an excellent fan, but I would not let her have it, for fear she would be always thinking of Zeb, if she had something to put her in mind of him. I never forgave the wolves this deed, and whenever I met one arterward, I wasted my last charge of powder on his pesky hide, till I built a monniment to Zeb's memory with wolf bones.

---

1839 Nashville, pp. 15, 17

# Buying a Horse

The Special Collections Library of The University of Tennessee, Knoxville

FIGURE 72. *Col. Crockett and the Yankee Horse Jockey*

There was a feller from down East, to a town called Varmount, that come into our parts to sell his hosses. He squinted with one eye, and the other kept looking up for rain. So my wife keered about him, and she was in a great flustification to go a shopping at the place where he was, and buy her a saddle hoss. So she went and got one. She paid forty dollars for it and brought it home, for I'm sure it couldn't bring her. My wife was never no judge of the article, though she could tell a bear from a panther by the feel of his bite, if it was so dark that she could n't hear herself talk. The hoss was lame in his fore legs and hind legs too, and he had a crook in his tail. He was blind of one eye and deaf of both ears. He couldn't stand up, he was so infirm, and he couldn't lay down becase his bowels were out of order. So the hoss-jockey was to come the next morning arter his money. I put a halter around the neck of the cre-tur and tied his head up to the limb of a tree. I put an old saddle on his back, and put a bridle on him. I fixed the bridle so that the least strain would break it off the bitts, by taking out the stitches. Then I went into the woods and got a hornets' neest, and stopped it up so that the creturs couldn't git out. In the morning the feller cum arter his pay. I begun to praise the hoss, and telled him the animal was so spirited, I did n't like for my wife to ride him. He said he was as gentle as a lamb. I axed him to get on and let me see how he would go. The jockey leeped up and got in the saddle. As soon as he had lighted on the beast, I beat in the hornets' neest, and flung it agin the hoss's backsides. The animal showed some spirit then, for the little varmints cum out, and spurred up the cretur most beautiful. He set out on the full run, and the bridle broke right off in the jockey's hand. The hoss then dug through the forest, without stopping to count the leaves, and the feller clung to the hoss's mane, like a chesnut burr to a bearskin. The last I heered of him, he was seen up by the fork of Duck River, going through the country like a runaway steamboat. He never cum back arter his money.

------

1839 Nashville, p. 19

# Crockett Rescuing a Captive Girl

The Special Collections Library of The University of Tennessee, Knoxville

FIGURE 73. *Crockett rescuing a captive girl*

One morning I sallied out into Breakneck Forest to try to ketch a Cata-mount or have a tussle with a bear or some other varmint, jest to give me an apetite for my breakfast. When I got as fur as the big fork of Rat river I thought I heered something coming over the dry leaves, and I squat down behind a stump and listened for the feller with one ear, while I kept the other open for varmints. I heered it come nearer and soon I seed it war a pesky

Injin a horseback. I squat so low that I war two inches shorter than nothin', and when he got to the place whar I war, I jest straitened up like a log stuck in the bottom of the Massissippy, and the Injin give a yell like a Painter with his tail in a Crocodile's mouth. Then I seed a little gal behind him with her hands tied, and I knowed that he had stolen the little she cretur, and my blood biled so, that the steam cum out of my nostrils. The etarnal redskin thought he war goin' to drive over me; but I put my feelers in his hoss's nose and held him fast, while I drew a lead on the copperhead, and drilled a hole through his countenance, so that his tongue stuck out a foot. I ketched the gal as she fell, and I rid home with her, for she war the darter to Hippopotamus Grim of Snake clearing. Hippopotamus swore it did him more good to git his gal than half a barrel of whiskey.

---

1850, p. [22]

# The Wife Swallowed

The Special Collections Library of The University of Tennessee, Knoxville

FIGURE 74. *The wife swallowed*

Thar war only one nigger that I ever pitied; for the creturs are so mean that I can't pity 'em any more than a skunk. This was a nigger named Bijah, that lived with Alpheus Dock. He fell in love with a big she nigger that lived near Roaring River, in Hemlock Hollow. He had pesky hard work to get her, as her master did'nt want to sell her, and his master didn't want to buy any she niggars; at last, he worked so smart, and behaved himself so well, that his master went and bought her for a high price; and Bijah went up the Roaring River to bring his wife home. He wouldn't let her walk so far, but put her into a wheelbarrow. Just as he got down by Pine Swamp with her, a pesky great alligator pushed his head up out of the mud, and took his wife into his jaws and swallowed her. He took her in head foremost, and the last that Bijah saw of his wife was her legs kicking up in the air, as she went down. Bijah sot right down and howled, and pulled his hair out by the roots. He went home, but he was never the same nigga again. He sot in the sun a week at a time, lookin as dumb as a stone, and nobody could make him get up, or speak a word. At last, an infernal slave trader cum along, and his master sold him. The trader tried to make something of him, and whipped him till he died under the lash without saying a word.

1850, p. [20]

# [Dancing Bears at a Wedding]

When Luke Wing's darter war married to Oak Staples, thar war two tame barrs brought in to dance at the wedding. A nigger wench happened to cum into the room at the time, and begun to cuff and scold at one of the barrs, as she thought it was her husband that had run away from her.

1850, p. [19]

# [Who Died for You?]

Some years since a sober, zealous Connecticut parson went to catechise a family in his parish, who were not so well versed in the rudiments of divinity as many are; when arrived, he thought proper to begin with Lois, the eldest daughter, a girl about 18, and buxom as May; whose charms had smitten the young village swains with an epidemic. "Well, Lois," said the parson, "I shall begin with you: come, tell me who died for you!" Lois, with a charming flush in her cheek, replied, "why nobody as I know on." The parson, rather surprised at her answer, repeated his question with increasing zeal. Lois, rather irritated at the inquisitive parson again replied, "why nobody, sir; there was Tom Dawson lay bed rid for me about six months, but folks say he has got about again."

1836, p. 21

# Young Lady's Diary

Arose at 11 A.M. Was dressed at twelve. Dropped in at Miss William's and learned the name of Margaret Flury's beau. At 2 stopped in at Jones's, and looked at several pieces of goods, together with ribbons without number. Threatened to call again. Shopkeeper very polite. Saw a handsome young man behind the counter. He looked like Sandy Jenkins. At 4 o'clock had a call from Mr. Fitz; he was very agreeble, and gave a full account of the ball at M——'s. Thought he should come again. At 6 prepared to go to the theatre. Went with our party, and was first bored with a tedious play written by that dull fellow, Shakspeare. After that came a new farce—I forget the name, but it was delightful, especially when one of the characters fell into a basket of crockery. Got my feet wet on the way home; but Mr. Brown, our beau, was very kind. He lent me his India-rubbers. They were too large for me, but as it was dark, no one could see the size of my feet. Got safe home, and went to bed. Lay awake till two o'clock, engaged in reading a sweet novel, by the dear, delightful Bulwer.* Went to sleep at last, and dreamed Mr. Fitz wanted to propose, and just as he was on the point, I was called to breakfast by Kitty. I will get ma' to turn off the impudent creature.

---

1841 Nashville, p. 15

*Edward Bulwer-Lytton (1803–73) was one of the most popular of the English novelists of the nineteenth century. He tried to translate the spirit and passions of Romantic poetry into an ideal and mythic vision in his fiction. Nearly twenty of his novels would have been available at this time.

# [A Yankee Help]

Library of Congress

FIGURE 75. *A Yankee Help*

W hy ma'am I'm rather delicate in health, and am very particular as to where I engage as lady's lady.—"

Certainly Miss you look very delicate indeed, but I assure you will find mine a very easy situation, little or nothing to do, a fine easy chair in the kitchen, and I put my *cooking* and *beds* out to make.

1842 Comic, p. [5]

# [The Poet Collins]*

Collins — This sweet poet was much attached to a young lady, who was born the day before him, and who did not return his passion. "Yours is a hard case," said a friend. "It is so, indeed," replied Collins, "for I came into the world a *day after the fair*."

———

1839, p. [14]

*The Collins in question may be William Collins (1721–59) whose pre-Romantic poetry was very popular well into the nineteenth century. Regarded as a cut below the major poets of his age, Collins's originality kept his reputation alive despite his completing less than two thousand lines of poetry in his short life.

# ["May I Be Married, Ma?"]

"May I be married, ma?" said a pretty brunette of sixteen to her mother. "What do you want to be married for?" replied the mother. "Why, ma, you know the *children* have never seen any body married, and I thought it might please 'em."

———

1836, p. 31

# Emigration

FIGURE 76. *Emigration*

Here's for America, there's no living in England thats flat, hang on old woman, take care of the young 'un, soon get there, happy country nothing to do but eat fat bacon, and swing on a gate all day long.

1842 Comic, p. [15]

# Declaration of Independence

FIGURE 77. *Declaration of Independence*

1842 Comic, p. [12]

Library of Congress

# The Rag Fair

FIGURE 78. *The rag fair*

The gals in Parson Longtext' church, got up a rag fair last fall, for the benefit of the poor. Made up a whole lot of odd contraptions, hearts stuck full of pins, paper baskets, and other queer notions, the consarnedest lot of trash you ever did see; then you see the chaps all went a shopping, paid a dollar for sixpence worth, and had a good stare in the bargain. Its a positive fact,

that forty-nine matches (not loco foco's,* but genewine love ones) were concluded on the strength of that 'are fair. Joe Lutestring[,] a dreadful nice young
man in the dry good's line, fastened on Old Sall Sparks kase he diskivered
[sh]e had a slick way of taking the flats in.—They do say her dad thought the
same thing, for the piece of goods had got kinder shop worn, and the old
man thought he'd never get her off his hands, but gals, keep up your hearts
gals, every Jack has his Jill.

---

1842 Comic, p. [14]

*A "locofoco" is a self-lighting cigar invented in 1834 by John Marck of New York that had
a match composition at its end. Locofocos became a slang term used to describe the anti-
monopolist wing of the New York City Democratic Party, because when in 1835 the regular or Tammany Democrats put out the lights of their meeting, they continued using the
light produced by candles and locofocos. Later, Whigs applied the term to any Democrat.

# Resignation

FIGURE 79. *Resignation*

Dew you see that 'are chap, aint he about as meechin and henpecked a looking critter as ever you'd wish to clap eyes on. I guess as how he's got for a worser half, about as damnified a tarter as ever Mr. Job had, twig her frontispiece, she's got her ebenezer up, and the way she looks awfully grand on Pilgarlic is almighty trying to his narvous system, and one can see she wears the breechelloons kase her petticoats arn't long enough to hide 'em, prehaps if she was my consarn, I would'nt take down her aproariousness a little quicker than no time, strap oil the genewine regulator or as the old song says,

> A woman, a dog, and a walnut tree,
> The more *you lick'em* the better they be.

1842 Comic, p. [9]

305

# [Sally Chatterwell]

Sally Chatterwell is the most loquatious of her sex, not that *ladies* are given to talking, but talking is certainly given to them; I verily believe her *rattle* like the snake's increases every year. "Bid me discourse!" is her favourite song, and proud of her eloquence, she boldly declares that nothing takes with the world so well as talk,—and no *belle*, without a clapper (except a *diving bell*) ever *went down*.

1842 Comic, p. [5]

# Kentucky Bluntness

An Englishman was travelling with his wife through the country in a gig. One day, after having journeyed as far as they intended, they stopped opposite to a house before which a bear swung on the sign. The gig had lost a step, and the husband jumping out, called to a young woman lounging at the door of the tavern, "Bring a chair here." The damsel addressed did not move. "Bring a chair here I say!" Still no indication of assistance. "D——n it, are you deaf? don't you hear? I say I want a chair to let my wife down, eh?" On this the landlord presents himself at the door—"Halloe, stranger, what's all this about?" We allow no swearing here; go along, sir! we take nobody in who swears or makes a noise here,"—and the poor Englishman was obliged to carry his spouse ten miles farther to another house of entertainment.

1838 Nashville, p. 36

# [Poor Shakem Nervous]

FIGURE 80. *Poor Shakem Nervous*

Poor Shakem Nervous went to a ball at Tammany Hall, walked home in thin pumps through a snow storm, went to bed, awoke at four in the morning with a violent ague fit. Sally the maid hearing his groans arose[,] made him a hot brandy sling, filled the warming pan with live hickory coals, and oh dire mishap, half asleep she run the scorching hot pan butt against his seat of honor. The fright and pain cured the ague, but it is a fact that he could not sit with any comfort for full a month afterwards.

1842 Comic, p. [8]

307

# The Fish Fag

FIGURE 81. *The fish fag*

U nfeeling woman, hast thou no compassion for the harmless creature thou art thus torturing alive?

Lord love your silly soul, to be sure it was sorter cruel at first, but I've [s]kinned 'em this ten years and now they are quite used to it.

Wast thou ever in a fish market? and didst ever see an old fish fag skinning eels. If you have not, then let me tell you that you've missed the sight of the most *selfish* and *scaly* of the fair sex, vain are the wriggles and squirming of the poor victims, she whips off their overcoats with out slightest compunction, and replies to all feeling enquiries, with—la! you would'nt eat 'em with their skins on would you?

1842 Comic, p. [16]

308

# A Fishing Smack

Library of Congress

FIGURE 82. *A fishing Smack*

1842 Comic, p. [5]

# Ben Harding's Account
# of a Shipwreck

FIGURE 83. *Ben Harding's account of a shipwreck*

One day Ben went out with me to tree a bear; and he got clear of us arter a queer fashion that I won't say nothing about, because the reader wants to hear Ben's story fust. Me and Ben sot down on a stump back to back, as there want room for us to set side by side, and he took out his pipe and begun to smoke. So as the smoke went up his nose, it give his brains a

The Special Collections Library of The University of Tennessee, Knoxville glister [sparkle] and his idees come out like he was speechifying in Congress. He told this story which I spose must be true, or he wood have forgot all about it, it was so long sense it happened. Says he—When I was a little shaver about as big as the Cappin's dog, I took a great noshun to go to sea, because I thought, d'ye see, that there was no work to be done, and that the sailors had nothing to do, but to set still and let the wind blow 'em along. But I always had to work where I was brought up—but I wan't brought up at all, I was dragged up—and so I meant to top my boom and be off like a rigger. Well I slept in the cockloft, and the sarvant gal slept there too, and I could-n't get out of the place without crawling over her, and I must go in the night if I went at all, for there war as many eyes on the look out for me in the day time as ever peeped over a cathead when the port was in sight. So I didn't know exactly how to work it. I had got me a little snug tarpaulin hat, that looked as bright as a new guinea, and a blue jacket that had belonged to an old boatswain, and fitted me as a purser's shirt fits a handspike. I had 'em all done up in a bundle and stowed away snug under my pillow. I laid awake till I thought it was about eight bells, and then I got up softly as a soger sliding down the gangway when all hands is called. I put on my rigging and then felt my way to the door. I knew when I got close to the door for the sarvant gal always slept right across the passage, and the smell of her breath come up like the steem from an old slush tub. I knew if I waked her up it was all day with me; and so I stood still to see if she war hard and fast. I knew by her breath-ing that she slept as solid as a marine on post, and then put my hands on the floor and felt my way to her. I first touched her bed clothes, and then her flipper; but it didn't wake her, and so I begun to get over her. She laid still till I had fairly got over her, and I thought I was safe, but my toe happened to get tangled in her hair and as it was never combed, it was hard work to get my mudplanter loosed. She woke up and jumped like a struck dolphin. I spose the way she opened her throat was never matched since Captin Kid hailed the flying Dutchman off the Cape of Good Hope. She only stopped squalling to take breath, and the way she puffed it out might have set a good example to a typhoon. I spose her master heard her, but as good luck would have it, he run up aloft to her while I was running doun to the door. When I got to the door, I found it was locked and barred. I unshipped the bar with one hand and turned the key with the other, and let moonshine into the entry before the old porpus could get doun stairs. He chased me on horseback, but I got into the bush, and had the fun of larfing at him as he cum back. I then made tracks for the seaport. Early in the morning, I went doun on the wharf. There was a smack there just going out on a fishing cruise. I stepped up to the cappin and doused my peak, and asked him if he wanted to ship a hand. He was a long-sided Yankee that had been one voyage round Cape Horn in a Nantucket whaleman. He had a jaw as long as a sword-fish's sword, and his head bobbed at the end of his long neck when he spoke, like a ship's cat-head riding at anchor in a heavy sea-way. He said he wanted a boy about my size, and asked me if I knew how to cook. I thort the feller was soft in his garret, for I had always seen the women folks do the cooking when I lived in the country, and I larfed in his face, and went off. The next craft I hauled my little carcase aboard of was a brig going to Norfolk. The cappin was a little black looking fellow with an eye like a scoured pump-bolt, and his head was as round as a bullet. He asked me where I cum from. I told him I belonged to Norfolk, and I gave him a name—I forget now what the name was—but it was the first one I could think of. He greed to take me. We hauled out of port in about two weeks afterwards. As soon as we got to sea, I felt rather qualmish, so to cure me, the mate sent me aloft to scrape doun the top-gallant-masts. I hadn't been up there long, when the wind begun to pipe. I hurried down, and it was well that I did, for the top-gallant-mast was hanging over the side, before my feet struck the deck. Here was the Devil to pay and no pitch hot. All hands was called to clear away the wreck; but it begun to blow like seven men. It would have done your heart good to hear the wind squalling amongst the rigging. It was worse than a camp-meeting. We laid aloft to take in sail. I got on the fore-top-sail yard close to the bunt, and the foot ropes was so long that my chin cum just up to the yard. All this time the wind was blowing so it took five men to hold the cappin's hair on. At last the ship cum up to the wind, and the sail flapped up and knocked me right off the yard. I went doun, head, neck, and shoulders, into the top, and went through the lubber holes, but I was brought up by the futtock shrouds, or I should have lost the number of my mess, as sure as the Devil's a nigger. The hands on the yard thought I had gone overboard, but they were in such a hurry they couldn't stop to see. They had got the sail almost furled, when the gale freshened, and it come down upon us like a rail harrycane. Away went the sail out of the bolt-ropes, and the men hurried down from aloft. I laid still where I was, as I knew there would be more hard work to do. Pretty soon I heard the pumps a going. I thought the brig had sprung a leak, and so I didn't want to be drouned alone, and I went down on deck. As soon as the Cappin saw me he put his speaking trumpet to my ear, and asked me where I had come from. I told him I had been overboard, but that I had been washed aboard again by a sea. He said I ought to be thankful for my providential deliverance. When he said that I begun to look wild, for I knew we must be in a very dangerous condition or else the Cappin would n't have talked about Providence. The Cappin was of the religion of a louse, when he was ashore—he only went to meeting when he was carried; and I knew when he begun to be gracious that we had sprung a leak or something worse. In a minute, the mate jerked me along by the arm and told me to take my turn at the pump and be d——d to me. I felt encouraged when I heard him swear; but just then, the brig pitched over on her beam ends, and two men went overboard. The rest of the men fell down on their knees and begun to pray. That made the mate as mad as a pea in a hot skillet, and he ordered them to get up and cut away the mast. He said it was the most unseamanlike conduct he ever heard of. The mast was cut away and the brig righted. We went afoul of the pumps again, but it was of no use. The hold and cabin were soon all afloat, and the Cappin's arm-chair came bobbing out of the companionway without being sent for. All this time the sea made a clean sweep over us, and another man was carried overboard. The long and short of it is that we found it of no use to man the pumps without we could pump the ocean dry, and we considered ourselves sunk. It come on night, and a pretty night it was. There war no more star-light than there is in an earthern jug. The sea made a clear breach right over us, and we expected to go doun every minute. Besides all this, there was a great many fleas aboard that plagued us confoundedly.

About day-light the Cappin called all hands to prayers, and we knelt doun while he prayed. But when he war in about the middle of his prayer, he got sight of a large ship that was coming right down to us. He jumped up off his knees, flung the prayer book into the lee scuppers, and bawled out, "By G——d! there's a sail!" The way we bundled into the stranger's boat, and the way we swallowed the prime West India when we got aboard the ship was enough to give old folks the horse distemper.

---

1840 Nashville, pp. 18, 19, 20

# The Jewesses

Fontanes* asked Chateaubriand,* if he could assign a reason why the women of the Jewish race were so much handsomer than the men? to which Chateaubriand gave the following truly poetical and Christian one: "The Jewesses," he said, "have escaped the curse which alighted upon their fathers, husbands, and sons. Not a Jewess was to be seen among the crowd of priests and rabbis who insulted the Son of God, scourged him, crowned him with thorns, and subjected him to ignominy, and the agony of the cross. The women of Judea believed in the Saviour, and assisted and soothed him under afflictions. A woman of Bethany poured on his head precious ointment, which she kept in a vase of alabaster. The Sinner anointed his feet with perfumed oil, and wiped them with her hair. Christ, on his part, extended his mercy to the Jewesses. He raised from the dead the son of the widow of Nain, and Martha's brother, Lazarus. He cured Simon's mother-in-law, and the woman who touched the hem of his garment. To the Samaritan woman he was a spring of living water, and a compassionate judge to the woman in adultery. The daughters of Jerusalem wept over him; the holy women accompanied him to Calvary, brought balm and spices, and weeping, sought him in the sepulchre. 'Woman, why weepest thou?' His first appearance, after the Resurrection, was to Mary Magdalen. He said to her, 'Mary.' At the sound of his voice, Mary Magdalen's eyes were opened, and she answered, 'Master.' The reflection of some very beautiful ray must have rested on the brow of the Jewesses.["]

---

1842, p. [14]

*Louis, Marquis de Fontanes (1757–1821), was a French nobleman and Neoclassical poet who was in exile in London during the French Revolution. There he met and became the friend of François-René de Chateaubriand (1768–1848), whom he helped upon his return to France. Fontanes held high official posts under Napoleon and Louis XVIII. Chateaubriand addressed his *Lettres à Fontanes sur la campagne romaine* (1804) to Fontanes. Chateaubriand became the outstanding French literary figure of the first half of the nineteenth century. He wrote in a huge range of genres and was a master of language and style, and his work still exerts a great influence upon French literature. His chef probably invented the beef dish that bears his name, in which a pocket is cut into a double-thick center cut of beef tenderloin and filled with various seasonings before grilling.

# A Mormon Preacher Is Treed
# in the Act of Making Love
# to a Beautiful Plantation Wench

Courtesy, American Antiquarian Society

FIGURE 84. *A Mormon preacher is treed in the act
of making love to a beautiful plantation wench*

A zealous Mormon Preacher, during his fanatical peregrinations in the West, was somewhat noted by many of his flock, for having a particular propensity for converting darkies into the sublime doctrines of Joe Smith: and many of the plantation overseers tolerated his visits within their precincts, merely for the sake of what they conceived to be a harmless eccentricity and

315

laughable folly, until one day they detected him in a kind of exhortation which they seemed to think did not properly belong to his mission.

He happened, one morning, to follow the footsteps of one of the fairest wenches of the sugar-cane field, and fancying that there was no one within hearing, he crept very cautiously behind a huge gum tree, from which protective point he commenced proclaiming the fervor of his passion—picturing to her the glorious wonders of the Mormon world—urging her to flee from the black and white devils that surrounded her, by seeking a Mormon heaven and safety, in his anxious arms. The simple negress seemed thoroughly subdued by his persuasive powers. "Come quick, my love," said he: "obey the command of the highest of all overseers, those of the prophet Joe Smith— who is now looking down in smiles from the limb of this gum tree, sacred to love and bliss. My fair fish, I've caught you," said he, chuckling to himself. "And I've caught *you*, my Mormon man!" cried an overseer, who, from the limb above, had been listening,—and, darting down upon the villian, made him make tracks without his *tracts*.

------

1853, p. [25]

# A Leap unto the Other Side of Jordan

FIGURE 85. *Jacob, there are serpents below, hadn't thee best jump back before thee lands?*

Parson Ponder, a Mormon preacher, one day went out into the field to rehearse his forthcoming sermon upon the superior beauties of the Mormon faith. He worked himself up to a great pitch of extacy, till the very frogs seemed moved to sympathy, and replied in strains of all-eye-croaker[.] At last, finding his store of breath and argument giving out, and his legs beginning to give in, he roared out at the top of his voice:

"*Brethren:* (He meant the frogs of course,) brethren, give me your hands;" at this moment a sister of the tribe, who had been watching his operations, saluted him with a loud clap of the hands, which so startled him that he gave one fearful spring, which landed his corpus in a deep ravine below, while the sister helping him out exclaimed, "Thou art leaping to the tother side of Jordan,[.]"

1855, p. [13]

# The Old Squaw Gumachaw
# Who Cooked and Eat the Prisoner's Horse

An old and fierce squaw in the Mormon settlement gradually found her collection of live stock to disappear, until she was left without a single pig or chicken, and suspecting that some of the Mormons had appropriated her property to their own use, she resolved upon a regular system of Indian retaliation, and she killed, cooked and eat everything belonging to them that she could lay her hands upon. Accordingly, the commissioners of the settlement found that their census of sheep, pigs and poultry were lessening daily— and some of the young Mormons were likewise among the missing. Suspicions were upon the panthers, wolves and bears that infested the country, and large parties were armed and placed upon the watch at all points. But nothing of the shape of the four legged intruders could be discovered.

At last, one of the elders, who had been extremely active in his efforts to annihilate the race of red skins in the neighborhood, found himself entrapped one evening by an Indian horse-snare. He was led by a party of savages to a hut in the depths of a forest, and on entering he beheld the head and shoulders of his favorite steed actually reasting [roasting] in a large fire, while an old squaw had the remaining extremes already half devoured. He made his escape during their preparations to cook him, and the Indians in that section remained undisturbed for some time.

1854, p. [12]

# The Indian Squaw, Who First Stole and Then Eat One of the Mormon's Horses

Courtesy, American Antiquarian Society

FIGURE 86. *The Indian squaw who first stole and then eat one of the Mormon's horses*

During the progress of a party of Mormons, under the celebrated leader, Strang, towards their new settlements in Deseret, one of their number, who had a magnificent horse, of which he was very proud, and of which he took a great deal of care, was exceedingly astonished, one fine morning, on discovering that the animal had been stolen. In company with some others he immediately set out in search of it. After following the tracks of the animal for several miles, they came to a pool of blood, after which no further traces of it could be found. Separating, and each one taking a different course, so as to meet at one common centre, they at last came upon an Indian camp: in the outskirts of it the amazed owner discovered the hind quarters of his noble beast suspended over a blazing fire, beside which was seated an old Indian squaw. She had stolen the horse, killed it, cut it up, and was then cooking it. Their first impulse was to kill the squaw; but, on reflecting that they were but few in number, and the Indians very numerous, they thought it best to pocket the insult and say nothing about it; resolving, in their own minds, that they would hereafter keep a more strict watch over their property.

1852, p. [7]

# [Why the Groom Avoids the Church]

A gentleman who had been a few months bound in Hymenial's silken fetters, after great exertion and trouble on his part to procure the fair lady's consent, found that he had "caught a tartar." His wife being shocked at the discovery that he had never gone to a place of worship since his marriage, expostulated with him for his conduct. "My dear," said he, "I have three very sufficient reasons for not complying with your wishes." After some persuasion he was induced to declare them:—"First, my love, I never can bear any society where one person monopolises the entire conversation." "Oh, you terrible man!" sighed the lady. "Then, I hate singing where there is no drinking!" "Dear me, shocking!" exclaimed his meek partner. "But above all, I was married to you there." "Oh, you vile wretch, you are lost!" sobbed his wife.

1839, p. 14

# My Idee of a Bloomer* Kuss-Tume

A Female with bishop sleeves on her legs, and a *corn-cake* on her head[.]

1855, p. [24]

*Amelia Jenks Bloomer (1818–94) attended the Seneca Falls meeting on women's rights in 1848 and, an ardent supporter of temperance, also supported women's rights issues through her paper, *The Lily.* Interestingly, she did not invent the costume that bears her name. That credit, as Bloomer in vain always insisted, belonged to Mrs. Elizabeth Smith Miller, a cousin of Elizabeth Cady Stanton, who created it for her honeymoon grand tour of Europe in 1850. The following February, Stanton adopted this sensible attire after seeing her cousin's freedom of movement, and she and her cousin strolled to the post office to show it to Bloomer, who herself adopted the costume in a few days and suggested that a nice round hat (the "*corn-cake*" cited above) would make the outfit unique. See Charles Neilson Gattey, *The Bloomer Girls* (New York: Coward-McCann, 1968), pp. 50–61).

# A Woman in California

The miner, notwithstanding his toil, has his fun and frolic, as well as *white men*. Early one Sunday, our mess was suddenly awakened by the discharge of a musket at our heads. Jumping up I exclaimed, "what's the matter; what has happened?"

"What's the matter!" shouted the stentorian voice of one of our neighbors, "turn out, turn out! new digging! a live woman came in last night!"

"A woman? oh, get out, you're joking."

"No, it's true as preaching. I was prospecting around the camp, and I'll be whipped if I did'nt see a petticoat hanging on a limb by a new tent on ———— Bar. I want to raise a company to go and look at the animal, for hang me if I've pluck enough to go alone."

"Cook, get breakfast just as quick as—"

"Blame the breakfast," replied our friend, "she may tote off to other diggins before you can fry a piece of pork, and you won't get sight at her."

We knew that delays were dangerous, so shouldering our picks and shovels, pistols and rifles, and taking a bottle or two of *aguadiente*, we marched to the new tent, in file, our leader whistling, "Come haste to the wedding," and gave three cheers and a discharge of fire-arms. The alarmed occupants rushed to the door to see what was up. Our captain mounted a rock and addressed the amazed husband in something like this strain—

"Stranger, we have been shut up here so long, that we don't know what is going on in the world, and we have nearly forgotten what it is made of. We have understood that our mothers were women, but it is so long since we have seen them, that we have forgotten how a woman looks, and being told that you have caught one, we are prospecting to get a glimpse."

The man, a sensible fellow by the way, entered into the heart of the joke, produced the *animal*, when, with nine cheers, a drink all round, and a few good natured jokes, we quietly dispersed.

———————
1854, p. [18]

# A Missourian's Opinion of His Neighbor

Jedediah Crawfish was very fond of his neighbor's wife, and went with his friend Elnathan to see her one afternoon. Jedediah went up stairs and left Elnathan below to watch. Presently the husband came home, and greeted Elnathan cordially. He told him that he had long suspected Jedediah of improper tenderness towards his wife, and said, 'As you are his intimate friend, you may tell me whether you think he is guilty.'

'I have known my friend Crawfish for twenty years,' replied Elnathan, 'and would not be afraid to stake my head that he is above doing a bad action.'

---

1836 Nashville, p. 13

# Recipes

# and

# Household

# Hints

# Davy Crockett's Recipe for Preserving Horseflesh amongst Wolves

Haven accasion to take a lot of cavalry horses through a great wolf settlement in Arkansas, where the wolves are squatted down about as thick as lies in Congress, one of Uncle Sam's officers bet me a thousand dollars agin an alligator supper, that the wolves would chaw up every crittur alive afore I got through. I won the wager in the following Crockettonian fashion:—In the first place, everybody knows that the hull and entire wolf creation is as feard of *iron* as a dandy is of common sense; and that every sucking wolf crittur smells *steel trap* as natrally in a piece of iron as a pig smells a tater patch. Well, I jist took particlar care for to sort out all my horses of the same coat an color, and I driv em all as cooly, safe and wholesome through that entire wolf population as I would send a bullet through a buzzard. So I wun the bet. Well, how do you think I done it? Why, I jist tuk care that all my horses were *iron greys*, so that the wolves dropt heads and tails an cut stick, thinkin they saw a *steel trap* in every horse-hide that went along.

1855, p. [24]

# Receipt for a Cold

The following reseet from my great aunt will be useful for the reeder, and he'd better tend to it. When you find you have got a cold, go into the forrest and find out a young painter that's about two years old. Chase him till you catch him; and then take off his hide, and lay it warm upon your bowels. Drink two pints of whiskey, and go to sleep. You may git up in the course of the night five or six times and scream. If that don't cure you, then you may say Davy Crockett never went to kongress, that's aul.

1841, p. [13]

326

# Crockett's Plan for Keeping Children from Getting the Measels

Them ere all-fired pineknots o' the face, called measels, are about as ugly things mongst children as the *tater rot* is among sheep; an my plan for preventen them from ketchin it when it comes about, is to lock em all up so fast that they'll have no chance to *break out*.

1855, p. [24]


# [Curing a Fever]

As far as my experience goes, it's not well to eat too much bear's fat when one's in a fever. Thar war a pashint [patient] at my house, who war very ill with the tipus fever, and wanted a swet. We giv him a smart chance of whiskey every morning, an brought on the sweat by setting him to climbing up a pine tree an sliding down agin. The whiskey and the climbing brought on the sweat, and then we put drafts on his feet maid of aqua fortis, and skunk's marrow, and that cured him.

1847, p. [8]

# [How to Cure a Cold]

When you have a cold and a sore throat, you can cure it in a minnit by binding a slice of a bars liver on it. It must be put on fresh and warm, right from the animal. Then drink a pint of whiskey, to keep your insides warm, and it will leave you instanterly. I have tried it a thousand times, and it never failed.

1851, p. [28]

# A Receipt for Cholera

Eat two cucumbers, dressed or raw, as you prefer; then take a quart of blackberries, four green corn, four young potatoes mashed, a lobster or crab, some ice water, and wash the whole down with a quart of buttermilk, and you will shortly have a touch of the real thing.

1836 Nashville, p. 47

# To Housewives*

Never allow ashes to be taken up in wood, or put into wood.—Always have your tinder-box and lamp ready for use, in case of sudden alarm.—Have important papers all together, where you can lay your hand on them at once, in case of fire.—Use hard soap to wash your clothes, and soft to wash your floors. Soft soap is so slippery, that it wastes a good deal in washing clothes.—Barley straw is the best for beds: dry corn husks, slit into threads, are still better.—Clean brass kettles, before using, with salt and vinegar.—Woollens should be washed in very hot suds, and not rinsed.

1842 Improved, p. 14

*This and the following item, "[Candles]," are included as a sample of the nonhumorous recipes and household hints that occasionally made their way into the Crockett Almanacs. They are often used as "filler."

# [Candles]

Those who make candles, will find it a great improvement to steep the wicks in lime water and saltpetre, and dry them. The flame will be clear, and the tallow will not "run."

1842 Improved, p. 26

# Crockett's Recipe for a Corn-Cake

Take a barrel of geese-eggs, and smash them up, shells and all; take five bushels of corn, and boil them, husks, cobs, and all. Thrash the whole together by a patent flail; bake over a volcano[,] spread with boiled sugar-cane, and swallow it smoking-hot.

---

1856, p. [32]

# Crockett's Recipe for Cooking Bear-Steaks

Salt 'em in a hail storm, pepper 'em with buckshot, an' then boil 'em with a flash o' lightnin'!

---

1854, p. [24]

# Appendix: The Sources of the Tales*

1835 Nashville    *Davy Crockett's Almanack, of Wild Sports of the West, and Life in the Backwoods. 1835. Calculated for All the States in the Union.* Nashville, Tenn.: Published by Snag & Sawyer, 1835.

1836 Nashville    *Davy Crockett's Almanack, of Wild Sports in the West, and Life in the Backwoods. Calculated for All the States in the Union. 1836.* Nashville, Tenn.: Published for the Author, 1836.

1836    *Crockett's Yaller Flower Almanac, for '36. The Ringtail Roarer! Ripsnorter! Circumflustercated Grinner's Guide!* Snagsville, Salt River [New York]: Published by Boon Crockett, and Squire Downing, Skunk's Misery, Down East [Elton], 1836.

1837 Nashville    *Davy Crockett's Almanack, of Wild Sports in the West, Life in the Backwoods, & Sketches of Texas. 1837.* Nashville, Tennessee: Published by the heirs of Col. Crockett, 1837.

1838 Nashville    *Davy Crockett's Almanack, of Wild Sports in the West, Life in the Backwoods, Sketches of Texas, and Rows on the Mississippi. 1838.* Nashville, Tennessee: Published by the heirs of Col. Crockett, 1838.

1839 Nashville    *The Crockett Almanac, 1839. Containing Adventures, Exploits, Sprees & Scrapes in the West, & Life and Manners in the Back-*

---

*There are different imprints for some of the Almanacs than those listed here. The "1842" noted above, for example, was also issued as "Baltimore: Turner, 1842." Most of these variant imprints do not change the tales, although occasionally a story is shifted to another page or, in rare instances, deleted to make room for advertising or other substituted material. This appendix contains only those Almanacs used to produce the texts for this edition. Note also that all almanacs were generally published in the fall of the year preceding their date, but conventional notation bears the year covered. The "Nashville" Almanacs were actually printed in Boston.

*woods*. Nashville, Tennessee: Published by Ben Harding, 1839.

1839              *Crockett Awl-Man-Axe for 1839*. New York: Turner & Fisher, 1839.

1840 Nashville    *The Crockett Almanac, 1840. Containing Adventures, Exploits, Sprees & Scrapes in the West, & Life and Manners in the Backwoods*. Nashville, Tennessee: Published by Ben Harding, 1840.

1841 Nashville    *The Crockett Almanac, 1841. Containing Adventures, Exploits, Sprees & Scrapes in the West, & Life and Manners in the Backwoods*. Nashville, Tennessee: Published by Ben Harding, 1841.

1841              *The Crockett Almanac, 1841. Containing Sprees and Scrapes in the West; Life and Manners in the Backwoods; and Exploits and Adventures on the Prairies*. Boston: Published by J. Fisher, 1841.

1842              *Ben Hardin's Crockett Almanac. 1842. With Correct Astronomical Calculations; For Each State in the Union—Territories and Canada. Rows—Sprees and Scrapes in the West: Life and Manners in the Backwoods: and Terrible Adventures on the Ocean*. New York and Philadelphia: Published by Turner & Fisher, 1842.

1842 Improved     *Crockett Almanac Improved, 1842. Improved Edition. Containing Real Stories*. Boston: Printed and published by S. N. Dickinson, 1842.

1842 Comic        *Crockett Comic Almanac Worser 1842. New Series, No. X. Lots of Funny Fun*. Gotham: Published by Doleful Serious, 1842.

1843              *Fisher's Crockett Almanac. 1843. Edited by Ben Hardin. Calendar for the Whole Country. With Rows, Sprees and Scrapes in the West: Life and Manners in the Backwoods: Terrible Bat-*

tles and Adventures on Sea and Land. New York: Published by Turner & Fisher, 1843.

1844          Davy Crockett's Almanac. 1844. For the Eastern, Northern and Middle States. Life and Manners in the Backwoods: Terrible Battles and Adventures of Border Life: With Rows, Sprees, and Scrapes in the West. Boston: Published by James Fisher, 1844.

1845          Davy Crockett's Almanac. 1845. Calendars Correct for the Entire Union, the Territories, Texas, and British Provinces. Boston: Published by James Fisher, 1845.

1847          Davy Crockett's Almanac. 1847. Daring Adventures in the Back Woods; Wonderful Scenes in River Life; Manners of Warfare in the West; Feats on the Prairies, in Texas and Oregon. Boston: James Fisher, 1847.

1848          Crockett's Almanac. 1848. Calculated for the Whole United States. Boston: James Fisher, 1848.

1849          Crockett Almanac, 1849. Calendar Calculated for the Whole United States. Boston: James Fisher, 1849.

1850          Crockett's Almanac. 1850. Containing Rows, Sprees, and Scrapes in the West; Life and Manners in the Backwoods, Adventures on the Ocean &c. New York, Philadelphia, and Boston: Fisher & Brothers (Successors to Turner & Fisher), 1850.

1851          Crockett's Almanac. 1851. Containing Life, Manners and Adventures in the Back Woods, and Rows, Sprees, and Scrapes on the Western Waters. Philadelphia, New York, and Boston: Fisher & Brother, Publishers, 1851.

1852          Crockett Almanac, 1852. Containing Life, Manners, and Adventures in the Back Woods, and Rows, Sprees, and Scrapes on the Western Waters. With Handsome Illustrations. Philadelphia, New York, Boston, and Baltimore: Fisher and Brother, 1852.

1853        *Crockett Almanac, 1853. Containing Life, Manners, and Adventures in the Back Woods, and Rows, Sprees, and Scrapes on the Western Waters. With Handsome Illustrations.* Philadelphia, New York, Boston, and Baltimore: Fisher & Brother, 1853.

1854        *Crockett Almanac, 1854. Containing Life, Manners and Adventures in the Backwoods, and Rows, Sprees, and Scrapes on the Western Waters.* Philadelphia, New York, Baltimore, and Boston: Fisher and Brother, 1854.

1855        *Crockett Almanac, 1855.* Philadelphia, New York, Boston, and Baltimore: Fisher & Brother, 1855.

1856        *Crockett Almanac, 1856.* Philadelphia, New York, Boston, and Baltimore: Fisher & Brother, 1856.